365
dish a day

365
dish a day

A RECIPE FOR EACH OF THE 365 DAYS IN A YEAR

+ ONE FOR A LEAP YEAR

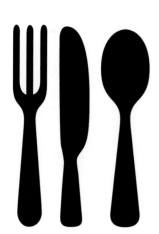

p

This is a Parragon Publishing Book
First published in 2006

Parragon Publishing
Queen Street House
4 Queen Street
Bath BA1 1HE, UK

ISBN: 1-40547-139-5

Printed in China

Produced by terryjeavons&company
Cover design by Talking Design

Notes for the Reader
This book uses imperial, metric, or US cup measurements. Follow the same
units of measurement throughout; do not mix imperial and metric. All spoon
measurements are level: teaspoons are assumed to be 5 ml, and tablespoons
are assumed to be 15 ml. Unless otherwise stated, milk is assumed to be
whole, eggs and individual vegetables such as potatoes are medium, and
pepper is freshly ground black pepper. Recipes using raw or very lightly
cooked eggs should be avoided by infants, the elderly, pregnant women,
convalescents, and anyone suffering from an illness.

contents

introduction

Cooking should be one of life's great joys, but when you're preparing meals day in, day out, just for yourself or for a hungry family, it can be hard to stay inspired or try something new. Whether you love food or have to drag yourself into the kitchen, *Dish a Day* gives a little daily inspiration to put delicious homemade food on your table. From revisiting well-loved classics to ideas for including today's new ingredients and tastes in your daily cooking, this is a book that will ensure your dish of the day is a treat both to cook and to eat.

The book is divided into twelve monthly chapters with a recipe for every day of the year. How you use the book is up to you. You might want to flick through the whole year first and get stuck into the most appealing recipes straight away, or perhaps turn over a page a day, using the book like a real-life food calendar. *Dish a Day* has also been organised in a way that makes a bit of forward planning easy. Simply scan a month ahead for seasonal ideas

and put together a shopping list straight from the pages. However you like to do things, you'll find a whole year's worth of great food ideas in one place.

Set up like a calendar, this is a book that follows the cook's year, guiding you through the freshest ingredients available each month. Every recipe has been specially selected to make the best use of our seasonal produce and to guarantee that you don't miss out on the month's best buys. Keep an eye out for wonderful ideas for using asparagus in May, blueberries in July, and wild mushrooms in October. By following the year's natural rhythms and using its seasonal produce, you'll find you get the finest flavors when they're at their most inexpensive. You'll also get a chance to enjoy cooking in the way our mothers and grandmothers did, using a glut of summer tomatoes for little tomato and zucchini tartlets or turning a fall harvest of pumpkins into delicious pumpkin chestnut risotto. Bring your cooking into line with the seasons and you will no longer find that the recipe you're shopping for in December requires the fruits of a hot summer or that you're a month too early for those fresh peaches or crop of new potatoes.

Ingredients aren't the only things that change for the cook as the year passes by. The way we want to eat and prepare food varies too. To reflect this, these recipes run from the warm, hearty comfort food of fall and winter to the light and refreshing dishes of spring and summer. So chilly January heats up with hot & spicy beef with toasted pine nuts, while easy-to-prepare dishes using the new season's vegetables, fresh fish, and eggs dominate our healthy springtime menus.

Summer takes us outside to enjoy main-course salads and some inspiration for weekend grilling, while winter reintroduces the joys of afternoon baking and the slow cooking of comfort food.

As befits an everyday cookery book, we've tried to keep things simple and most of the recipes make an ideal after work supper or no-fuss dessert or afternoon treat. However, with every day of the year covered, there's room for those special food days too, so if you fancy making apricot-stuffed roast duck for New Year's Eve, eating the ultimate cheeseburger on July the fourth, or welcoming in the Chinese New Year with a dish of ginger chicken with toasted sesame seeds, you'll find these here too. Let *Dish a Day* breathe new life into your everyday cooking and start enjoying the best our seasons have to offer.

January

JANUARY
1

SERVES 4

ingredients

5 tbsp. fresh brown bread crumbs

½ cup fromage blanc or
   unsweetened yogurt

5 tbsp. chopped fresh parsley

5 tbsp. chopped fresh chives

salt and pepper

4 baby chickens

1 tbsp. sunflower oil

1½ lb. young spring vegetables
   such as carrots, zucchini, sugar
   snap peas, corn, and turnips, cut
   into small chunks

½ cup boiling chicken stock

2 tsp. cornstarch

⅔ cup dry white wine

poussins with herbs & wine

In a bowl, mix together the bread crumbs, one-third of the fromage blanc or unsweetened yogurt and 2 tablespoons each of parsley and chives. Season well with salt and pepper then spoon into the neck ends of the baby chickens. Place the chickens on a rack in a roasting pan, brush with oil and season well.

Roast in a preheated oven, 425°F/220°C, for 30–35 minutes or until the juices run clear, not pink, when the chickens are pierced with a skewer.

Place the vegetables in a shallow flameproof dish in one layer and add half the remaining herbs with the chicken stock. Cover and bake for 25–30 minutes until tender. Strain the vegetables, reserving the cooking juices, and keep warm.

Lift the chickens on to a serving plate and skim any fat from the juices in the pan. Add the reserved vegetable juices.

Blend the cornstarch with the wine and whisk into the sauce with the remaining fromage blanc or unsweetened yogurt. Whisk until boiling, then add the remaining herbs. Season to taste. Spoon the sauce over the chickens and serve with the vegetables.

cabbage soup with sausage

Put the sausages in water to cover generously and bring to a boil. Reduce the heat and simmer until firm. Drain the sausages and, when cool enough to handle, remove the skin, if you wish, and slice thinly.

Heat the oil in a large saucepan over a medium heat, add the onion, leek and carrots and cook for 3–4 minutes, stirring frequently, until the onion starts to soften.

Add the tomatoes, cabbage, garlic, thyme, stock, and sausages. Bring to a boil, reduce the heat to low and cook gently, partially covered, for about 40 minutes until the vegetables are tender.

Taste the soup and adjust the seasoning, if necessary. Ladle into warm bowls and serve with Parmesan cheese.

ingredients

12 oz. lean sausages, preferably
    highly seasoned
2 tsp. oil
1 onion, finely chopped
1 leek, halved lengthwise and thinly
    sliced
2 carrots, halved and thinly sliced
14 oz. can chopped tomatoes
12 oz. young green cabbage, cored
    and coarsely shredded
1–2 garlic cloves, finely chopped
pinch dried thyme
6¼ cups chicken or meat stock
salt and pepper
freshly grated Parmesan cheese,
    to serve

pasta with prosciutto

Trim off the fat from the prosciutto, then finely chop both the fat and the lean meat, keeping them separate. Melt the butter in a heavy-bottom skillet. Add the prosciutto fat and onion and cook over low heat, stirring occasionally, for 10 minutes.

Meanwhile, bring a large heavy-bottom pan of lightly salted water to a boil. Add the pasta, return to a boil, and cook for 8–10 minutes, or until tender but still firm to the bite. Add the lean prosciutto to the skillet and cook, stirring occasionally, for 2 minutes. Stir in the cream, then season to taste with pepper and heat through gently.

Drain the pasta and transfer to a warmed serving dish. Add the prosciutto mixture and toss well, then stir in the grated Parmesan cheese. Serve immediately.

ingredients

4 oz. prosciutto
4 tbsp. unsalted butter
1 small onion, finely chopped
salt and pepper
12 oz. dried green and white
    tagliatelle
2/3 cup heavy cream or panna
    da cucina
½ cup freshly grated Parmesan
    cheese

SERVES 6

tenderloin steak with bleu cheese sauce

Preheat the broiler or barbecue. Tie the tenderloin widthwise at regular intervals with string to form a neat shape. Put the butter into a small bowl and beat with a wooden spoon until softened. Spread 2 tablespoons of the softened butter evenly all over the tenderloin. Season to taste with pepper.

Put the tenderloin onto an oiled broiler or grill rack and cook under or over high heat, turning frequently, until browned on all sides, then cook at medium heat for 18–25 minutes, according to your taste, turning frequently.

Meanwhile, add the bleu cheese to the remaining softened butter and blend together until the mixture is smooth.

Put the shallot and Madeira into a pan, bring to a boil, and boil until reduced to about 2 tablespoons. Stir in the cream, then let simmer for 3 minutes. Add the cheese mixture, a little at a time, whisking after each addition until the sauce is smooth. Remove from the heat and season with salt and pepper.

Transfer the tenderloin to a warmed serving dish and let rest for 5 minutes. Slice into steaks and serve with green beans and the bleu cheese sauce drizzled over, garnished with chopped parsley. Serve any remaining sauce in a pitcher.

ingredients

1 tenderloin steak, about 3 lb.

5 tbsp. butter

salt and pepper

olive or vegetable oil, for oiling

4½ oz. bleu cheese, crumbled

1 shallot, minced

generous ⅓ cup Madeira or
    dry sherry

⅔ cup heavy cream

chopped fresh parsley, to garnish

freshly cooked green beans,
    to serve

peach & pecan empanadas

Preheat the oven to 400°F/200°C. Roll out the pastry on a lightly floured counter. Using a 6-inch saucer as a guide, cut out 8 circles.

Cut a small cross in the stem end of each peach. Lower them into a pan of boiling water and let stand for 10–30 seconds, depending on ripeness. Drain and cool under cold running water to prevent further cooking. Peel using a small knife.

Place a spoonful of sour cream on the center of each pastry circle and top with a few peach slices. Sprinkle over a little brown sugar and nuts. Brush each edge with a little beaten egg, fold the pastry over the filling, and press the edges together to seal. Crimp the edges and prick the tops.

Place on a baking sheet, brush with egg, and sprinkle with the sugar. Bake for 20 minutes, or until golden. Serve warm.

ingredients

all-purpose flour, for dusting

12 oz. ready-made puff pastry, thawed if frozen

3 fresh peaches

2/3 cup sour cream

4 tbsp. brown sugar

4 tbsp. pecan halves, toasted and finely chopped

beaten egg, to glaze

superfine sugar, for sprinkling

sweet potato & cheese soup

Melt the butter in a large pan over medium heat. Add the onion and leeks and cook, stirring, for about 3 minutes, until slightly softened. Add the sweet potatoes and cook for another 5 minutes, stirring, then pour in the stock, add the parsley and the bay leaf, and season with pepper. Bring to a boil, then lower the heat, cover the pan, and simmer for about 30 minutes.

Remove from the heat and let cool for 10 minutes. Remove and discard the bay leaf. Transfer half of the soup into a food processor and blend until smooth. Return to the pan with the rest of the soup, stir in the cream, and cook for another 5 minutes.

Gradually stir in the crumbled cheese until melted (do not let the soup boil). Remove from the heat and ladle into serving bowls. Garnish with finely crumbled bleu cheese and serve with slices of fresh bread.

ingredients

4 tbsp. butter

1 large onion, chopped

2 leeks, trimmed and sliced

6 oz. sweet potatoes, peeled and diced

3½ cups vegetable stock

1 tbsp. chopped fresh parsley

1 bay leaf

pepper

2/3 cup heavy cream

5½ oz. bleu cheese, crumbled

2 tbsp. finely crumbled bleu cheese,

thick slices of fresh bread, to serve

SERVES 4

lone star chili

Dry-fry the cumin seeds in a heavy-bottom skillet over medium heat, shaking the skillet, for 3–4 minutes until lightly toasted. Let cool, then crush in a mortar with a pestle. Alternatively, use a coffee grinder.

Toss the beef in the seasoned flour to coat. Melt the fat in a large, heavy-bottom pan. Add the beef, in batches, and cook until browned on all sides. Remove the beef with a slotted spoon and set aside.

Add the onions and garlic to the pan and cook gently for 5 minutes, or until softened. Add the cumin, oregano, paprika, and chilies and cook, stirring, for 2 minutes. Return the beef to the pan, pour over the lager, then add the chocolate. Bring to a boil, stirring, then reduce the heat, cover, and let simmer for 2–3 hours until the beef is very tender, adding more lager if necessary.

Serve with warmed flour tortillas and some sour cream to douse the flames. Wash it down with some additional ice-cold beer of your choice.

ingredients

1 tbsp. cumin seeds

1 lb. 7 oz. rump steak, cut into
   1-inch cubes

all-purpose flour, well seasoned with
   salt and pepper, for coating

3 tbsp. beef dripping, bacon fat,
   or vegetable oil

2 onions, finely chopped

4 garlic cloves, finely chopped

1 tbsp. dried oregano

2 tsp. paprika

4 dried red chilies, such as ancho
   or pasilla, crushed, or to taste

1 large bottle of South American
   lager

4 squares semisweet chocolate

TO SERVE

warmed flour tortillas

sour cream

steak waldorf salad

Heat a thick, cast-iron stove-top pan or heavy-bottom skillet over medium heat. Brush each steak with oil and season to taste with pepper. When hot, add the steaks to the pan, and cook for 6–7 minutes for rare or 8–10 minutes for medium, turning the steaks frequently and brushing once or twice with oil. Remove from the pan and set aside.

Meanwhile, stir the mustard into the mayonnaise. Put the lemon juice into a large bowl. Peel and core the apples, then cut them into small chunks and immediately toss them in the lemon juice. Stir in the mustard mayonnaise. Add the celery and walnuts to the apples and toss together.

Arrange the salad greens on 4 plates, then divide the apple mixture between them. Very thinly slice the steaks, arrange on top of the salad, and serve immediately.

ingredients

2 tenderloin steaks, about
    6 oz. each and 1-inch thick
olive or sunflower-seed oil,
    for brushing
1 tbsp. whole grain mustard
2/3 cup mayonnaise
1 tbsp. lemon juice
1 lb. 2 oz. eating apples
4 celery stalks, thinly sliced
generous 3/8 cup walnut halves,
    broken into pieces
3½ oz. mixed salad greens
pepper

breadcrumbed chicken morsels

Preheat the oven to 400°F/200°C. Put the bread crumbs into a large, shallow bowl. Add the romano cheese and mixed herbs and season well with salt and pepper. Mix together well. Beat the egg in a separate bowl. Dip the chicken strips into the beaten egg, then coat them in the bread crumb mixture. Arrange on a cookie sheet, then transfer to the preheated oven. Bake for 30 minutes until golden.

Meanwhile, to make the tartare sauce, put the mayonnaise into a bowl and stir in the lemon juice and chives. Add the garlic, capers, shallots, dill pickles, and olives and mix together well. Arrange the mixed salad greens on a large serving platter.

Remove the chicken from the oven and arrange over the salad greens. Garnish with lemon wedges and serve with the tartare sauce.

ingredients

1¾ cups fresh white or
   whole-wheat bread crumbs

3 tbsp. grated romano cheese

1 tbsp. dried mixed herbs

salt and pepper

1 egg

4 skinless chicken breasts, cut
   into thick strips

TARTARE SAUCE

generous ¾ cup mayonnaise

1 tbsp. lemon juice

2 tbsp. chopped fresh chives

1 garlic clove, finely chopped

1 tbsp. capers, chopped

2 shallots, finely chopped

1¾ oz. dill pickles, chopped

6 black olives, pitted and
   finely chopped

wedges of lemon, to garnish

fresh mixed salad greens, to serve

ginger pears with chocolate sauce

Peel the pears, leaving the stalks intact. Cut the base of each pear so that it sits upright. Carefully remove as much of the core as possible with a small spoon.

Place the water, sugar, gingerroot, cinnamon stick, and lemon juice in a small, heavy-bottom pan. Bring to a boil and boil for 5 minutes. Stand the pears upright in the pan and cook, turning occasionally, for 15–20 minutes, or until softened. Place each pear on a serving plate.

To make the chocolate sauce, place the cream and chocolate in a heatproof bowl and set over a pan of gently simmering water until the chocolate has melted. Stir until smooth. Transfer to a pitcher and serve immediately with the warm pears.

ingredients

4 dessert pears

2 cups water

generous ¾ cup golden
   superfine sugar

4-inch piece fresh gingerroot,
   peeled and sliced

½ cinnamon stick

dash of lemon juice

SAUCE

4 tbsp. light cream

7 oz. semisweet chocolate,
   broken into pieces

carrots à la grecque

Cut the carrots in half and then into quarters to form fingers of equal thickness. Put the carrots and all the remaining ingredients in a large saucepan and bring to a boil, then simmer, uncovered, for about 20 minutes until the carrots are tender.

Using a slotted spoon, transfer the carrots to a serving dish. Return the cooking liquid to a boil and boil until reduced by about half.

Strain the cooking liquid over the carrots and let cool. When cool, chill in the fridge for 3–4 hours or overnight. Serve at room temperature, garnished with chopped fresh herbs.

ingredients

1 lb. 9 oz. young carrots

1¼ cup olive oil

1¾ cups dry white wine

1 tbsp. Greek honey

2 sprigs fresh thyme

6 sprigs fresh parsley

1 bay leaf

2 garlic cloves, chopped finely

1 tbsp. coriander seeds, crushed
   lightly

salt and pepper

chopped fresh herbs, to garnish

JANUARY

12

SERVES 4

hot & spicy beef with toasted pine nuts

To make the marinade, mix the soy sauce with the cornstarch and water in a medium bowl. Add the beef and stir until the meat is well coated. Cover the bowl with plastic wrap and chill in the refrigerator for 1 hour.

Spread the pine nuts on a cookie sheet and toast under a broiler. Mix the lime juice, soy sauce, vinegar, cornstarch and 1 tablespoon of the peanut oil in a small bowl and set aside.

Heat the remaining peanut oil in a wok or large skillet. Stir-fry the gingerroot, chilies, and leek for 2 minutes. Add the beef and the marinade and stir-fry for 1 minute. Stir in the carrots, asparagus, and shallots and cook for 7 minutes, or until the beef is cooked through. Add the lime mixture, reduce the heat and simmer until the liquid thickens. Remove from the heat, sprinkle with the pine nuts, and serve with noodles.

ingredients

MARINADE

2 tbsp. soy sauce

1 tbsp. cornstarch

1 tbsp. water

STIR-FRY

1 lb. rump steak, cut into thin strips

1/3 cup pine nuts

1 lime, juiced

1 tbsp. soy sauce

2 tbsp. white wine vinegar

1 tsp. cornstarch

2 tbsp. peanut oil

3 tsp. grated fresh gingerroot

2 red, hot chilies, chopped finely

1 leek, sliced thinly

2 carrots, sliced thinly

3 1/2 oz. fine tip asparagus

3 shallots, sliced thinly

cooked noodles, to serve

ingredients

5 tbsp. oil

2 onions, sliced

1 lb. ground lamb

2 tbsp. yogurt

1 tsp. chili powder

1 tsp. finely chopped fresh
gingerroot

1 tsp. fresh garlic, crushed

1 tsp. salt

1½ tsp. garam masala

½ tsp. ground allspice

2 fresh green chilies

fresh cilantro leaves

salad greens, to serve

TO GARNISH

fresh cilantro leaves, chopped

1 lemon, cut into wedges

broiled ground lamb

Heat the oil in a pan. Add the sliced onions and cook over low heat until golden brown.

Place the ground lamb in a large bowl. Add the yogurt, chili powder, gingerroot, garlic, salt, garam masala, and ground allspice and mix to combine. Add the lamb mixture to the fried onions and stir-fry for 10–15 minutes. Remove the mixture from the heat and set aside.

Meanwhile, place the chilies and half of the cilantro leaves in a food processor and process. Alternatively, finely chop the chilies and cilantro with a sharp knife. Set aside until required.

Put the ground lamb mixture in a food processor and process. Alternatively, place in a large bowl and mash with a fork. Mix the lamb mixture with the chilies and cilantro and blend well.

Transfer the mixture to a shallow heatproof dish. Cook under a preheated medium-hot broiler for about 10–15 minutes, moving the mixture about with a fork. Watch it carefully to prevent it from burning.

Garnish with cilantro leaves and lemon wedges and serve with salad greens.

chicken & corn empanadas

Preheat the oven to 400°F/200°C. Place the chicken, corn, onion, olives, cilantro, Tabasco, cinnamon, and salt and pepper to taste in a bowl and mix together.

Roll out the pastry on a lightly floured work surface. Using a 6-inch saucer as a guide, cut out 4 rounds.

Place an equal quantity of filling on 1 half of each pastry round. Brush the edge of each round with beaten egg, fold the pastry over the filling, and press the edges together to seal. Crimp the edges with a fork and prick the tops.

Place on a baking sheet, brush with beaten egg and sprinkle lightly with salt. Bake in the preheated oven for 20 minutes, or until golden brown and hot in the centre.

ingredients

14 oz. cooked chicken, diced

14 oz. canned creamed-style
    corn kernels

1 small onion, finely chopped

8 pimento-stuffed green olives,
    finely chopped

2 tbsp. finely chopped fresh cilantro

1 tsp. Tabasco sauce, or to taste

1 tsp. cinnamon

salt and pepper

12 oz. ready-made puff pastry,
    thawed if frozen

all-purpose flour, for dusting

beaten egg, for sealing and glazing

ginger marmalade loaf

JANUARY
15

SERVES 6

Preheat the oven to 350°F/180°C. Grease and line the bottom and ends of a 2-lb. loaf pan. Place 1 tablespoon of the ginger marmalade in a small pan and reserve. Place the remaining marmalade in a bowl with the butter, sugar, and eggs. Sift in the flour, baking powder, and ground ginger and beat together until smooth. Stir in three-fourths of the nuts.

Spoon the mixture into the prepared loaf pan and smooth the top. Sprinkle with the remaining nuts and bake in the preheated oven for 1 hour, or until well risen and a skewer inserted into the center comes out clean. Let cool in the pan for 10 minutes, then turn out and peel off the lining paper. Transfer to a wire rack to cool until warm.

Set the pan of reserved marmalade over low heat to warm, then brush over the loaf and serve in slices.

ingredients

⅓ cup butter, softened, plus
    extra for greasing
⅓ cup ginger marmalade
scant 1 cup brown sugar
3 eggs, beaten
generous 1½ cups self-rising flour
½ tsp. baking powder
1 tsp. ground ginger
⅔ cup coarsely chopped pecans

COOK'S TIP
If the loaf begins to brown too much before it has cooked, lightly cover with a piece of foil.

vegetarian fajitas

SERVES 4

Heat the oil in a heavy-bottomed skillet. Add the onions and garlic and cook over a low heat, stirring occasionally, for 5 minutes, or until softened. Stir in the green and red bell peppers, chilies and cilantro and cook, stirring occasionally, for 10 minutes.

Meanwhile, dry-fry the tortillas, one at a time, for 30 seconds on each side in a separate skillet. Alternatively, stack the tortillas and heat in a microwave oven according to the packet instructions.

Add the mushrooms to the vegetable mixture and cook, stirring constantly, for 1 minute. Season to taste with salt and pepper. Divide the vegetables among the tortillas, roll up and serve immediately.

ingredients

2 tbsp. corn oil

2 onions, thinly sliced

2 garlic cloves, finely chopped

2 green bell peppers and 2 red bell peppers, seeded and sliced

4 fresh green chilies, seeded and sliced

2 tsp. chopped fresh cilantro

12 wheat tortillas

8 oz. mushrooms, sliced

salt and pepper

glazed turnips

SERVES 4–6

ingredients

2 lb. young turnips, peeled and quartered

2 tbsp. butter

1 tbsp. brown sugar

2/3 cup vegetable stock

1 sprig fresh rosemary

salt and pepper

Put the turnip into a pan of boiling salted water, bring back to a boil and simmer for 10 minutes. Drain well.

Melt the butter in the rinsed-out pan over a gentle heat, add the turnip and sugar and mix to coat well.

Add the stock with the rosemary and bring to a boil. Reduce the heat and simmer for 15–20 minutes with the lid off the pan so that the juices reduce and the turnips are tender and well glazed.

Remove the pan from the heat, discard the rosemary and season with salt and pepper to taste.

Serve immediately with roasted lamb, pork, or duck.

balti shrimp

SERVES 4

Seed and thinly slice 2 of the chilies and set aside for the garnish. Place the whole chilies, onions, lemon juice, tomato paste, 2 tablespoons of the fresh cilantro, the ground coriander, chili powder, turmeric, and salt in a food processor and process until a smooth paste forms. If necessary, thin with the water.

Heat the corn oil in a preheated wok or large, heavy-bottom skillet. Add the spice paste and cook, stirring constantly, for 4 minutes, or until thickened.

Add the shrimp and cook, stirring constantly, for 4–5 minutes, or until they have changed color. Transfer to a warmed serving plate, garnish with the sliced chilies and remaining fresh cilantro, and serve immediately.

ingredients

4 fresh green chilies

2 onions, coarsely chopped

2 tbsp. lemon juice

2 tbsp. tomato paste

3 tbsp. chopped fresh cilantro

1 tsp. ground coriander

1 tsp. chili powder

½ tsp. ground turmeric

pinch of salt

1 tbsp. water (optional)

3 tbsp. corn oil

32 large raw shrimp, shelled
and deveined

COOK'S TIP
For a cucumber raita,
beat 1¼ cups plain yogurt,
then stir in ¼ diced
cucumber, 1 chopped
fresh chili, ¼ teaspoon
ground cumin and salt
to taste. Let chill in the
refrigerator before serving.

SERVES 4

cauliflower cheese

Cook the cauliflower in a pan of boiling salted water for 4–5 minutes. It should still be firm. Drain, place in a hot 3-pint gratin dish and keep warm.

Melt the butter in the rinsed-out pan over a medium heat and stir in the flour. Cook for 1 minute, stirring continuously.

Remove from the heat and stir in the milk gradually until you have a smooth consistency.

Return to a low heat and continue to stir while the sauce comes to a boil and thickens. Reduce the heat and simmer gently, stirring constantly, for about 3 minutes until the sauce is creamy and smooth.

Remove from the heat and stir in the Cheddar cheese and a good grating of the nutmeg. Taste and season well with salt and pepper.

Pour the hot sauce over the cauliflower, top with the Parmesan, and place under a hot broiler to brown. Serve with perhaps a tomato, green salad, and some crusty bread.

ingredients

1 cauliflower, trimmed and cut into
    florets (1½ lb. prepared weight)
2 tbsp. butter
¼ cup all-purpose flour
2 cups milk
1 cup finely grated Cheddar cheese
whole nutmeg, for grating
salt and pepper
1 tbsp. grated Parmesan cheese

TO SERVE
1 small tomato
green salad
crusty bread

tagliarini with gorgonzola

Melt the butter in a heavy-based pan. Stir in 6 oz. of the cheese and melt, over a low heat, for about 2 minutes.

Add the heavy cream, wine, and cornstarch and beat with a whisk until fully incorporated.

Stir in the sage and season to taste with salt and white pepper. Bring to a boil over a low heat, whisking constantly, until the sauce thickens. Remove from the heat and set aside while you cook the pasta.

Bring a large saucepan of lightly salted water to a boil. Add the tagliarini and 1 tbsp. of the olive oil. Cook the pasta for 8–10 minutes, or until just tender, drain thoroughly and toss in the remaining olive oil. Transfer the pasta to a serving dish and keep warm.

Reheat the sauce over a low heat, whisking constantly. Spoon the Gorgonzola sauce over the tagliarini, then generously sprinkle over the remaining cheese and serve immediately.

ingredients

2 tbsp butter

8 oz. Gorgonzola cheese, coarsely crumbled

2/3 cup heavy cream

2 tbsp. dry white wine

1 tsp. cornstarch

4 fresh sage sprigs, finely chopped

salt and white pepper

14 oz. dried tagliarini

2 tbsp. olive oil

COOK'S TIP

When buying Gorgonzola, always check that it is creamy yellow with delicate green veining. Avoid hard or discolored cheese. It should have a rich, piquant aroma, not a bitter smell.

chicken-noodle soup

Put the chicken breasts and water in a pan over a high heat and bring to a boil. Lower the heat to its lowest setting and simmer, skimming the surface until no more foam rises. Add the onion, garlic, gingerroot, peppercorns, cloves, star anise, and a pinch of salt and continue to simmer for 20 minutes, or until the chicken is tender and cooked through. Meanwhile, grate the carrot along its length on the coarse side of a grater so you get long, thin strips.

Strain the chicken, reserving about 2 pints stock, but discarding any flavoring ingredients. (At this point you can leave the stock to cool and refrigerate overnight, so any fat solidifies and can be lifted off and discarded.) Return the stock to the rinsed-out pan with the carrot, celery, baby corncobs, and scallions and bring to a boil. Boil until the baby corncobs are almost tender, then add the noodles and continue boiling for 2 minutes.

Meanwhile, chop and add the chicken to the pan and continue cooking for about 1 minute longer until the chicken is reheated and the noodles are soft. Add seasoning to taste.

ingredients

2 skinless chicken breasts

3½ pints water

1 onion, with skin left on, cut in half

1 large garlic clove, cut in half

½-inch piece fresh gingerroot, peeled and sliced

4 black peppercorns, lightly crushed

4 cloves

2 star anise

salt and pepper

1 carrot, peeled

1 celery stalk, chopped

3½ oz. baby corncobs, cut in half lengthwise and chopped

2 scallions, finely shredded

4 oz. dried rice vermicelli noodles

grilled pork with orange sauce

Mix the orange juice, vinegar and garlic together in a shallow, nonmetallic dish and season to taste with pepper. Add the pork, turning to coat. Cover and leave in the refrigerator to marinate for up to 3 hours.

Meanwhile, mix all the gremolata ingredients together in a small mixing bowl, cover with plastic wrap and let chill in the refrigerator until required.

Heat a nonstick grill pan and brush lightly with olive oil. Remove the pork from the marinade, add to the pan and cook over a medium–high heat for 5 minutes on each side, or until the juices run clear when the meat is pierced with a skewer.

Meanwhile, pour the marinade into a small saucepan and simmer over a medium heat for 5 minutes, or until slightly thickened. Transfer the pork to a serving dish, pour the orange sauce over it and sprinkle with the gremolata. Serve immediately.

ingredients

4 tbsp. freshly squeezed orange
    juice
4 tbsp. red wine vinegar
2 garlic cloves, finely chopped
pepper
4 pork steaks, trimmed of all
    visible fat
olive oil, for brushing

GREMOLATA

3 tbsp. finely chopped fresh parsley
grated rind of 1 lime
grated rind of ½ lemon
1 garlic clove, very finely chopped

bœuf stroganof

Heat the oil in a large, nonstick skillet. Add the onion and cook, stirring, for 5 minutes, until softened and lightly colored.

Add the mushrooms and mustard to the skillet and cook, stirring occasionally, for a further 4-5 minutes, or until lightly colored. Add the beef to the skillet and cook, stirring occasionally, for 5 minutes, or until tender. Add the sour cream and salt and pepper, then heat, stirring constantly, until hot. Serve garnished with chopped parsley.

ingredients

2 tbsp. vegetable oil

1 onion, sliced coarsely

3¼ cups thinly sliced white
   mushrooms

1 tsp. French mustard

1 lb. round or sirloin steak, sliced
   thinly

1¼ cups sour cream

salt and pepper

chopped fresh parsley, to garnish

garlic-crusted fish with potatoes

Preheat the oven to 450°F/230°C.

Cut the potatoes into chunks and cook in a pan of lightly salted water for 15 minutes, or until tender. Drain well. Cream in the pan until smooth. Set over a low heat and beat in the milk, butter, and salt and pepper to taste.

Put the fish fillets in a roasting pan and brush the fish with the oil. Sprinkle the garlic on top, add salt and pepper to taste, then spread with the creamed potatoes. Roast in the oven for 8–10 minutes, or until the fish is just tender.

Meanwhile, preheat the broiler. Transfer the fish to the broiler and cook for about 2 minutes, or until golden brown. Sprinkle with the parsley and serve immediately.

ingredients

2 lb. mealy potatoes

salt and pepper

½ cup milk

2 tbsp. butter

4 white fish fillets, about 8 oz. each

1 tbsp. corn oil

4 garlic cloves, finely chopped

2 tbsp. chopped fresh parsley,
   to garnish

VARIATION

If you prefer, you can cook the potatoes unpeeled, but do scrub them first. Peel them as soon as they are cool enough to handle, then cream as above. This helps to preserve the vitamins and minerals that lie just beneath the skin.

creamed swede & potato

Cook the swedes and potatoes in a large pan of boiling salted water for 20 minutes until soft. Test with the point of a knife and if not cooked return to the heat for a further 5 minutes.

Drain well, return to the rinsed-out pan and heat for a few moments to ensure they are dry. Cream using a potato creamer until smooth. Season well with the salt and pepper and add the butter. Grate in as much of the nutmeg as you like and serve hot, garnished with the parsley.

ingredients

1 lb. swedes, peeled and diced

9 oz. mealy potatoes, peeled
   and diced

salt and pepper

2 tbsp. butter

whole nutmeg, for grating

fresh parsley sprigs, to garnish

sunshine risotto

Place the sun-dried tomatoes in a heatproof bowl and pour over enough boiling water to cover. Set aside to soak for 30 minutes, or until soft and supple. Drain and pat dry with paper towels, then shred finely and set aside.

Bring the stock to a boil in a pan, then reduce the heat and keep simmering gently over a low heat while you are cooking the risotto.

Heat the olive oil in a deep pan over a medium heat. Add the onion and cook, stirring occasionally, for 2 minutes, or until beginning to soften. Add the garlic and cook for a further 15 seconds.

Reduce the heat, add the rice and mix to coat in the oil. Cook, stirring constantly, for 2–3 minutes, or until the grains are translucent.

Gradually add the hot stock, a ladle at a time. Stir constantly and add more liquid as the rice absorbs each addition. Increase the heat to medium so that the liquid bubbles. After about 15 minutes, stir in the sun-dried tomatoes.

Continue adding the stock, stirring constantly, until the risotto has been cooking for 20 minutes, or until all the liquid is absorbed and the rice is creamy.

Remove the pan from the heat and stir in the chopped parsley and half the romano cheese. Spoon the risotto onto 6 warmed plates. Drizzle with extra virgin olive oil and sprinkle the remaining romano cheese on top. Serve immediately.

ingredients

about 12 sun-dried tomatoes

2¾ pints chicken or vegetable stock

2 tbsp. olive oil

1 large onion, finely chopped

4–6 garlic cloves, finely chopped

14 oz. risotto rice

2 tbsp. chopped fresh parsley

4 oz. freshly grated aged romano cheese

extra virgin olive oil, for drizzling

ingredients

3 tbsp. olive oil

1 onion, chopped

1 red bell pepper, seeded and diced

1 orange bell pepper, seeded and
    diced

1 lb. 12 oz. canned chopped
    tomatoes

1 tbsp. sun-dried tomato paste

1 tsp. paprika

8 oz. pepperoni sausage, sliced

2 tbsp. chopped fresh flat-leaf
    parsley, plus extra to garnish

salt and pepper

1 lb. dried garganelli

mixed salad greens, to serve

SERVES 4–5

pepperoni pasta

Heat 2 tablespoons of the olive oil in a large heavy-bottom skillet. Add the onion and cook over low heat, stirring occasionally, for 5 minutes, or until softened. Add the red and orange bell peppers, the tomatoes and their can juices, the sun-dried tomato paste, and paprika and bring to a boil. Add the pepperoni and parsley and season to taste with salt and pepper. Stir well, bring to a boil, then reduce the heat and let simmer for 10–15 minutes.

Meanwhile, bring a large heavy-bottom pan of lightly salted water to a boil. Add the pasta, return to a boil, and cook for 8–10 minutes, or until tender but still firm to the bite. Drain well and transfer to a warmed serving dish. Add the remaining olive oil and toss. Add the sauce and toss again. Sprinkle with parsley and serve immediately with mixed salad greens.

scallops with herb butter

Cut away any discolored parts from the scallops. Dry well and season with salt and pepper.

Heat a heavy-bottom skillet and brush with the oil. When the oil is smoking, add the scallops and cook for 1 minute, then turn and cook on the other side for 1 minute. It is a good idea to cook the scallops in 2 batches as, if you try to cook them all at once, you might end up with them stewing rather than pan-frying. The scallops should have a good golden color and a slight crust at the edges. Transfer to a warm plate and keep warm.

To make the herb butter, melt the butter in a pan and fry the garlic for a few seconds. Add the parsley and, while still foaming, pour over the scallops.

Serve at once with plenty of bread to mop up the juices.

ingredients

12 large shelled scallops, cleaned

salt and pepper

1 tbsp. vegetable oil

crusty bread, to serve

HERB BUTTER

1 tbsp. unsalted butter

2 garlic cloves, finely chopped

2 tbsp. chopped fresh parsley

bread & butter dessert

Preheat the oven to 350°F/180°C.

Use a little of the butter to grease an 8 x 10-inch baking dish and butter the slices of bread. Cut the bread into quarters and arrange half, overlapping, in the dish.

Scatter over half the fruit and peel, cover with the remaining bread slices and add the remaining fruit and peel.

In a bowl, whisk the eggs well and mix in the milk, cream and sugar. Pour this over the pudding and let stand for 15 minutes to allow the bread to soak up some of the egg mixture. Tuck in most of the fruit as you don't want it to burn in the oven. Grate the nutmeg over the top, according to taste, and sprinkle over the raw sugar.

Place the dessert on a baking sheet and bake at the top of the oven for 30–40 minutes until just set and golden brown.

Remove from the oven and serve warm with a little cream.

ingredients

3 tbsp. butter, softened

6 slices of thick white bread

2 oz. mixed fruit (golden raisins, currants and raisins)

1 oz. candied peel

3 large eggs

1¼ cups milk

⅔ cup heavy cream

¼ cup superfine sugar

whole nutmeg, for grating

1 tbsp. raw sugar

cream, to serve

VARIATIONS

Try dried apricots instead of mixed fruit and spread apricot jelly on the buttered bread. Alternatively, add a sliced banana and sprinkle with cinnamon or add sliced pear to slices of panettone, mixing a little vanilla extract into the egg.

SERVES 4

chicken & vegetable casserole

To make the filling, pour the stock into a large pan and bring to a boil. Add the chicken and mushrooms, lower the heat, cover the pan, and simmer for 25–30 minutes. Grease a 2-pint flameproof pie pan with butter. Remove the pan from the heat. Lift out the chicken and mushrooms and place in the prepared pie pan. Reserve the stock.

Preheat the oven to 400°F/200°C. In a bowl, mix the cornstarch with enough of the milk to make a smooth paste, then stir in the remaining milk. Stir into the stock. Pour into the pie pan, add the carrots and rosemary, and season well.

To make the topping, put the potatoes into a bowl. Add the onion and half the cheese, and mix. Spoon the mixture over the chicken, level the surface, then scatter over the remaining cheese. Bake for 30 minutes until golden. Remove from the oven, garnish with rosemary, and serve with vegetables.

ingredients

1¼ cups chicken stock

1 lb. boneless chicken, chopped

3½ oz. white mushrooms

1 tbsp. butter, for greasing

1 tbsp. cornstarch

⅔ cup milk

7 oz. carrots, peeled, blanched, and chopped

1 tbsp. chopped fresh rosemary

salt and pepper

TOPPING

2 lb. potatoes, peeled, cooked, and mashed

1 onion, grated

1 cup grated Cheddar cheese

sprigs of fresh rosemary, to garnish

SERVES 6

braised beef in red wine

Put the flour and pepper in a polythene bag, add the meat and shake well to coat each piece. Heat the oil in a large flameproof casserole. Add the meat and fry, in batches, for 5–10 minutes, stirring constantly, until browned on all sides. Remove with a slotted spoon and set aside.

Add the whole onions, the garlic and carrots to the casserole and fry for 5 minutes until beginning to soften. Return the meat to the casserole.

Pour in the wine, stirring in any glazed bits from the bottom, then add the stock, the tomatoes with their juice, lemon rind, bay leaf, parsley, basil, thyme, salt and pepper. Bring to a boil then cover the casserole.

Cook in a preheated oven, 350°F/180°C, for about 2 hours, until the meat is tender. Serve hot with rice.

ingredients

4 tbsp. all-purpose flour

salt and pepper

2 lb. stewing beef, cubed

4 tbsp. olive oil

12 oz. pearl onions

2 garlic cloves, chopped finely

2 cups sliced carrots

1¼ cups dry red wine

⅔ cup beef or chicken stock

14 oz. canned chopped tomatoes with herbs in juice

pared rind of 1 lemon

1 bay leaf

1 tbsp. chopped fresh flat-leaf parsley

1 tbsp. chopped fresh basil

1 tsp. chopped fresh thyme

boiled rice, to serve

CHAPTER

2

February

quick clam chowder

Heat the oil in a heavy-bottom pan. Add the bacon and cook over medium heat, stirring, for 5 minutes, or until the fat runs and it begins to crisp. Remove from the pan, drain on paper towels, and reserve.

Add the butter to the pan and stir to melt. Add the onion, celery, and potatoes with a pinch of salt. Cover and cook over low heat, stirring occasionally, for 10 minutes, or until soft. Stir in the leeks, the tomatoes and their juices, and 2 tablespoons of the parsley. Pour in the stock, bring to a boil, reduce the heat, and simmer for 10–15 minutes, or until the vegetables are tender. Season to taste with salt and pepper and stir in the clams.

Heat the soup through gently for 2–3 minutes, then ladle into warmed bowls, garnish with the remaining parsley and reserved bacon, and serve.

ingredients

2 tsp. corn oil

4 oz. rindless lean bacon, diced

2 tbsp. butter

1 onion, chopped

2 celery stalks, chopped

2 potatoes, chopped

salt and pepper

2 leeks, sliced

14 oz. canned chopped tomatoes

3 tbsp. chopped fresh parsley

5 cups fish stock

1 lb. 4 oz. canned clams, drained
    and rinsed

veal with prosciutto & sage

Place the veal scallops between 2 sheets of plastic wrap and pound with the flat end of a meat mallet or the side of a rolling pin until very thin. Transfer to a plate and sprinkle with the lemon juice. Set aside for 30 minutes, spooning the juice over them occasionally.

Pat the scallops dry with paper towels, season with salt and pepper, and rub with half the sage. Place a slice of prosciutto on each scallop and secure with a toothpick.

Melt the butter in a large, heavy-bottom skillet. Add the remaining sage and cook over low heat, stirring constantly, for 1 minute. Add the scallops and cook for 3–4 minutes on each side, until golden brown. Pour in the wine and cook for an additional 2 minutes.

Transfer the scallops to a warmed serving dish and pour the pan juices over them. Remove and discard the toothpicks and serve immediately.

ingredients

4 veal scallops

2 tbsp. lemon juice

salt and pepper

1 tbsp. chopped fresh sage leaves

4 slices prosciutto

2 oz. unsalted butter

3 tbsp. dry white wine

hot cheese soup

Melt the butter in a large, heavy-bottom pan. Sprinkle in the flour and cook, stirring constantly, for 1 minute. Remove the pan from the heat and gradually stir in the chicken stock and milk. Return to the heat and bring to a boil, stirring constantly, then let simmer for 3–4 minutes, or until the soup is thickened and smooth.

Add the grated carrots and let simmer for 3 minutes, then stir in the grated cheese. When the cheese has melted, season to taste with salt and pepper. Ladle the soup into warmed soup bowls and serve immediately with crusty bread.

ingredients

2 oz. butter

⅜ cup all-purpose flour

scant 2 cups chicken stock

1¼ cups milk

2 carrots, grated

6 oz. Cheddar cheese, grated

salt and pepper

crusty bread, to serve

beef stew with herb dumplings

Preheat the oven to 300°F/150°C.

Heat 1 tablespoon of the oil in a large skillet and fry the onion and garlic until soft and brown. Remove from the pan using a slotted spoon and place in a large casserole dish.

Trim the meat and cut into thick strips. Using the remaining oil, fry the meat in the skillet over a high heat, stirring well until it is brown all over. Sprinkle in the flour and stir well to prevent lumps. Season well.

Over a medium heat, pour in the stock, stirring all the time to make a smooth sauce, then continue to heat until boiling.

Carefully turn the contents of the skillet into the casserole dish. Add the bouquet garni and the wine. Cover and cook gently for 2–2½ hours.

Start making the dumplings 20 minutes before the stew is ready. Place all the ingredients except the water in a bowl and mix well. Just before adding the dumplings to the stew, add enough of the water to the mixture to form a firm but soft dough. Break the dough into 12 pieces and roll them into round dumplings (you might need some flour on your hands for this).

Remove the stew from the oven, check the seasoning, discard the bouquet garni and add the dumplings, pushing them down under the liquid. Cover and return the dish to the oven, continuing to cook for 15 minutes until the dumplings have doubled in size.

Serve piping hot with the parsley scattered over the top.

ingredients

3 tbsp. olive oil

2 onions, finely sliced

2 garlic cloves, chopped

2 lb. 4 oz. good-quality braising steak

2 tbsp. all-purpose flour

salt and pepper

300 ml/½ pint beef stock

bouquet garni (bunch of mixed fresh herbs)

1¼ cups red wine

1 tbsp. chopped fresh parsley, to garnish

HERB DUMPLINGS

4 oz. self-rising flour, plus extra for shaping

2 oz. suet

1 tsp. mustard

1 tbsp. chopped fresh parsley

1 tsp. chopped fresh sage

salt and pepper

4 tbsp. cold water

chicken liver pâté

Melt half the butter in a large frying pan over a medium heat and cook the onion for 3–4 minutes until soft and transparent. Add the garlic and continue to cook for a further 2 minutes.

Check the chicken livers and remove any discolored parts using a pair of scissors. Add the livers to the frying pan and cook over quite a high heat for 5–6 minutes until they are brown in color.

Season well with salt and pepper and add the mustard and brandy, if using.

Process the pâté in a blender or food processor until smooth. Add the remaining butter cut into small pieces and process again until creamy.

Press the pâté into a serving dish or 4 small ramekins, smooth the surface and cover. If it is to be kept for more than 2 days, you could cover the surface with a little clarified butter. Serve accompanied by toast fingers.

ingredients

5 oz. butter

1 onion, finely chopped

1 garlic clove, finely chopped

9 oz. chicken livers

salt and pepper

½ tsp. Dijon mustard

2 tbsp. brandy (optional)

brown toast fingers, to serve

ingredients

4 tbsp. butter, plus extra for
   greasing
2 lb. white fish fillets, such
   as plaice, skinned
salt and pepper
²/₃ cup dry white wine
1 tbsp. chopped fresh parsley,
   tarragon or dill
6 oz. small mushrooms, sliced
6 oz. cooked peeled shrimp
¼ cup all-purpose flour
½ cup heavy cream
2 lb. mealy potatoes, peeled
   and cut into chunks

fisherman's pie

Preheat the oven to 350°F/180°C. Butter a 3-pint baking dish.

Fold the fish fillets in half and place in the dish. Season well with salt and pepper, pour over the wine, and scatter over the herbs.

Cover with foil and bake for 15 minutes until the fish starts to flake. Strain off the liquid and reserve for the sauce. Increase the oven temperature to 425°F/220°C.

Sauté the mushrooms in a skillet with 1 tablespoon of the butter and spoon over the fish. Scatter over the shrimp.

Heat 2 tablespoons of the butter in a pan and stir in the flour. Cook for a few minutes without browning, remove from the heat, then add the reserved cooking liquid gradually, stirring well between each addition.

Return to the heat and gently bring to a boil, still stirring to ensure a smooth sauce. Add the cream and season to taste with salt and pepper. Pour over the fish in the dish and smooth over the surface.

Make the creamed potato by cooking the potatoes in boiling salted water for 15–20 minutes. Drain well and cream with a potato creamer until smooth. Season to taste with salt and pepper and add the remaining butter, stirring until melted.

Pile or pipe the potato onto the fish and sauce and bake for 10–15 minutes until golden brown.

salmon ramen

While you heat a broiler to high, bring the stock to a boil with the garlic clove and soy sauce in a pan, and bring another pan of water to a boil for cooking the noodles.

Mix the ingredients for the teriyaki glaze together and brush one surface of each salmon fillet with the glaze. Lightly brush the broiler rack with oil and broil the salmon fillets for 4 minutes on one side only. The flesh should flake easily and the centre should remain a bright pink. Remove the fish from the broiler and set aside.

Boil the noodles for 3 minutes until soft. Alternatively, cook according to the packet instructions. Drain and rinse.

Remove the garlic from the stock, then bring the stock back to a boil. Drop in the spinach leaves and scallions and leave them to boil until the leaves are just wilted. Use a slotted spoon to remove the spinach and scallions and divide them among 4 large bowls. Divide the noodles among the bowls, then add a salmon fillet to each. Carefully pour the boiling stock into each bowl.

Sprinkle with the bean sprouts, chili slices and cilantro leaves to serve.

ingredients

4 cups fish or vegetable stock

1 large garlic clove

½ tsp. light soy sauce

4 salmon fillets, 5 oz. each, skinned

peanut or corn oil, for broiling

5 oz. dried ramen or thin Chinese
 egg noodles

3½ oz. baby spinach leaves

4 scallions, chopped

TERIYAKI GLAZE

2½ tbsp. sake

2½ tbsp. dark soy sauce

2 tbsp. mirin or sweet sherry

½ tbsp. brown sugar

½ garlic clove, very finely chopped

¼-inch piece fresh gingerroot,
 peeled and very finely chopped

TO SERVE

3½ oz. bean sprouts

1 fresh green chili, seeded
 and sliced

fresh cilantro leaves

FEBRUARY

7

SERVES 4

COOK'S TIP

Dried ramen noodles are the ones you find wrapped together in tight bundles, often labeled simply as 'stir-fry noodles'. But, if you can't find any, just substitute any Japanese or Chinese egg noodles.

maple pecan pies

To make the pastry, sift the flour into a mixing bowl and rub in the butter with the fingertips until the mixture resembles bread crumbs. Add the sugar and egg yolks and mix to form a soft dough. Wrap the dough and chill in the refrigerator for 30 minutes. Preheat the oven to 400°F/200°C.

On a lightly floured work surface, roll out the pastry thinly, cut out 12 circles and use to line 12 tartlet pans. Prick the bases with a fork. Line each pan with parchment paper and fill with dried beans or pie weights. Bake in the preheated oven for 10–15 minutes until light golden. Remove the paper and beans and bake for a further 2–3 minutes. Let cool on a cooling rack.

Mix half the maple syrup and half the cream in a bowl. Put the sugar, cream of tartar and water in a pan and heat gently until the sugar dissolves. Bring to a boil and boil until light golden. Remove from the heat and stir in the maple syrup and cream mixture.

Return the pan to the heat and cook to the soft ball stage (240°F/116°C): that is, when a little of the mixture dropped into a bowl of cold water forms a soft ball. Stir in the remaining cream and leave until cool. Brush the remaining maple syrup over the edges of the pies. Put the chopped pecans in the pastry cases and spoon in the toffee. Top each pie with a pecan half. Let cool completely before serving.

ingredients

PASTRY

1 cup all-purpose flour, plus
    extra for dusting

3 tablespoons butter, cut into
    small pieces

¼ cup superfine sugar

2 egg yolks

FILLING

2 tbsp. maple syrup

⅔ cup heavy cream

½ cup superfine sugar

pinch of cream of tartar

6 tbsp. water

4 oz. shelled pecans, chopped

12 pecan halves, to decorate

cheese toasts

Toast the bread under the medium broiler on one side only.

Put the cheese into a pan and add the butter and beer. Heat slowly over a low heat, stirring continuously. Add some salt and pepper and the mustard powder and stir well until the mixture is thick and creamy. Allow to cool slightly before adding the egg.

Spread the mixture over the untoasted side of the bread and place under the hot broiler until golden and bubbling. Serve at once.

ingredients

4 slices of bread

8 oz. mature Cheddar cheese, grated

1 tbsp. butter

3 tbsp. beer

salt and pepper

½ tsp. dry mustard powder

1 egg, beaten

chicken with pistachio nuts

Combine the chicken stock, soy sauce, and sherry with 1 teaspoon of cornstarch. Stir well and set aside. Combine the egg white, salt, 2 tablespoons of the oil, and 2 teaspoons of cornstarch. Toss the chicken in the mixture to coat.

In a wok or skillet, heat the remaining vegetable oil until hot. Add the chicken in batches and stir-fry until golden. Remove from the wok and drain on paper towels, then set aside to keep warm. Add more oil to the wok if needed and stir-fry the mushrooms, then add the broccoli and cook for 2–3 minutes.

Return the chicken to the wok and add the beansprouts, water chestnuts, and pistachio nuts. Stir-fry until all the ingredients are thoroughly warm. Add the chicken stock mixture and cook, stirring continuously until thickened. Serve immediately over a bed of rice, garnished with pistachios.

ingredients

¼ cup chicken stock

2 tbsp. soy sauce

2 tbsp. dry sherry

3 tsp. cornstarch

1 egg white, beaten

½ tsp. salt

4 tbsp. peanut or vegetable oil

1 lb. chicken breast, cut into strips

1 lb. mushrooms, sliced thinly

1 head of broccoli, cut into florets

5½ oz. beansprouts

3½ oz. canned water chestnuts, drained and sliced thinly

generous 1 cup pistachio nuts, plus extra to garnish (optional)

boiled white rice, to serve

SERVES 4

ginger chicken with toasted sesame seeds

In a medium dish, combine the soy sauce with 4 tablespoons of water. Toss and coat the chicken strips in the sauce. Cover the dish with plastic wrap and refrigerate for 1 hour. Remove the chicken from the marinade with a slotted spoon.

Heat the oil in a wok or skillet, and stir-fry the chicken and leek until the chicken is browned and the leek is beginning to soften. Stir in the vegetables, gingerroot, and wine. Reduce the heat, cover and simmer for 5 minutes.

Place the sesame seeds on a cookie sheet under a hot broiler. Stir them once to make sure they toast evenly. Set aside to cool.

In a small bowl, combine the cornstarch with the water and whisk until smooth. Gradually add the liquid to the wok, stirring constantly until thickened. Pile on a bed of hot rice and top with the sesame seeds, then serve.

ingredients

MARINADE

4 tbsp. soy sauce

4 tbsp. water

STIR-FRY

1 lb 2 oz. chicken breasts, skinned, cut into strips

2 tbsp. peanut oil

1 leek, sliced thinly

1 head of broccoli, cut into small florets

2 carrots, sliced thinly

½ cauliflower, cut into small florets

1 tsp. grated fresh gingerroot

5 tbsp. white wine

2 tbsp. sesame seeds

1 tbsp. cornstarch

1 tbsp. water

cooked rice, to serve

broiled mushroom & spinach-stuffed trout

Clean the trout, trim the fins with a pair of scissors and wipe the inside of the fish with paper towels. Leave the head and tail on and slash the skin of each fish on both sides about 5 times. Brush with the oil and season well with salt and pepper, both inside and out.

To make the stuffing, melt the butter in a small pan and gently soften the shallots for 2–3 minutes. Add the mushrooms and continue to cook for a further 2 minutes. Add the spinach and heat until it is just wilted.

Remove from the heat and add the herbs, lemon rind and a good grating of nutmeg. Allow to cool.

Fill the trout with the mushroom and spinach stuffing, then reshape them as neatly as you can.

Broil under a medium broiler for 10–12 minutes, turning once. The skin should be brown and crispy.

To make the tomato salsa, mix together all the ingredients.

Serve the trout hot with the tomato salsa spooned over them.

ingredients

2 whole trout, about 12 oz. each

1 tbsp. vegetable oil

salt and pepper

STUFFING

1 tablespoon butter

2 shallots, finely chopped

2 oz. mushrooms, finely chopped

2 oz. baby spinach

1 tbsp. chopped fresh parsley
   or tarragon

grated rind of 1 lemon

whole nutmeg, for grating

TOMATO SALSA

2 tomatoes, peeled, seeded
   and finely diced

4-inch piece of cucumber, finely
   diced

2 scallions, finely chopped

1 tbsp. olive oil

salt and pepper, to taste

quick pork & pasta stir-fry

Heat the oil in a wok or large skillet over a medium heat and add the chili powder, garlic, and red cabbage. Stir-fry for 2–3 minutes.

Stir in the rest of the vegetables and cook for another 2 minutes. Add the meat, then increase the heat and stir-fry for 5 minutes, or until the pork is well cooked and the dish is piping hot. Serve immediately over fettucine or vermicelli.

ingredients

1 tbsp. peanut oil

½ tsp. chili powder, or to taste

2 garlic cloves, crushed

½ red cabbage, shredded

2 leeks, sliced thinly

1 orange bell pepper, sliced thinly

1 carrot, sliced thinly

1 zucchini, sliced thinly

12 oz. pork tenderloin, cubed

cooked fettucine or vermicelli,
  to serve

vanilla hearts

Lightly grease a cookie sheet with a little butter. Strain the flour into a large mixing bowl and rub in the butter with your fingertips until the mixture resembles fine bread crumbs.

Stir in the superfine sugar and vanilla extract and bring the mixture together with your hands to make a smooth firm dough.

On a lightly floured surface, roll out the dough to a thickness of 1 inch. Stamp out 12 hearts with a heart-shaped cookie cutter measuring about 2 inches across and 1 inch deep.

Arrange the hearts on the prepared cookie sheet. Bake in a preheated oven, 350°F/180°C, for 15–20 minutes until the hearts are a light golden color.

Transfer the vanilla hearts to a wire rack and let cool. Dust the cookies with a little superfine sugar just before serving.

ingredients

⅔ cup butter, cut into small pieces,
  plus extra for greasing

2 cups all-purpose flour

½ cup superfine sugar, plus extra
  for dusting

1 tsp vanilla extract

COOK'S TIP

Place a fresh vanilla pod in your sugar and keep it in a storage jar for several weeks to give the sugar a delicious vanilla flavor .

southwestern seafood stew

SERVES 4

Preheat the oven to 400°F/200°C. Place the bell pepper quarters skin side up in a roasting pan with the tomatoes, chilies, and garlic. Sprinkle with the dried oregano and drizzle with oil. Roast in the oven for 30 minutes, or until the bell peppers are well browned and softened.

Remove the roasted vegetables from the oven and let stand until cool enough to handle. Peel off the skins from the bell peppers, tomatoes, and chilies and chop the flesh. Finely chop the garlic.

Heat the oil in a large pan. Add the onion and cook for about 5 minutes, or until softened. Add the bell peppers, tomatoes, chilies, garlic, stock, lime rind and juice, chopped cilantro, bay leaf, and salt and pepper to taste. Bring to a boil, then stir in the seafood. Reduce the heat, cover, and let simmer gently for 10 minutes, or until the seafood is just cooked through. Discard the bay leaf, then garnish with chopped cilantro before serving with warmed flour tortillas.

ingredients

1 each of yellow, red, and orange
   bell peppers, cored, seeded,
   and quartered
1 lb. ripe tomatoes
2 large fresh mild green chilies,
   such as poblano
6 garlic cloves, peeled
2 tsp. dried oregano or dried
   mixed herbs
2 tbsp. olive oil, plus extra
   for drizzling
1 large onion, finely chopped
2 cups fish, vegetable, or chicken
   stock
finely grated rind and juice of 1 lime
2 tbsp. chopped fresh cilantro,
   plus extra to garnish
1 bay leaf
salt and pepper
1 lb. red snapper fillets, skinned and
   cut into chunks
8 oz. raw shrimp, shelled
8 oz. cleaned squid, cut into rings
warmed flour tortillas, to serve

rigatoni with spicy bacon & tomato sauce

Heat the oil and garlic in a large skillet over a medium-low heat. Cook until the garlic is just beginning to color. Add the bacon and cook until browned. Stir in the tomatoes and chili flakes. Season with a little salt and pepper. Bring to a boil, then simmer over a medium-low heat for 30–40 minutes, or until the oil separates from the tomatoes.

Cook the pasta in plenty of boiling salted water until al dente. Drain and transfer to a warm serving dish. Pour the sauce over the pasta. Add the basil and romano, then toss well to mix. Serve at once.

ingredients

6 tbsp. olive oil

3 garlic cloves, sliced thinly

scant ⅓ cup lean bacon, chopped

1 lb 12 oz. canned chopped
   tomatoes

½ tsp. dried chili flakes

salt and pepper

4 cups rigatoni

10 fresh basil leaves, shredded

2 tbsp freshly grated romano

guinea fowl with cabbage

Preheat the oven to 475°F/240°C.

Rub the guinea fowl with the oil and season to taste inside and out with salt and pepper. Add the apple and parsley sprigs to the guinea fowl's cavity and truss to tie the legs together. Place the guinea fowl in a roasting pan and roast in the oven for 20 minutes to color the breasts. When the guinea fowl is brown, reduce the oven temperature to 325°F/160°C.

Meanwhile, bring a large pan of salted water to a boil. Add the cabbage and blanch for 3 minutes. Drain, rinse in cold water and pat dry.

Place the lardons in a flameproof casserole dish over a medium-high heat and sauté until they give off their fat. Use a slotted spoon to remove the lardons from the casserole and set aside.

Add the onion to the fat left in the casserole and cook, stirring frequently, for 5 minutes, or until the onion is tender, but not brown. Stir the bouquet garni into the casserole with a very little salt and a pinch of pepper, then return the lardons to the casserole.

Remove the guinea fowl from the oven. Add the cabbage to the casserole, top with the guinea fowl and cover the surface with a piece of wet waxed paper. Cover the casserole and put it in the oven for 45 minutes–1 hour, or until the guinea fowl is tender and the juices run clear when a skewer is inserted into the thickest part of the meat.

Remove the guinea fowl from the casserole and cut into serving portions. Stir the parsley into the cabbage and onion, then taste and adjust the seasoning if necessary. Serve the guinea fowl portions on a bed of cabbage and onion.

ingredients

1 oven-ready guinea fowl, weighing 2 lb. 12 oz.

½ tbsp. corn oil

salt and pepper

½ apple, peeled, cored and chopped

several fresh flat-leaf parsley sprigs, stems bruised

1½ tbsp. chopped fresh flat-leaf parsley

1 large savoy cabbage, coarse outer leaves removed, cored and quartered

1 thick piece of smoked belly of pork, weighing about 5 oz., rind removed and cut into thin lardons, or 5 oz. unsmoked lardons

1 onion, sliced

1 bouquet garni

COOK'S TIP

It is important not to add too much salt to the onion as the lardons will be salty.

jelly roll

Sift the flour into a mixing bowl and add the salt and suet. Mix together well. Stir in the lemon rind and the sugar.

Make a well in the centre and add the liquid to give a light, elastic dough. Knead lightly until smooth. If you have time, wrap the dough in plastic wrap and leave it to rest for 30 minutes.

Roll the dough into an 8 x 10-inch rectangle.

Spread the jelly over the dough, leaving a ½ inch border. Brush the border with the milk and roll up the dough carefully from one short end. Seal the ends.

Wrap the roll loosely in waxed paper and then in foil, sealing the ends well.

Prepare a steamer by half filling it with water and putting it on to boil. Place the roll in the steamer and steam over rapidly boiling water for 1½–2 hours, making sure you top up the water from time to time.

When cooked, remove from the steamer, unwrap and serve on a warm plate, cut into slices, with cream.

ingredients

8 oz. self-rising flour

pinch of salt

4 oz. suet

grated rind of 1 lemon

1 tbsp. sugar

½ cup mixed milk and water

4–6 tbsp. strawberry jelly

2 tbsp. milk

cream, to serve

tarragon chicken

Season the chicken with salt and pepper and place in a single layer in a large, heavy-bottom skillet. Pour in the wine and enough chicken stock just to cover and add the garlic and dried tarragon. Bring to a boil, reduce the heat, and poach gently for 10 minutes, or until the chicken is cooked through and tender. Remove the chicken with a slotted spoon or tongs, cover, and keep warm.

Strain the poaching liquid into a clean skillet and skim off any fat from the surface. Bring to a boil and cook until reduced by about two-thirds. Stir in the cream, return to a boil, and cook until reduced by about half. Stir in the fresh tarragon.

Slice the chicken breasts and arrange on warmed plates. Spoon over the sauce, garnish with tarragon sprigs, and serve immediately.

ingredients

4 skinless, boneless chicken
    breasts, about 6 oz. each
salt and pepper
½ cup dry white wine
1–1¼ cups chicken stock
1 garlic clove, finely chopped
1 tbsp dried tarragon
¾ cup heavy cream
1 tbsp chopped fresh tarragon
fresh tarragon sprigs, to garnish

italian sole

Melt the butter in a large pan, stirring over low heat. Remove the pan from the heat and add the bread crumbs, walnuts, the zest and juice of 1 lemon, half of the rosemary, and half of the parsley.

Gently press the bread crumb mixture over the top of the sole fillets. Place the sole fillets in a shallow, foil-lined roasting pan.

Bake in a preheated oven, 400°F/200°C, for 25–30 minutes.

Mix the garlic, the remaining lemon zest and juice, rosemary, parsley, and the chili in a bowl. Beat in the walnut oil and mix well to combine. Drizzle the dressing over the sole fillets as soon as they are cooked.

Transfer the fish to serving plates and serve immediately with salad greens.

ingredients

2 tbsp. butter

1 cup whole-wheat bread crumbs

3 tbsp. chopped walnuts

grated zest and juice of 2 lemons

2 sprigs rosemary, stalks removed

2 tbsp. chopped parsley

4 sole fillets, each about 5½ oz.

1 garlic clove, crushed

1 small red chili, diced

3 tbsp. walnut oil

salad greens, to serve

VARIATION

If preferred, the walnuts may be omitted from the crust. In addition, extra-virgin olive oil can be used instead of walnut oil, if you prefer.

sweet-&-sour red cabbage

Cut the cabbage into fourths, remove the center stalk and shred finely.

Pour the oil into a large pan and add the red cabbage, onion, garlic, and apple.

Sprinkle on the sugar, cinnamon, and juniper berries and grate a quarter of the nutmeg into the pan.

Pour over the red wine vinegar and orange juice and add the orange rind. Stir well and season with the salt and pepper. The pan will be quite full but the volume of the cabbage will reduce during cooking.

Cook over medium heat, stirring well from time to time, until the cabbage is just tender but still has 'bite'. This will take 10–15 minutes depending on how finely the cabbage is sliced.

Stir in the red currant jelly and add more salt and pepper if necessary. Serve hot.

ingredients

1 red cabbage, about 1 lb. 10 oz.

2 tbsp. olive oil

2 onions, finely sliced

1 garlic clove, chopped

2 small cooking apples, peeled, cored and sliced

2 tbsp. muscovado sugar

½ tsp. ground cinnamon

1 tsp. crushed juniper berries

whole nutmeg, for grating

2 tbsp. red wine vinegar

grated rind and juice of 1 orange

salt and pepper

2 tbsp. red currant jelly

COOK'S TIP

Red cabbage is a traditional accompaniment for game and meat dishes. It is also truly delicious served with sausages for a simple supper.

creamy carrot & parsnip soup

Melt the butter in a large pan over low heat. Add the onion and cook, stirring, for 3 minutes, until slightly softened. Add the carrots and parsnips, cover the pan, and cook, stirring occasionally, for about 15 minutes, until the vegetables have softened a little. Stir in the gingerroot, orange zest, and stock. Bring to a boil, then reduce the heat, cover the pan, and simmer for 30–35 minutes, until the vegetables are tender. Remove the soup from the heat and let cool for 10 minutes.

Transfer the soup into a food processor and blend until smooth (you may need to do this in batches). Return the soup to the pan, stir in the cream, and season well with salt and pepper. Warm through gently over low heat. Remove from the heat and ladle into soup bowls. Garnish each bowl with a swirl of cream and a sprig of cilantro and serve with crusty rolls.

ingredients

4 tbsp. butter

1 large onion, chopped

1 lb. carrots, peeled and chopped

2 large parsnips, peeled and chopped

1 tbsp. grated fresh gingerroot

1 tsp. grated orange zest

2½ cups vegetable stock

½ cup light cream

salt and pepper

fresh crusty rolls, to serve

GARNISH

light cream

sprigs of fresh cilantro

spicy corn fritters

Place the corn, chilies, garlic, lime leaves, cilantro, egg, and cornmeal in a large mixing bowl, and stir to combine. Add the green beans to the ingredients in the bowl and mix well, using a wooden spoon.

Divide the mixture into small, evenly sized balls. Flatten the balls of mixture between the palms of your hands to form rounds. Heat a little peanut oil in a preheated wok or large skillet until really hot. Cook the fritters, in batches, until brown and crispy on the outside, turning occasionally.

Leave the fritters to drain on paper towels while cooking the remaining fritters. Transfer the drained fritters to warm serving plates and serve immediately.

ingredients

¾ cup canned or frozen corn kernels

2 red chilies, seeded and very finely chopped

2 cloves garlic, crushed

10 lime leaves, finely chopped

2 tbsp. chopped fresh cilantro

1 large egg

½ cup cornmeal

3½ oz. fine green beans, finely sliced

peanut oil

quick chocolate mousse

Heat the cream in a pan over a low heat for about 3–4 minutes until almost boiling.

Break up or chop the chocolate into small pieces and place in a blender.

Pour the hot cream into the blender and then blend together until smooth.

Pour in the eggs and blend again until well mixed. Add the Marsala and give the mixture a final blend.

Pour into 6 ramekin dishes and allow to cool. Cover with plastic wrap and chill for about 2 hours. Serve decorated with the grated white chocolate.

ingredients

1¼ cups light cream

7 oz. bittersweet chocolate (should have at least 52% cocoa solids)

2 eggs, lightly beaten

2 tbsp. Marsala

2 tbsp. grated white chocolate, to decorate

lamb tagine

Heat the corn oil in a large, heavy-bottom skillet or flameproof casserole. Add the onion and lamb cubes and cook over medium heat, stirring frequently, for 5 minutes, or until the meat is lightly browned all over. Add the chopped garlic, vegetable stock, orange rind and juice, honey, cinnamon stick, and gingerroot. Bring to a boil, then reduce the heat, cover with a lid and let simmer for 45 minutes.

Using a sharp knife, halve the eggplant lengthwise and slice thinly. Add to the skillet with the chopped tomatoes and apricots. Cover and cook for an additional 45 minutes, or until the lamb is tender. Stir in the cilantro, season to taste with salt and pepper and serve immediately, straight from the skillet, with the freshly cooked couscous.

ingredients

½-inch piece fresh gingerroot, finely chopped

1 eggplant

4 tomatoes, peeled and chopped

⅔ cup no-soak dried apricots

2 tbsp. chopped fresh cilantro

salt and pepper

freshly cooked couscous, to serve

moules marinières

Clean the mussels by scrubbing or scraping the shells and pulling off any beards. Discard any with broken shells or any that refuse to close when tapped with a knife. Rinse the mussels under cold running water.

Pour the wine into a large, heavy-bottom pan, add the shallots and bouquet garni and season to taste with pepper. Bring to a boil over a medium heat. Add the mussels, cover tightly and cook, shaking the pan occasionally, for 5 minutes. Remove and discard the bouquet garni and any mussels that remain closed.

Divide the mussels between 4 soup plates with a slotted spoon. Tilt the pan to let any sand settle, then spoon the cooking liquid over the mussels and serve immediately with crusty bread.

ingredients

4 lb. 8 oz. live mussels

1¼ cups dry white wine

6 shallots, finely chopped

1 bouquet garni

pepper

crusty bread, to serve

COOK'S TIP
Never eat mussels that you have collected from the beach yourself, as they may have been polluted and could cause serious illness.

peanut butter cookies

Preheat the oven to 350°F/180°C, then grease 3 cookie sheets. Place the butter and peanut butter in a bowl and beat together. Beat in the sugars, then gradually beat in the egg and vanilla. Sift the flour, baking soda, baking powder, and salt into the bowl and stir in the oats.

Drop spoonfuls of the mixture on to the cookie sheets, spaced well apart to allow for spreading. Flatten slightly with a fork. Bake in the oven for 12 minutes, or until lightly browned. Let cool on the cookie sheets for 2 minutes, then transfer to wire racks to cool completely.

MAKES 26

ingredients

½ cup butter, softened, plus extra
   for greasing
scant ½ cup crunchy peanut butter
generous ½ cup golden superfine
   sugar
generous ½ cup brown sugar
1 egg, beaten
½ tsp. vanilla extract
⅔ cup all-purpose flour
½ tsp. baking soda
½ tsp. baking powder
pinch of salt
1½ cups rolled oats

lemon & ricotta pancakes

Place the ricotta cheese, sugar, and egg yolks in a large bowl and mix together. Stir in the lemon rind and melted butter. Strain in the flour and fold in.

Place the egg whites in a separate, spotlessly clean bowl and whisk until soft peaks form. Gently fold the egg whites into the ricotta mixture.

Set a large, nonstick skillet over medium heat and add heaped tablespoonfuls of batter, allowing room for them to spread. Cook for 1–2 minutes, or until the underside is colored, then turn over with a spatula and cook on the other side for an additional 2 minutes. Wrap in a clean dish towel to keep warm until all the pancakes are cooked. Serve with the warmed jelly.

ingredients

scant 1¼ cups ricotta cheese

5 tbsp. golden superfine sugar

3 large eggs, separated

finely grated rind of 1 lemon

2 tbsp. melted butter

6 tbsp. all-purpose flour

warmed cherry or blueberry jelly, to serve

COOK'S TIP

Do not spread the pancake batter too thinly in the skillet. The finished pancakes should measure about 4–5 inches across.

macaroni with sausage, pepperoncini & olives

Heat the oil in a large skillet over a medium heat. Add the onion and cook for 5 minutes until soft. Add the garlic and cook for a few seconds, until just beginning to color. Add the sausage and cook until evenly browned. Stir in the pepperoncini, tomatoes, oregano, and stock. Season with salt and pepper. Bring to a boil, then simmer over a medium heat for 10 minutes, stirring occasionally.

Cook the macaroni in plenty of boiling salted water until al dente. Drain and transfer to a warm serving dish.

Add the olives and half the cheese to the sauce, then stir until the cheese has melted. Pour the sauce over the pasta. Toss well to mix. Sprinkle with the remaining cheese and serve at once.

ingredients

1 tbsp. olive oil

1 large onion, chopped finely

2 garlic cloves, chopped very finely

2 cups pork sausage, peeled and chopped coarsely

3 canned pepperoncini, or other hot red peppers, drained and sliced

14 oz. canned chopped tomatoes

2 tsp. dried oregano

½ cup chicken stock or red wine

salt and pepper

4 cups dried macaroni

12–15 black olives, pitted and cut into fourths

⅔ cup freshly grated cheese, such as Gruyère

CHAPTER

3

March

pot roasted leg of lamb

Wipe the lamb all over with paper towels, trim off any excess fat and season to taste with salt and pepper, rubbing well in. Lay the sprigs of rosemary over the lamb, cover evenly with the bacon strips, and tie securely in place with kitchen string.

Heat the oil in a skillet and fry the lamb over a medium heat for about 10 minutes, turning several times. Remove from the skillet.

Preheat the oven to 325°F/160°C. Transfer the oil from the skillet to a large flameproof casserole dish and cook the garlic and onions for 3–4 minutes until the onions are beginning to soften. Add the carrots and celery and cook for a further few minutes.

Lay the lamb on top of the vegetables and press down to partly submerge. Pour the wine over the lamb, add the tomato paste, and simmer for 3–4 minutes. Add the stock, tomatoes, and herbs and season to taste with salt and pepper. Return to a boil for a further 3–4 minutes.

Cover the casserole tightly and cook in the oven for 2–2½ hours until very tender.

Remove the lamb from the casserole and, if you like, remove the bacon and herbs together with the string. Keep the lamb warm. Strain the juices, skimming off any excess fat, and serve separately. The vegetables may be put around the joint or in a dish. Garnish with sprigs of rosemary.

ingredients

1 leg of lamb, weighing 3 lb. 8 oz.

salt and pepper

3–4 fresh rosemary sprigs

4 oz. lean bacon strips

4 tbsp. olive oil

2–3 garlic cloves, crushed

2 onions, sliced

2 carrots, sliced

2 celery stalks, sliced

1¼ cups dry white wine

1 tbsp. tomato paste

1¼ cups lamb or chicken stock

3 medium tomatoes, peeled, quartered and seeded

1 tbsp. chopped fresh parsley

1 tbsp. chopped fresh oregano or marjoram

fresh rosemary sprigs, to garnish

chocolate fondue

Prepare the fruit according to type, cutting it into bite-size pieces. Brush apples, pears, and bananas with a little lemon juice to prevent them discoloring. Cut the sponge cake into cubes. Arrange the fruit and cake on several serving plates.

Place the chocolate and cream in the top of a double boiler and heat gently, stirring constantly, until melted and smooth. Alternatively, melt the chocolate and cream in a heatproof bowl set over a pan of barely simmering water. Remove the pan or bowl from the heat. Stir in the rum and sugar. Pour the mixture into a ceramic fondue pot set over a burner and hand the fruit and cake separately. Each guest can then spear their chosen piece and dip it in the hot chocolate mixture.

ingredients

selection of fresh fruit, such as
    apples, bananas, pears, seedless
    grapes, peaches, and oranges
juice of 1 lemon (optional)
small sponge or Madeira cake
8 oz. semisweet chocolate, broken
    into pieces
6 tbsp. heavy cream
2 tbsp. dark rum
½ cup confectioners' sugar

COOK'S TIP
Make sure that the chocolate is melted over very low heat. If the chocolate is too hot, then it may burn and turn grainy. Do not let any water splash on to the chocolate, otherwise it will seize and is unsuable.

VARIATION
Use white chocolate instead of the semisweet chocolate and use other types of fruit, such as strawberries or pineapple chunks.

chickpeas & chorizo

Heat the oil in a large, heavy-bottom skillet over medium heat. Add the onion and garlic and cook, stirring occasionally, until the onion is softened, but not browned. Stir in the chorizo and continue cooking until it is heated through.

Tip the mixture into a bowl and stir in the chickpeas and peppers. Splash with sherry vinegar and season with salt and pepper to taste. Serve hot or at room temperature, generously sprinkled with parsley, with plenty of crusty bread.

ingredients

4 tbsp. olive oil

1 onion, chopped finely

1 large garlic clove, crushed

9 oz. chorizo sausage, casing removed and cut into ½-in. dice

14 oz. canned chickpeas, drained and rinsed

6 pimientos del piquillo, drained, patted dry, and sliced

1 tbsp. sherry vinegar, or to taste

salt and pepper

finely chopped fresh parsley, to garnish

crusty bread slices, to serve

COOK'S TIP

If you can't find these pimientos del piquillo you can roast the peppers yourself. Use 6 of the long, sweet Mediterranean variety if possible.

broiled herring with lemon sauce

Peel the lemon. Remove all the bitter pith and discard. Using a small, serrated knife, cut between the membranes and ease out the flesh segments, discarding any seeds. Chop finely and set aside.

Melt 1 tablespoon of the butter in a small pan and season with salt and pepper. Brush the herring all over with the melted butter and cook under a preheated broiler, turning once, for 5–6 minutes, until cooked through.

Meanwhile, melt the remaining butter, then remove the pan from the heat. Stir in the chopped lemon and fennel.

Transfer the herring to a warmed platter, pour the sauce over them, and serve immediately.

ingredients

1 large lemon

3 tbsp. unsalted butter

salt and pepper

20 fresh herring, cleaned and heads removed

1 tbsp. chopped fresh fennel leaves

roast chicken with oregano

To calculate the cooking time, allow 20 minutes per 1 lb., plus 20 minutes.

Grate the rind from the lemon and cut the lemon in half. Put the chicken in a large roasting pan and squeeze the lemon juice from 1 lemon half into the cavity. Add the lemon rind, 3 tablespoons of the oregano, and the garlic. Rub the butter, the juice from the remaining lemon half, and the oil over the chicken. Sprinkle with the remaining oregano, salt, and pepper. Put the squeezed lemon halves inside the chicken cavity.

Roast the chicken in a preheated oven, 375°F/190°C, for the calculated cooking time, basting occasionally, until golden brown and tender. (To test if the chicken is cooked, pierce the thickest part of a thigh with a skewer. If the juices run clear it is ready.)

Allow the chicken to rest in a warm place for 5–10 minutes then carve into slices or serving pieces. Stir the remaining juices in the pan and serve spooned over the chicken.

ingredients

3½–4 lb. whole chicken

1 lemon

4 tbsp. chopped fresh oregano

1 garlic clove, crushed

2 tbsp. butter

3 tbsp. olive oil

salt and pepper

SERVES 4

beef & pea soup

Heat the oil in a large pan over a medium heat. Add the onion and garlic and cook, stirring frequently, for 5 minutes, or until softened. Add the bell pepper and carrots and cook for a further 5 minutes.

Meanwhile, drain the peas, reserving the liquid from the can. Place two-thirds of the peas, reserving the remainder, in a food processor or blender with the peas liquid and process until smooth.

Add the beef to the pan and cook, stirring constantly, to break up any lumps, until well browned. Add the spices and cook, stirring, for 2 minutes. Add the cabbage, tomatoes, stock and puréed peas and season to taste with salt and pepper. Bring to a boil, then reduce the heat, cover and simmer for 15 minutes, or until the vegetables are tender.

Stir in the reserved peas, cover and simmer for a further 5 minutes. Ladle the soup into warmed soup bowls and serve.

ingredients

2 tbsp. vegetable oil

1 large onion, finely chopped

2 garlic cloves, finely chopped

1 green bell pepper, seeded
   and sliced

2 carrots, sliced

14 oz. canned black-eyed peas

8 oz. ground beef

1 tsp. each of ground cumin, chili
   powder and paprika

¼ cabbage, sliced

8 oz. tomatoes, peeled and chopped

2 cups beef stock

salt and pepper

lobster risotto

To prepare the lobster, remove the claws by twisting them. Crack the claws using the back of a large knife and set aside. Split the body lengthwise. Remove and discard the intestinal vein, the stomach sac and the spongy gills. Remove the meat from the tail and roughly chop. Set aside with the claws.

Bring the stock to a boil in a pan, then reduce the heat and keep simmering gently over a low heat while you are cooking the risotto.

Heat the oil with half the butter in a large pan over a medium heat. Add the onion and cook, stirring occasionally, for 5 minutes until softened. Add the garlic and cook for a further 30 seconds. Stir in the thyme.

Reduce the heat, add the rice and mix to coat in butter and oil. Cook, stirring constantly, for 2–3 minutes, or until the grains are translucent.

Stir in the wine and cook, stirring constantly, for 1 minute until reduced. Gradually add the hot stock, a ladle at a time. Stir constantly and add more liquid as the rice absorbs each addition. Increase the heat to medium so that the liquid bubbles. Cook for 20 minutes, or until all the liquid is absorbed and the rice is creamy.

Five minutes before the end of cooking time, add the lobster meat and claws.

Remove the pan from the heat and stir in the peppercorns, remaining butter and the parsley. Spoon onto warmed plates and serve immediately.

ingredients

1 cooked lobster, about 14 oz.–1 lb.

2½ cups fish stock

1 tbsp. olive oil

2 tbsp. butter

½ onion, finely chopped

1 garlic clove, finely chopped

1 tsp. chopped fresh thyme leaves

6 oz. risotto rice

⅔ cup sparkling white wine

1 tsp. green or pink peppercorns
  in brine, drained and roughly
  chopped

1 tbsp. chopped fresh parsley

VARIATION

For a slightly less extravagant version, you could substitute 1 lb. shrimp for the lobster. If you peel them yourself, you can use the heads and shells to make a delicately flavored shellfish stock.

tiny meatballs with tomato sauce

MAKES ABOUT 60

Heat 1 tablespoon of oil in a skillet. Add the onion and cook for 5 minutes, stirring until soft, but not brown. Remove the skillet from the heat and let cool. Add the onion to the lamb with the egg, lemon juice, cumin, cayenne, mint, and salt and pepper in a large bowl. Use your hands to squeeze all the ingredients together. Cook a little of the mixture and taste to see if the seasoning needs adjusting. With wet hands, shape into about 60 ¾-inch balls. Place on a baking sheet and chill for at least 20 minutes.

To make the tomato sauce, heat the oil in a flameproof casserole dish over a medium heat. Add the garlic, shallots and bell peppers and fry for 10 minutes, stirring occasionally, until the peppers are soft, but not brown. Add the tomatoes and juices, orange rind and salt and pepper and bring to a boil. Reduce the heat to as low as possible and simmer, uncovered, for 45 minutes, or until the sauce thickens. Purée the sauce through a mouli or in a food processor, then use a wooden spoon to press through a fine strainer. Taste and adjust the seasoning if necessary.

When ready to cook, heat a small amount of oil in one or two large skillets. Arrange the meatballs in a single layer, without overcrowding the skillet, and cook over medium-high heat for 5 minutes until brown on the outside but still pink inside. Work in batches if necessary, keeping the cooked meatballs warm while you cook the remainder. Gently reheat the sauce and serve with the meatballs for dipping.

COOK'S TIP

This is an ideal tapas to serve at a drinks party because the meatballs can be made ahead and both the sauce and meatballs can be served at room temperature. If you freeze the meatballs, allow 3 hours for them to thaw at room temperature.

ingredients

olive oil

1 red onion, chopped very finely

2¼ cups ground lamb

1 large egg, beaten

2 tsp. freshly squeezed lemon juice

½ tsp. ground cumin

pinch of cayenne pepper, to taste

2 tbsp. finely chopped fresh mint

salt and pepper

TOMATO SAUCE

2 tbsp. olive oil

5 large garlic cloves

2½ oz. shallots, chopped

2 red bell peppers, cored, seeded and chopped

1lb. 5 oz. good-quality canned chopped tomatoes

2 thin strips pared orange rind

breakfast muffins

Preheat the broiler. Cut the muffins in half and lightly toast them for 1–2 minutes on the open side. Set aside and keep warm.

Trim off all visible fat from the bacon and broil for 2–3 minutes on each side until cooked through. Drain on absorbent paper towels and keep warm. Place 4 egg-poaching rings in a skillet and pour in enough water to cover the base of the pan. Bring to a boil and reduce the heat to a simmer. Carefully break one egg into each ring and poach gently for 5–6 minutes until set.

Meanwhile, cut the tomatoes into 4 thick slices each and arrange on a piece of kitchen foil on the broiler rack. Broil for 2–3 minutes, until just cooked. Season to taste.

Peel and thickly slice the mushrooms. Place in a saucepan with the stock, bring to a boil, cover, and simmer for 4–5 minutes until cooked. Drain thoroughly, set aside and keep warm until ready to serve.

To serve, arrange the tomato and mushroom slices on the toasted muffins and top each with 2 slices of bacon. Carefully arrange an egg on top of each and sprinkle with a little pepper. Garnish with snipped fresh chives and serve at once.

ingredients

2 whole-wheat English muffins

8 slices lean bacon

4 medium eggs

2 large tomatoes

2 large flat mushrooms

4 tbsp fresh vegetable stock

salt and pepper

1 small bunch fresh chives, snipped,
    to garnish

VARIATION

Omit the bacon for a vegetarian version and use more tomatoes and mushrooms instead. Alternatively, include a broiled low-fat tofu or soy protein burger.

raisin coleslaw & tuna-filled pita breads

Mix the carrot, cabbage, yogurt, vinegar, and raisins together in a bowl. Lightly stir in the tuna and half the pumpkin seeds and season to taste with pepper.

Lightly toast the pita breads under a preheated broiler or in a toaster, then let cool slightly. Using a sharp knife, cut each pita bread in half. Divide the filling evenly among the pita breads and sprinkle the remaining pumpkin seeds over the filling. Core and cut the apples into wedges, then serve immediately with the filled pita breads.

ingredients

3 oz. grated carrot

2 oz. white cabbage, thinly sliced

⅓ cup low-fat plain yogurt

1 tsp. cider vinegar

1 oz. raisins

7 oz. canned tuna steak in water, drained

2 tbsp. pumpkin seeds

freshly ground black pepper

4 wholemeal or white pita breads

4 dessert apples, to serve

noodles with chicken satay sauce

Heat the oil in a large skillet over a medium heat. Add the chicken and cook for 5–7 minutes until no longer pink. Add the bell pepper and scallions. Cook for 3 minutes, or until just soft. Remove from the heat.

Cook the pasta in plenty of boiling salted water until al dente. Drain and return to the pan. Put the peanut butter, gingerroot, soy sauce, and chicken stock in a large pan. Simmer over a medium-low heat, stirring, until bubbling. Add the cooked vegetables, chicken, and pasta to the peanut mixture. Toss gently until coated with the sauce. Transfer to a warm serving dish and serve immediately.

ingredients

2 tbsp. vegetable oil

1 lb. boneless, skinless chicken breasts, cubed

1 red bell pepper, seeded and sliced

4 scallions, green part included, sliced diagonally

pinch of salt

8 oz. dried vermicelli or spaghettini

½ cup smooth peanut butter

1 tsp. grated fresh gingerroot

2 tbsp. soy sauce

½ cup chicken stock

rhubarb crumble

Preheat the oven to 375°F/190°C.

Cut the rhubarb into 1-inch lengths and place in a 3-pint flameproof dish with the sugar and the orange rind and juice.

Make the crumble by placing the flour in a mixing bowl and rubbing in the butter until the mixture resembles bread crumbs. Stir in the brown sugar and the ginger.

Spread the crumble evenly over the fruit and press down lightly using a fork.

Bake in the centre of the oven on a baking sheet for 25–30 minutes until the crumble is golden brown.

Serve warm with cream or yogurt.

ingredients

2 lb. rhubarb

½ cup superfine sugar

grated rind and juice of 1 orange

2½ cups plain or wholemeal flour

4 tbsp. butter

⅔ cup brown sugar

1 tsp. ground ginger

cream or yogurt, to serve

SERVES 6

sausages with lentils

Heat the oil in a large, preferably nonstick, lidded skillet over medium-high heat. Add the sausages and cook, stirring frequently, for about 10 minutes until they are brown all over and cooked through; remove from the skillet and set aside.

Pour off all but 2 tablespoons of oil from the skillet. Add the onions and bell peppers and cook for about 5 minutes until soft, but not brown. Add the lentils and thyme or marjoram and stir until coated with oil.

Stir in the stock and bring to a boil. Reduce the heat, cover, and let simmer for about 30 minutes until the lentils are tender and the liquid is absorbed; if the lentils are tender, but too much liquid remains, uncover the skillet and let simmer until it evaporates. Season to taste with salt and pepper.

Return the sausages to the skillet and reheat. Stir in the parsley. Serve the sausages with lentils on the side, then splash a little red wine vinegar over each portion.

ingredients

2 tbsp. olive oil

12 merguez sausages

2 onions, chopped finely

2 red bell peppers, cored, seeded, and chopped

1 orange or yellow bell pepper, cored, seeded. and chopped

scant 1½ cups small green lentils, rinsed

1 tsp. dried thyme or marjoram

2 cups vegetable stock

salt and pepper

4 tbsp. chopped fresh parsley

red wine vinegar, to serve

bacon & cornmeal muffins

Preheat the oven to 400°F/200°C and preheat the broiler to medium. Line 12 holes of 1 or 2 muffin pans with paper muffin cases. Cook the pancetta under the preheated broiler until crisp, then crumble into pieces and reserve until required.

Sift the flour, baking powder, and salt into a bowl, then stir in the cornmeal and sugar. Place the butter, eggs, and milk in a separate bowl. Add the wet ingredients to the dry ingredients and mix until just blended. Fold in the pancetta, then divide the mixture between the paper cases and bake in the preheated oven for 20–25 minutes, or until risen and golden. Serve the muffins warm or cold.

ingredients

5½ oz. pancetta

generous 1 cup self-rising flour

1 tbsp. baking powder

1 tsp. salt

1⅔ cups fine cornmeal

¼ cup golden granulated sugar

scant ½ cup butter, melted

2 eggs, beaten

1¼ cups milk

COOK'S TIP

Pancetta is thin Italian bacon. If it is unavailable, you can use thinly sliced strips of lean bacon instead.

clam & leek linguine

Drain the clams, reserving the liquid from the jar. Heat the oil in a large skillet over a medium-low heat. Add the leeks and garlic, then cook gently for 3–4 minutes, or until the leeks are tender-crisp. Stir in the wine and cook for 1–2 minutes, or until evaporated. Add the bay leaf, clams, and the reserved liquid. Season with salt and pepper. Simmer for 5 minutes, then remove from the heat.

Cook the pasta in plenty of boiling salted water until al dente. Drain and transfer to a warm serving dish. Briefly reheat the sauce and pour over the pasta. Add the parsley and toss well to mix. Serve immediately.

ingredients

14 oz. clams in brine (in jar)

3 tbsp. olive oil

2 large leeks (white part only), sliced
    lengthwise and cut into thin
    2 inch strips

2 garlic cloves, chopped very finely

4 tbsp. dry white wine

1 bay leaf

salt and pepper

12 oz. dried spaghetti or linguine

3 tbsp. chopped fresh flatleaf
    parsley, to garnish

cappuccino squares

Preheat the oven to 350°F/180°C. Grease and line the bottom of a shallow 11 x 7-inch pan. Sift the flour, baking powder, and cocoa into a bowl and add the butter, superfine sugar, eggs, and coffee. Beat well, by hand or with an electric whisk, until smooth, then spoon into the pan and smooth the top. Bake in the oven for 35–40 minutes, or until risen and firm. Let cool in the pan for 10 minutes, then turn out on to a wire rack and peel off the lining paper. Let cool completely.

To make the frosting, place the chocolate, butter, and milk in a bowl set over a pan of simmering water and stir until the chocolate has melted. Remove the bowl from the pan and strain in the confectioners' sugar. Beat until smooth, then spread over the cake. Dust the top of the cake with strained cocoa, then cut into squares.

ingredients

1 cup butter, softened, plus extra
    for greasing
generous 1½ cups self-rising flour
1 tsp. baking powder
1 tsp. unsweetened cocoa, plus
    extra for dusting
generous 1 cup golden superfine
    sugar
4 eggs, beaten
3 tbsp. instant coffee powder
    dissolved in 2 tbsp. hot water
WHITE CHOCOLATE FROSTING
4 oz. white chocolate, broken
    into pieces
¼ cup butter, softened
3 tbsp. milk
1¾ cups confectioners' sugar

irish soda bread

Preheat the oven to 450°F/230°C, then dust a cookie sheet with flour. Sift the white flour, whole-wheat flour, baking soda, and salt into a bowl and stir in the sugar. Make a well in the center and pour in enough of the buttermilk to make a dough that is soft but not too wet and sticky. Add a little more buttermilk, if necessary.

Turn the dough out on to a floured counter and knead very briefly into a large circle, 2 inches thick. Dust lightly with flour and, using a sharp knife, mark the top of the loaf with a deep cross.

Place the loaf on the cookie sheet and bake in the preheated oven for 15 minutes. Reduce the oven temperature to 400°F/200°C and bake for an additional 20–25 minutes, or until the loaf sounds hollow when tapped on the bottom. Transfer to a wire rack to cool, and eat while still warm.

ingredients

2 cups white all-purpose flour,
    plus extra for dusting
2 cups whole-wheat flour
1½ tsp. baking soda
1 tsp. salt
1 tsp. brown sugar
generous 1¾ cups buttermilk

COOK'S TIP
Buttermilk is available in
most large food stores,
but if you cannot find it,
you can substitute ordinary
milk instead.

leek & potato soup

Melt the butter in a large pan over a medium heat, add the prepared vegetables and sauté gently for 2–3 minutes until soft but not brown. Pour in the stock, bring to a boil, then reduce the heat and simmer, covered, for 15 minutes.

Remove from the heat and blend the soup in the pan using a hand-held stick blender if you have one. Otherwise, pour into a blender, blend until smooth and return to the rinsed-out pan.

Heat the soup, season with salt and pepper to taste, and serve in warm bowls, swirled with the cream, if using, and garnished with chives.

ingredients

2 tbsp. butter

1 onion, chopped

3 leeks, sliced

8 oz. potatoes, peeled and
   cut into ¾-inch cubes

3½ cups vegetable stock

salt and pepper

⅔ cup light cream, optional

2 tbsp. snipped fresh chives,
   to garnish

chicken, tomato & onion casserole

Melt the butter with the olive oil in a flameproof casserole dish. Add the chicken pieces and cook, turning frequently, for 5–10 minutes, until golden brown all over. Transfer the pieces to a plate, using a slotted spoon.

Add the onions and garlic to the casserole and cook over low heat, stirring occasionally, for 10 minutes, until golden. Add the tomatoes with the juice from the can, the parsley, basil leaves, tomato paste, and wine, and season to taste with salt and pepper. Bring to a boil, then return the chicken pieces to the casserole, pushing them down into the sauce.

Cover and cook in a preheated oven, 325°F/160°C, for 50 minutes. Add the mushrooms and cook for an additional 10 minutes, until the chicken is cooked through and tender. Serve immediately.

ingredients

1½ tbsp. unsalted butter

2 tbsp. olive oil

4 lb. skinned chicken portions, bone in

2 red onions, sliced

2 garlic cloves, chopped finely

14 oz. canned tomatoes, chopped

2 tbsp. chopped fresh flat-leaf parsley

6 fresh basil leaves, torn

1 tbsp. sun-dried tomato paste

⅔ cup red wine

salt and pepper

8 oz. mushrooms, sliced

VARIATION
Substitute Marsala for the red wine and add 1 green bell pepper, seeded and sliced, with the onion in step 2.

springtime pasta

Fill a bowl with cold water and add the lemon juice. Prepare the artichokes one at a time. Cut off the stems and trim away any tough outer leaves. Cut across the tops of the leaves. Slice in half lengthwise and remove the central fibrous chokes, then cut lengthwise into ¼-inch thick slices. Immediately place the slices in the bowl of acidulated water to prevent discoloration.

Heat 5 tablespoons of the olive oil in a heavy-bottom skillet. Drain the artichoke slices and pat dry with paper towels. Add them to the skillet with the shallots, garlic, parsley, and mint, and cook over low heat, stirring frequently, for 10–12 minutes, until tender.

Meanwhile, bring a large pan of lightly salted water to a boil. Add the pasta, bring back to a boil, and cook for 8–10 minutes, until tender, but still firm to the bite.

Shell the shrimp, cut a slit along the back of each, and remove and discard the dark vein. Melt the butter in a small skillet, cut the shrimp in half, and add them to the skillet. Cook, stirring occasionally, for 2–3 minutes, until they have changed color. Season to taste with salt and pepper.

Drain the pasta and tip it into a bowl. Add the remaining olive oil and toss well. Add the artichoke mixture and the shrimp and toss again. Serve immediately.

ingredients

2 tbsp. lemon juice

4 baby globe artichokes

7 tbsp. olive oil

2 shallots, chopped finely

2 garlic cloves, chopped finely

2 tbsp. chopped fresh flat-leaf
    parsley

2 tbsp. chopped fresh mint

12 oz. dried rigatoni or other
    tubular pasta

12 large uncooked shrimp

1 tbsp unsalted butter

salt and pepper

COOK'S TIP

The large Mediterranean shrimp, known as gamberoni *in Italy, have a superb flavor and texture that is superior to that of the very big jumbo shrimp, but they may be difficult to obtain.*

spicy chickpea snack

SERVES 4

Using a sharp knife, cut the potatoes into dice. Place them in a pan, add water just to cover, and bring to a boil. Cover and simmer over medium heat for 10 minutes until cooked through. Test by inserting the tip of a knife into the potatoes. They should feel soft and tender. Drain and set aside.

Using a sharp knife, finely chop the onion. Set aside until required. Put the chickpeas into a bowl.

Combine the tamarind paste and water. Add the chili powder, sugar, and 1 teaspoon salt and mix again. Pour the mixture over the chickpeas.

Add the onion and the diced potatoes to the chickpeas and stir to mix. Season to taste with pepper.

Transfer to a serving bowl and garnish with tomatoes, chilies and cilantro leaves.

ingredients

2 medium potatoes

1 medium onion

14 oz. canned chickpeas, drained

2 tbsp. tamarind paste

6 tbsp. water

1 tsp. chili powder

2 tsp. sugar

salt and pepper

TO GARNISH

1 tomato, sliced

2 fresh green chilies, chopped

fresh cilantro leaves

amaretto coffee

Pour the Amaretto into the cup of coffee and stir so the flavor mixes in well with the coffee.

Hold a teaspoon, rounded side upward, against the side of the cup with the tip just touching the surface of the coffee. Pour the cream over the back of the spoon so that it floats on top of the coffee. Serve immediately.

ingredients

1 fl oz. Amaretto

1 cup hot black coffee

1 tbsp. heavy cream

MARCH
22

SERVES 1

roasted sea bass

Preheat the oven to 400°F/200°C.

Remove any scales from the fish and rinse it thoroughly both inside and out. If you like, trim off the fins with a pair of scissors. Using a sharp knife, make five or six cuts diagonally into the flesh of the fish on both sides. Season well with salt and pepper, both inside and out.

Mix the onion, garlic, herbs, and anchovies together in a bowl.

Stuff the fish with half the mixture and spoon the remainder into a roasting pan. Place the sea bass on top.

Spread the butter over the fish, pour over the wine, and place in the oven. Roast for 30–35 minutes until the fish is cooked through and the flesh flakes easily.

Using a spatula, carefully remove the sea bass from the pan to a warmed serving platter. Place the roasting pan over a medium heat and stir the onion mixture and juices together. Add the sour cream, mix well and pour into a warmed serving bowl.

Serve the sea bass whole and divide at the table. Spoon a little sauce on the side.

ingredients

1 whole sea bass, about 3–4 lb.,
    cleaned

salt and pepper

1 small onion, finely chopped

2 garlic cloves, finely chopped

2 tbsp. finely chopped fresh
    herbs, such as parsley, chervil
    and tarragon

1 oz. anchovy fillets, finely chopped

25 g/1 oz butter

2/3 cup white wine

2 tbsp. sour cream

MARCH
23

SERVES 4

ingredients

two cans sweetened condensed
   milk, about 14 fl oz. each
6 tbsp. butter, melted
5½ oz. graham crackers, crushed
   into crumbs
⅓ cup almonds, toasted
   and ground
⅓ cup hazelnuts, toasted
   and ground
4 ripe bananas
1 tbsp. lemon juice
1 tsp. vanilla extract
2¾ oz. chocolate, grated
scant 2 cups thick heavy
   cream, whipped

banoffee pie

Place the cans of milk in a large pan and cover them with water. Bring to a boil, then reduce the heat and simmer for 2 hours, topping up the water level regularly to keep the cans covered. Carefully lift out the hot cans and let cool.

Preheat the oven to 350°F/180°C. Grease a 9-inch tart pan with butter. Put the remaining butter into a bowl and add the crackers and nuts. Mix together well, then press the mixture evenly into the bottom and sides of the tart pan. Bake for 10–12 minutes, then remove from the oven and let cool.

Peel and slice the bananas and put them into a bowl. Sprinkle over the lemon juice and vanilla extract and mix gently. Spread the banana mixture over the cracker layer in the pan, then open the cans of condensed milk and spoon the contents over the bananas. Sprinkle over 1¾ oz of the chocolate, then top with a thick layer of whipped cream. Scatter over the remaining chocolate and serve.

peking duck salad

Begin by preparing the Peking duck. Remove the crisp skin and cut it into thin strips, then slice the meat and set both aside separately. The noodles won't need any cooking, but rinse them under warm water to separate them, then leave them to drain. Meanwhile, mix the hoisin and plum sauces together in a large bowl and add the noodles after any excess water has dripped off. Add the duck skin to the bowl, and stir together.

Cut the cucumber in half lengthwise, then use a teaspoon to scoop out the seeds, cut into half-moon slices, and add to the noodles. Next slice the scallions on the diagonal and add to the bowl. Use your hands to mix all the ingredients together until they are well coated with the sauce.

Transfer the noodles to a large platter and arrange the duck meat on top.

SERVES 4

ingredients

½ Peking duck, bought from
    a Chinese take-out

1 lb. fresh Hokkien noodles

5 tbsp. bottled hoisin sauce

5 tbsp. bottled plum sauce

1 small cucumber

4 scallions

COOK'S TIP

If you can't find Hokkien noodles, any thick noodles, such as udon or many brands of ready-to-use noodles sold in Asian food stores, are equally suitable. Or boil dried thick Chinese egg noodles for 5 minutes, or according to the packet instructions, and use them.

lemon curd

You will need 2 medium jars or 3–4 small jars with lids and waxed disks. To sterilise the jars, make sure they are washed in soapy water and rinsed well and then heat in a moderate oven for 5 minutes.

Carefully grate the rind from each of the lemons using a fine grater. Make sure you only take the yellow rind and not the bitter white pith.

Cut the lemons in half and squeeze out all the juice, then strain to remove the seeds. Place a medium heatproof bowl over a pan of simmering water and add the lemon rind, juice and sugar. Mix together well until the sugar has dissolved.

Add the eggs and the butter cut into small pieces and continue to stir for 25–30 minutes until the butter has melted and the mixture begins to thicken. Beat well and turn into the jars. Cover and label before storing. Once opened the lemon curd will keep for up to 2 months in the refrigerator.

ingredients

3 unwaxed lemons

1½ cups caster sugar

3 eggs, beaten

6 tbsp. butter

VARIATIONS

To make orange curd, use 3 oranges instead of the lemons, and for lime prepare 5 limes for the same amount of the other ingredients. Black currants can also be made into curd by stewing the fruit first and straining to make a purée.

ingredients

2 tbsp. olive oil, plus extra for
    greasing
2 cups white bread flour
½ tsp. salt
1 envelope active dry yeast
generous 1 cup lukewarm water
1 cup pitted green or black olives,
    halved

TOPPING

2 red onions, sliced
2 tbsp. olive oil
1 tsp. sea salt
1 tbsp. fresh thyme leaves

VARIATION
Use this quantity of dough to make
1 large focaccia, if you prefer.

mini focaccia

Lightly oil several cookie sheets. Sift the flour and salt into a large mixing bowl, then stir in the yeast. Pour in the olive oil and lukewarm water and mix everything together to form a dough.

Turn the dough out onto a lightly floured counter and knead it for about 5 minutes. Alternatively, use an electric mixer with a dough hook.

Place the dough in a greased bowl, cover, and set aside in a warm place for about 1–1½ hours or until it has doubled in size. Punch down the dough by kneading it again for 1–2 minutes.

Knead half of the olives into the dough. Divide the dough into quarters and then shape the quarters into rounds. Place them on the cookie sheets and push your fingers into the dough to create a dimpled effect.

To make the topping, sprinkle the red onions and remaining olives over the rounds. Drizzle the oil over the top and sprinkle with the sea salt and thyme leaves. Cover and set aside to rise for 30 minutes.

Bake in a preheated oven, 375°F/190°C, for 20–25 minutes or until the focaccia are golden. Transfer to a wire rack to cool completely before serving.

goujons with garlic mayonnaise

Combine the mayonnaise and garlic in a small dish. Cover with plastic wrap and chill in the refrigerator while you cook the fish. Cut the fish into 1 inch strips. Dip in the egg, then drain, and dredge in flour.

Meanwhile heat the oil. Fry the pieces of fish quickly in the oil until golden brown. This should take only 3–4 minutes. Remove the cooked fish from the oil and drain on a dish lined with paper towels. Remove the garlic mayonnaise from the refrigerator and stir once. Set the drained fish on an attractive dish, garnish with lemon wedges, and serve with the mayonnaise on the side for dipping.

ingredients

6 tbsp mayonnaise

2 garlic cloves, peeled and crushed

2 large white fish fillets, skinned

1 egg, beaten

3 heaping tbsp. all-purpose flour

oil for deep-frying

lemon wedges, to garnish

chinese-style marinated beef with vegetables

To make the marinade, mix the sherry, soy sauce, cornstarch, sugar, garlic, and sesame oil in a bowl. Add the beef to the mixture, cover with plastic wrap and let marinate for about 30 minutes.

Heat 1 tablespoon of the sesame oil in a wok or skillet. Stir-fry the beef without its marinade for 2 minutes, or until medium-rare. Discard the marinade. Remove the beef from the wok and set aside.

Combine the cornstarch and soy sauce in a bowl and set aside. Pour the remaining 2 tablespoons of sesame oil into the wok, add the broccoli, carrots, and snow peas and stir-fry for 2 minutes. Add the stock, then cover the pan and steam for one minute. Stir in the spinach, beef, and the cornstarch mixture. Cook until the juices boil and thicken. Serve over white rice or noodles and garnish with fresh cilantro.

ingredients

MARINADE

1 tbsp. dry sherry

½ tbsp. soy sauce

½ tbsp. cornstarch

½ tsp. superfine sugar

2 garlic cloves, chopped finely

1 tbsp. sesame oil

STIR-FRY

1 lb. 2 oz. rump steak, cut into strips

3 tbsp. sesame oil

½ tbsp. cornstarch

½ tbsp. soy sauce

3 tbsp. sesame oil

1 head of broccoli, cut into florets

2 carrots, cut into thin strips

1¼ cups snow peas

½ cup beef stock

9 oz. baby spinach, shredded

fresh cilantro, to garnish

cooked rice or noodles, to serve

gnocchi with tuna, garlic, lemon, capers, & olives

Cook the gnocchi in plenty of boiling salted water. Drain and return to the pan.

Heat the olive oil and half the butter in a skillet over a medium-low heat. Add the garlic and cook for a few seconds until just beginning to color. Reduce the heat to low. Add the tuna, lemon juice, capers, and olives. Stir gently until all the ingredients are heated through.

Transfer the pasta to a warm serving dish. Pour the tuna mixture over the pasta. Add the parsley and remaining butter. Toss well to mix. Serve immediately.

ingredients

12 oz. gnocchi

4 tbsp. olive oil

4 tbsp. butter

3 large garlic cloves, sliced thinly

7 oz. canned tuna, drained
  and broken into chunks

2 tbsp. lemon juice

1 tbsp. capers, drained

10–12 black olives, pitted and sliced

2 tbsp. chopped fresh flat-leaf
  parsley, to serve

MARCH
31

MAKES 10–12 SLICES

ingredients

generous ½ cup raisins

finely grated rind and juice of
  1 orange

6 oz. butter, diced, plus extra for
  greasing the pan

3½ oz. semisweet chocolate, at
  least 70% cocoa solids, broken up

4 large eggs, beaten

½ cup superfine sugar

1 tsp. vanilla extract

⅜ cup all-purpose flour

generous ½ cup ground almonds

½ tsp. baking powder

pinch salt

scant ½ cup blanched almonds,
  toasted and chopped

confectioners' sugar, sifted, to
  decorate

rich chocolate cake

Put the raisins in a small bowl, add the orange juice, and let soak for 20 minutes. Line a deep 10-inch round cake pan with a removable bottom with waxed paper and grease the paper; set aside.

Melt the butter and chocolate together in a small pan over medium heat, stirring. Remove from the heat and set aside to cool.

Using an electric mixer beat the eggs, sugar, and vanilla together for about 3 minutes until light and fluffy. Stir in the cooled chocolate mixture.

Drain the raisins if they haven't absorbed all the orange juice. Sift over the flour, ground almonds, baking powder, and salt. Add the raisins, orange rind, and almonds, and fold everything together.

Spoon into the cake pan and smooth the surface. Bake in a preheated oven, 350°F/180°C, for about 40 minutes, or until a toothpick inserted into the center comes out clean and the cake starts to come away from the sides of the pan. Let cool in the pan for 10 minutes, then remove from the pan and let cool completely on a wire rack. Dust the surface with confectioners' sugar before serving.

CHAPTER

4

April

easter cookies

Preheat the oven to 350°F/180°C, then grease 2 large cookie sheets. Place the butter and sugar in a bowl and beat until light and fluffy. Gradually beat in the egg and milk. Stir in the candied peel and currants, then sift in the flour and allspice. Mix together to make a firm dough. Knead lightly until smooth. On a floured counter, roll out the dough to ¼ inch thick and use a 2-inch round cookie cutter to stamp out the cookies. Re-roll the dough trimmings and stamp out more cookies until the dough is used up.

Place the biscuits on the cookie sheets and bake in the preheated oven for 10 minutes. Remove from the oven to glaze. Brush with the egg white and sprinkle with the superfine sugar, then return to the oven for an additional 5 minutes, or until lightly browned. Cool on the cookie sheets for 2 minutes, then transfer to wire racks to cool completely.

ingredients

¾ cup butter, softened, plus extra for greasing

generous ¾ cup golden superfine sugar

1 egg, beaten

2 tbsp milk

¼ cup chopped candied peel

generous ⅔ cup currants

2½ cups all-purpose flour, plus extra for dusting

1 tsp. allspice

GLAZE

1 egg white, lightly beaten

2 tbsp. golden superfine sugar

spaghetti with parsley chicken

Heat the olive oil in a heavy-bottom pan. Add the lemon rind and cook over low heat, stirring frequently, for 5 minutes. Stir in the gingerroot and sugar, season to taste with salt, and cook, stirring constantly, for an additional 2 minutes. Pour in the chicken stock, bring to a boil, then cook for 5 minutes, or until the liquid has reduced by half.

Meanwhile, bring a large heavy-bottom pan of lightly salted water to a boil. Add the pasta, return to a boil, and cook for 8-10 minutes, or until tender but still firm to the bite.

Meanwhile, melt half the butter in a skillet. Add the chicken and onion and cook, stirring frequently, for 5 minutes, or until the chicken is light brown all over. Stir in the lemon and gingerroot mixture and cook for 1 minute. Stir in the parsley leaves and cook, stirring constantly, for an additional 3 minutes. Drain the pasta and transfer to a warmed serving dish, then add the remaining butter and toss well. Add the chicken sauce, toss again, and serve.

ingredients

1 tbsp. olive oil

thinly pared rind of 1 lemon, cut into julienne strips

1 tsp. finely chopped fresh gingerroot

1 tsp. sugar

salt

1 cup chicken stock

9 oz. dried spaghetti

4 tbsp. butter

8 oz. skinless, boneless chicken breasts, diced

1 red onion, finely chopped

leaves from 2 bunches of flat-leaf parsley

ingredients

2 lb. 4 oz. fresh spinach, coarse
    stalks removed
1½ cups ricotta cheese
1 cup freshly grated Parmesan
    cheese
3 eggs, beaten lightly
pinch of freshly grated nutmeg
salt and pepper
generous ¾ cup all-purpose flour,
    plus extra for dusting

FOR THE HERB BUTTER

4 oz. unsalted butter
2 tbsp. chopped fresh oregano
2 tbsp chopped fresh sage

APRIL

3

SERVES 4

spinach & ricotta dumplings

Wash the spinach, then place it in a pan with just the water clinging to its leaves. Cover and cook over low heat for 6–8 minutes, until just wilted. Drain well and set aside to cool.

Squeeze or press out as much liquid as possible from the spinach, then chop finely or process in a food processor or blender. Place the spinach in a bowl and add the ricotta, half the Parmesan, the eggs, and nutmeg, and season to taste with salt and pepper. Beat until thoroughly combined. Start by sifting in ¾ cup of the flour and lightly work it into the mixture, adding more, if necessary, to make a workable mixture. Cover with plastic wrap and let chill for 1 hour.

With floured hands, break off small pieces of the mixture and roll them into walnut-size balls. Handle them as little as possible, as they are quite delicate. Lightly dust the dumplings with flour.

Bring a large pan of lightly salted water to a boil. Add the dumplings and cook for about 2–3 minutes, until they rise to the surface. Remove them from the pan with a slotted spoon, drain well, and set aside.

Meanwhile, make the herb butter. Melt the butter in a large, heavy-bottom skillet. Add the oregano and sage and cook over low heat, stirring frequently, for 1 minute. Add the dumplings and toss gently for 1 minute to coat. Transfer to a warmed serving dish, sprinkle with the remaining Parmesan, and serve.

COOK'S TIP

A good way to remove the liquid from cooked spinach is to put it in a strainer and use a potato creamer to press out the unwanted water.

anchovy & potato casserole

SERVES 4

Preheat the oven to 400°F/200°C. Generously grease a flameproof dish with butter. Cut each anchovy fillet into 4 pieces. Layer the grated potatoes, onion slices, garlic, parsley, and anchovies in the dish, ending with a layer of potatoes, seasoning each layer with pepper.

Pour half the cream over the top and dot with the butter. Bake in the preheated oven for 35–40 minutes, or until the potatoes are just colored, then pour over the remaining cream and bake for an additional 20–25 minutes, or until the topping is golden and tender. Serve immediately, garnished with parsley sprigs.

ingredients

3 tbsp. butter, plus extra for greasing
14 anchovy fillets
1 lb. potatoes, grated
2 onions, sliced
1 garlic clove, finely chopped
1 tbsp. chopped fresh parsley
pepper
1¼ cups light cream
fresh parsley sprigs, to garnish

COOK'S TIP

If you use canned anchovy fillets, you can drizzle a little of the oil over the potatoes before adding the cream in Step 2. If using salted anchovy fillets, soak them in water or milk before filleting them.

ingredients

2 tbsp. butter

2 carrots, cut into thin sticks

1 small onion, finely chopped

8 oz. skinless, boneless chicken
    breast, diced

8 oz. mushrooms, quartered

½ cup dry white wine

½ cup chicken stock

2 garlic cloves, finely chopped

salt and pepper

2 tbsp. cornstarch

4 tbsp. water

2 tbsp. light cream

½ cup plain yogurt

2 tsp. fresh thyme leaves

2½ cups arugula

12 oz. dried penne

fresh thyme sprigs, to garnish

SERVES 3–4

penne with chicken & arugula

Melt the butter in a heavy-bottom skillet. Add the carrots and cook over medium heat, stirring frequently, for 2 minutes. Add the onion, chicken, mushrooms, wine, chicken stock, and garlic, and season to taste with salt and pepper. Mix the cornstarch and water together in a bowl until a smooth paste forms, then stir in the cream and yogurt.

Stir the cornstarch mixture into the skillet with the thyme, cover, and let simmer for 5 minutes. Place the arugula on top of the chicken, but do not stir in, cover and cook for 5 minutes, or until the chicken is tender. Strain the cooking liquid into a clean pan, then transfer the chicken and vegetables to a dish and keep warm. Heat the cooking liquid, whisking occasionally, for 10 minutes, or until reduced and thickened.

Meanwhile, bring a large heavy-bottom pan of lightly salted water to a boil. Add the pasta, return to a boil and cook for 8–10 minutes, or until tender but still firm to the bite. Return the chicken and vegetables to the thickened cooking liquid and stir to coat. Drain the pasta well, transfer to a warmed serving dish, and spoon the chicken and vegetable mixture on top. Garnish with thyme sprigs and serve immediately.

VARIATION
Replace the arugula with the same amount of fresh watercress or baby spinach, if you prefer.

chorizo & scallop soup

Put the chorizo in a clean, dry skillet and cook over medium heat for about 5–8 minutes. Lift out with a perforated spoon and drain on paper towels. Put the peas in a strainer and rinse under cold running water. Let drain.

Heat the oil in a large pan over medium heat. Add the shallots and cook for about 4 minutes, until slightly softened. Add the carrots, leeks, and garlic, and cook for another 3 minutes. Add the drained peas to the pan, then the stock and oregano. Bring to a boil, then add the chorizo and season with salt and pepper. Lower the heat, cover, and simmer for 1–1¼ hours.

Just before the end of the cooking time, add the scallops and cook for about 2 minutes. Remove the pan from the heat. Ladle the soup into serving bowls, garnish with chopped fresh parsley, and serve with slices of fresh whole-wheat bread.

ingredients

4½ oz. lean chorizo, skinned and chopped

1 lb. yellow field peas

1 tbsp. vegetable oil

2 shallots, chopped

2 carrots, chopped

2 leeks, trimmed and chopped

2 garlic cloves, chopped

6¼ cups vegetable stock

½ tsp. dried oregano

salt and pepper

8 oz. scallops

fresh flat-leaf parsley, chopped, to garnish

slices of fresh whole-wheat bread, to serve

tuna casserole

Preheat the oven to 350°F/180°C. Melt the butter in a large, heavy-bottom pan. Sprinkle in the flour and cook, stirring constantly, for 1 minute. Remove the pan from the heat and gradually whisk in the milk. Return to the heat, bring to a boil, and cook, whisking constantly, for 2 minutes. Remove the pan from the heat and stir in the grated cheese.

Flake the tuna and add it to the mixture with the oil from the can. Stir in the corn and season to taste with salt and pepper. Lightly grease a large flameproof dish. Line the dish with the tomato slices, then spoon in the tuna mixture. Crumble the potato chips over the top and bake in the preheated oven for 20 minutes. Serve.

ingredients

2 tbsp. butter, plus extra for greasing

scant ¼ cup all-purpose flour

1¼ cups milk

2 oz. Cheddar cheese, grated

7 oz. canned tuna in oil

11½ oz. canned corn, drained

salt and pepper

2 tomatoes, thinly sliced

2½ oz. plain potato chips

roast lamb with orzo

If necessary, untie the leg of lamb and open out. Place the lemon slices down the middle, sprinkle over half the oregano, the chopped garlic, salt and pepper. Roll up the meat and tie with string. Using the tip of a sharp knife, make slits in the lamb, and insert the garlic slices.

Calculate the cooking time, allowing 25 minutes per 1 lb. plus 25 minutes.

Put the tomatoes and their juice, $^2/_3$ cup cold water, the remaining oregano, sugar, and the bay leaf in a large roasting tin. Place the lamb on top, drizzle over the olive oil, and season with salt and pepper.

Roast the lamb in a preheated oven, 350°F/180°C, for the calculated cooking time. Fifteen minutes before the lamb is cooked, stir $^2/_3$ cup boiling water and the orzo into the tomatoes. Add a little extra water if the sauce seems too thick. Return to the oven for a further 15 minutes, until the lamb and orzo are tender and the tomatoes reduced to a thick sauce.

To serve, carve the lamb into slices and serve hot with the orzo and tomato sauce.

ingredients

1 lb. 10 oz. boned leg or shoulder
   of lamb
½ lemon, sliced thinly
1 tbsp. chopped fresh oregano
4 large garlic cloves, 2 chopped
   finely and 2 sliced thinly
salt and pepper
1 lb. 12 oz. canned chopped
   tomatoes in juice
pinch of sugar
1 bay leaf
2 tbsp. olive oil
1⅓ cups orzo or short grain rice

SERVES 4

ingredients

4 salmon fillets, about 7 oz. each

½ cup teriyaki marinade

1 shallot, sliced

¾-inch piece fresh gingerroot, finely chopped

2 carrots, sliced

4 oz. white mushrooms, sliced

5 cups vegetable stock

9 oz. dried medium egg noodles

4 oz. frozen peas

6 oz. Napa cabbage, shredded

4 scallions, sliced

teriyaki salmon fillets with chinese noodles

Wipe off any fish scales from the salmon skin. Arrange the salmon fillets, skin-side up, in a dish just large enough to fit them in a single layer. Mix the teriyaki marinade with the shallot and gingerroot in a small bowl and pour over the salmon. Cover and let marinate in the refrigerator for at least 1 hour, turning the salmon over halfway through the marinating time.

Put the carrots, mushrooms, and stock into a large pan. Arrange the salmon, skin-side down, on a shallow baking sheet. Pour the fish marinade into the pan of vegetables and stock and bring to a boil. Reduce the heat, cover, and simmer for 10 minutes.

Meanwhile, preheat the broiler to medium. Cook the salmon under the preheated broiler for 10–15 minutes, depending on the thickness of the fillets, until the flesh turns pink and flakes easily. Remove from the broiler and keep warm.

Add the noodles and peas to the stock and return to a boil. Reduce the heat, cover, and simmer for 5 minutes, or until the noodles are tender. Stir in the Napa cabbage and scallions and heat through for 1 minute.

Carefully drain off 1¼ cups of the stock into a small heatproof bowl and reserve. Drain and discard the remaining stock. Divide the noodles and vegetables between 4 warmed serving bowls and top each with a salmon fillet. Pour the reserved stock over each meal and serve immediately.

phyllo chicken pie

Put the chicken in a large pan and add the halved onion, carrot, celery, bay leaf, lemon rind, and peppercorns. Pour in enough cold water to just cover the chicken legs and bring to a boil. Cover with a lid and simmer for about 1 hour. (To test if the chicken is cooked, pierce a thigh with a skewer. If the juices run clear it is ready.) Remove the chicken from the saucepan and set aside to cool.

Bring the cooking liquid to a boil and boil until reduced to 2½ cups. Strain and reserve the stock. When the chicken is cool enough to handle, remove the flesh, discarding the skin and bones. Cut the flesh into small bite-size pieces.

To make the filling, heat 2 oz. of the butter in a saucepan, add the chopped onions, and fry for 5–10 minutes, until softened. Stir in the flour and cook gently, stirring, for 1–2 minutes. Remove from the heat and gradually stir in the reserved stock and the milk. Return to the heat, bring to a boil, stirring, then simmer for 1–2 minutes until thick and smooth.

Remove the pan from the heat, stir in the chicken, and season with salt and pepper. Let cool. When the mixture has cooled, stir the cheese and eggs into the sauce and mix well together.

Melt the remaining 3½ oz of butter and use a little to lightly grease a deep 12 x 8-inch metal baking pan.

Cut the pastry sheets in half widthwise. Take one sheet of pastry and cover the remaining sheets with a damp dish towel. Use the sheet to line the pan and brush with a little of the melted butter. Repeat with half of the pastry sheets, brushing each with butter.

Spread the chicken filling over the pastry, then top with the remaining pastry sheets, brushing each with butter and tucking down the edges. Using a sharp knife, score the top layers of the pastry into 6 squares.

Bake in a preheated oven, 375°F/190°C, for 50 minutes, until golden brown. Remove from the oven and leave in a warm place for 5–10 minutes then serve hot, cut into squares.

SERVES 6–8

ingredients

3 lb. 5 oz. whole chicken

1 small onion, halved, and 3 large onions, chopped finely

1 carrot, sliced thickly

1 celery stalk, sliced thickly

1 bay leaf

pared rind of 1 lemon

10 peppercorns

5½ oz. butter

scant ½ cup all-purpose flour

⅔ cup milk

salt and pepper

⅓ cup kefalotiri or pecorino cheese, grated

3 eggs, beaten

8 oz. phyllo pastry sheets

APRIL

11

SERVES 4–6

ingredients

2 tbsp. olive oil

1 onion, chopped finely

2 garlic cloves, chopped finely

1 lb. 7 oz. lean ground lamb or beef

14 oz. canned chopped tomatoes in juice

pinch of sugar

2 tbsp. chopped fresh flat-leaf parsley

1 tbsp. chopped fresh marjoram

1 tsp. ground cinnamon

½ tsp. grated nutmeg

¼ tsp. ground cloves

salt and pepper

8 oz. long, hollow Greek macaroni or
   other short pasta

2 eggs, beaten

1¼ cups Greek yogurt

2 oz. Greek feta cheese, grated

1 oz. kefalotiri or pecorino cheese, grated

baked pasta with spicy meat sauce

Heat the oil in a pan, add the onion and garlic, and fry for 5 minutes, until softened. Add the lamb or beef and fry for about 5 minutes, until browned all over, stirring frequently and breaking up the meat.

Add the tomatoes to the pan, with the sugar, parsley, marjoram, cinnamon, nutmeg, cloves, salt, and pepper. Bring to a boil then simmer, uncovered, for 30 minutes, stirring occasionally.

Meanwhile, cook the macaroni in a large pan of boiling salted water for 10–12 minutes or as directed on the package, until tender, then drain well. Beat together the eggs, yogurt, and feta cheese. Season with salt and pepper.

When the meat is cooked, transfer it to a large flameproof dish. Add the macaroni in a layer to cover the meat then pour over the sauce. Sprinkle over the kefalotiri or pecorino cheese.

Bake in a preheated oven, 375°F/190°C, for 30–45 minutes, until golden brown. Serve hot or warm, cut into portions.

roast angler fish with romesco sauce

Preheat the oven to 425°F/220°C. To make the sauce, put the bell pepper, garlic, and tomatoes in a roasting pan and toss with 1 tablespoon of the oil. Roast in the oven for 20–25 minutes, then remove from the oven, cover with a dish towel and set aside for 10 minutes. Peel off the skins and place the vegetables in a food processor.

Heat 1 tablespoon of the remaining oil in a skillet. Add the bread cubes and almonds and cook over a low heat, stirring frequently, until golden. Remove with a slotted spoon and drain on paper towels. Add the chili, shallots, and paprika to the skillet and cook, stirring occasionally, for 5 minutes.

Transfer the bread and chili mixture to the food processor, add the vinegar, sugar, and water and process to a paste. With the motor running, add the remaining oil through the feeder tube. Set aside.

Reduce the oven temperature to 400°F/200°C. Remove the thin membrane covering the angler fish, then rinse the tail and pat it dry. Wrap the ham around the angler fish and rub lightly with oil. Season with salt and pepper. Put on a baking sheet.

Roast the angler fish in the preheated oven for 20 minutes until the flesh is opaque and flakes easily: test by lifting off the ham along the central bone and cut a small amount of the flesh away from the bone to see if it flakes.

Cut through the ham to remove the central bone and produce 2 thick fillets. Cut each fillet into 2 or 3 pieces and arrange on a plate with a spoonful of romesco sauce. Serve at once.

ingredients

2 lb. angler fish in 1 piece
2–3 slices serrano ham or prosciutto
olive oil
salt and pepper

ROMESCO SAUCE
1 red bell pepper, halved and
   seeded
4 garlic cloves, unpeeled
2 tomatoes, halved
½ cup olive oil
1 slice white bread, diced
4 tbsp. blanched almonds
1 fresh red chili, seeded and
   chopped
2 shallots, chopped
1 tsp. paprika
2 tbsp. red wine vinegar
2 tsp. sugar
1 tbsp. water

SERVES 4

pan-fried pork with mozzarella

Trim any excess fat from the meat, then slice it crosswise into 12 pieces, each about 1 inch thick. Stand each piece on end and beat with the flat end of a meat mallet or the side of a rolling pin until thoroughly flattened. Rub each piece all over with garlic, transfer to a plate, and cover with plastic wrap. Set aside in a cool place for 30 minutes to 1 hour.

Cut the mozzarella into 12 slices. Season the pork to taste with salt and pepper, then place a slice of cheese on top of each slice of meat. Top with a slice of prosciutto, letting it fall in folds. Place a sage leaf on each portion and secure with a toothpick.

Melt the butter in a large, heavy-bottom skillet. Add the pork, in batches if necessary, and cook for 2–3 minutes on each side, until the meat is tender and the cheese has melted. Remove with a slotted spoon and keep warm while you cook the remaining batch.

Remove and discard the toothpicks. Transfer the pork to 4 warmed individual plates, garnish with parsley and lemon slices, and serve immediately with mostarda di Verona.

ingredients

1 lb. loin of pork

2–3 garlic cloves, chopped finely

6 oz. mozzarella di bufala, drained

salt and pepper

12 slices prosciutto

12 fresh sage leaves

2 oz. unsalted butter

mostarda di Verona, to serve
   (optional)

TO GARNISH

flat-leaf parsley sprigs

lemon slices

COOK'S TIP

Mostarda di Verona *is made with applesauce and is available from some good Italian delicatessens.*

marinated raw beef

Using a very sharp knife, cut the beef fillet into wafer-thin slices and arrange on 4 individual serving plates.

Pour the lemon juice into a small bowl and season to taste with salt and pepper. Whisk in the olive oil, then pour the dressing over the meat. Cover the plates with plastic wrap and set aside for 10–15 minutes to marinate.

Remove and discard the plastic wrap. Arrange the Parmesan shavings in the center of each serving and sprinkle with parsley. Garnish with lemon slices and serve with fresh bread.

ingredients

7 oz. fillet of beef, in 1 piece

2 tbsp. lemon juice

salt and pepper

4 tbsp. extra virgin olive oil

2 oz. Parmesan cheese, shaved thinly

4 tbsp. chopped fresh flat-leaf parsley

lemon slices, to garnish

ciabatta or focaccia, to serve

SERVES 4

COOK'S TIP

You need extremely thin slices of meat for this recipe. If you place the beef in the freezer for about 30 minutes, you will find it easier to slice.

VARIATION

To make Carpaccio di Tonno, substitute fresh, uncooked tuna for the fillet of beef. Do not use thawed frozen fish, and eat on the day of purchase.

warm chicken liver salad

Arrange the salad greens on serving plates. Heat the oil in a nonstick skillet, add the onion, and cook for 5 minutes, or until softened. Add the chicken livers, tarragon, and mustard and cook for 3–5 minutes, stirring, until tender. Put on top of the salad greens.

Add the vinegar, salt, and pepper to the skillet and heat, stirring constantly, until all the sediment has been lifted from the skillet. Pour the dressing over the chicken livers and serve warm.

ingredients

salad greens

1 tbsp. olive oil

1 small onion, chopped finely

1 lb. frozen chicken livers, thawed

1 tsp. chopped fresh tarragon

1 tsp. wholegrain mustard

2 tbsp. balsamic vinegar

salt and pepper

french country casserole

Preheat the oven to 350°F/180°C. Heat the oil in a large, flameproof casserole dish. Add the lamb in batches and cook over medium heat, stirring, for 5–8 minutes, or until browned. Transfer to a plate.

Add the sliced leeks to the casserole and cook, stirring occasionally, for 5 minutes, or until softened. Sprinkle in the flour and cook, stirring, for 1 minute. Pour in the wine and stock and bring to a boil, stirring. Stir in the tomato paste, sugar, chopped mint, and apricots and season to taste with salt and pepper. Return the lamb to the casserole and stir.

Arrange the potato slices on top and brush with the melted butter. Cover and bake in the preheated oven for 1½ hours.

Increase the oven temperature to 400°F/200°C, uncover the casserole, and bake for an additional 30 minutes, or until the potato topping is golden brown. Serve immediately, garnished with fresh mint sprigs.

ingredients

2 tbsp. corn oil

4 lb. 8 oz. boneless leg of lamb,
    cut into 1-inch cubes

6 leeks, sliced

1 tbsp. all-purpose flour

2/3 cup rosé wine

1¼ cups chicken stock

1 tbsp. tomato paste

1 tbsp. sugar

2 tbsp. chopped fresh mint

4 oz. dried apricots, chopped

salt and pepper

2 lb. 4 oz. potatoes, sliced

3 tbsp. melted unsalted butter

fresh mint sprigs, to garnish

VARIATION
Use a light red wine instead of rosé if you would prefer a slightly heavier flavor in this country casserole.

COOK'S TIP
It is always a good idea to fry off meat to brown it before adding it to a casserole. This will ensure that it has an appetising color in the finished dish.

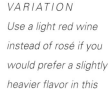

ingredients

4 bananas

VANILLA ICE CREAM

1¼ cups milk

1 tsp. vanilla extract

3 egg yolks

½ cup superfine sugar

1¼ cups heavy cream, whipped

CHOCOLATE RUM SAUCE

4½ oz. semisweet chocolate,
   broken into small pieces

2½ tbsp. butter

6 tbsp. water

1 tbsp. rum

6 tbsp. chopped mixed nuts,
   to decorate

banana splits

To make the ice cream, heat the milk and vanilla extract in a pan until almost boiling.
In a bowl, beat together the egg yolks and sugar. Remove the milk from the heat
and stir a little into the egg mixture. Transfer the mixture to the pan. Stir over low
heat until thick. Do not boil. Remove from the heat. Cool for 30 minutes, fold in the
cream, cover with plastic wrap, and chill for 1 hour. Transfer into an ice cream maker
and process for 15 minutes. Alternatively, transfer into a freezerproof container and
freeze for 1 hour, then place in a bowl and beat to break up the ice crystals. Put
back in the container and freeze for 30 minutes. Repeat twice more, freezing for
30 minutes and whisking each time.

To make the sauce, melt the chocolate and butter with the water together in a pan,
stirring. Remove from the heat and stir in the rum. Peel the bananas, slice them
lengthwise, and arrange on 4 serving dishes. Top with ice cream and nuts and serve
with the sauce.

flounder packets with fresh herbs

Preheat the oven to 375°F/190°C. Cut 4 large squares of aluminum foil, each large enough to hold a fish and form a packet, and spray with oil.

Place each fish fillet on a foil sheet and sprinkle them with the herbs, lemon rind and juice, onion, capers (if using), salt, and pepper.

Fold the foil to make a secure packet and place on a cookie sheet. Bake the packets in the oven for 15 minutes, or until tender. Serve the fish hot, in their loosely opened packets.

ingredients

vegetable oil

4 flounder fillets, skinned

6 tbsp. chopped fresh herbs, such as dill, parsley, chives, thyme, or marjoram

finely grated rind and juice of 2 lemons

1 small onion, sliced thinly

1 tbsp. capers, rinsed (optional)

salt and pepper

chicken with bok choy

Break the broccoli into small florets and cook in a pan of lightly salted boiling water for 3 minutes. Drain and reserve.

Heat a wok or large skillet over a high heat until almost smoking, add the oil and then add the gingerroot, chili, and garlic. Stir-fry for 1 minute. Add the onion and chicken and stir-fry for a further 3–4 minutes, or until the chicken is sealed on all sides.

Add the remaining vegetables, including the broccoli, and stir-fry for about 3–4 minutes, or until tender.

Add the soy and Thai fish sauces and stir-fry for a further 1–2 minutes, then serve immediately sprinkled with the cilantro and sesame seeds.

ingredients

6 oz. broccoli

1 tbsp. peanut oil

1-inch piece fresh gingerroot, finely grated

1 fresh red Thai chili, seeded and chopped

2 garlic cloves, crushed

1 red onion, cut into wedges

1 lb. skinless, boneless chicken breast, cut into thin strips

6 oz. bok choy, shredded

4 oz. baby corncobs, halved

1 tbsp. light soy sauce

1 tbsp. Thai fish sauce

1 tbsp. chopped fresh cilantro

1 tbsp. toasted sesame seeds

ingredients

MARINADE

⅓ cup vegetable stock

2 tsp. cornstarch

2 tbsp. soy sauce

1 tbsp. superfine sugar

pinch of chili flakes

STIR-FRY

9 oz. firm bean curd, rinsed and
drained thoroughly and cut into
½ inch cubes

4 tbsp. peanut oil

1 tbsp. grated fresh gingerroot

3 garlic cloves, crushed

4 scallions, sliced thinly

1 head of broccoli, cut into florets

1 carrot, cut into batons

1 yellow bell pepper, sliced thinly

5 cups shiitake mushrooms,
sliced thinly

steamed rice, to serve

spicy bean curd

Blend the vegetable stock, cornstarch, soy sauce, sugar, and chili flakes together
in a large bowl. Add the bean curd and toss well to coat. Set aside to marinate for
20 minutes.

In a wok or large skillet, heat 2 tablespoons of the peanut oil and stir-fry the bean
curd with its marinade until brown and crispy. Remove from the wok and set aside.
Heat the remaining 2 tablespoons of peanut oil in the wok and stir-fry the gingerroot,
garlic, and scallions for 30 seconds. Add the broccoli, carrot, yellow bell pepper, and
mushrooms to the wok and cook for 5–6 minutes. Return the bean curd to the wok
and stir-fry to reheat. Serve immediately over steamed rice.

ingredients

6 oz. cherry tomatoes

8 oz. mixed mushrooms, such as
    white, crimini, shiitake, and oyster

4 tbsp. vegetable stock

small bunch of fresh thyme

4 eggs, separated

½ cup water

4 egg whites

4 tsp. olive oil

1 oz. arugula leaves

salt and pepper

fresh thyme sprigs, to garnish

soufflé omelet

Halve the tomatoes and place them in a pan. Wipe the mushrooms with paper towels, trim if necessary, and slice if large. Place the mushrooms in the pan with the tomatoes.

Add the stock and thyme, still tied together, to the pan. Bring to a boil, cover, and simmer for 5–6 minutes until tender. Drain, remove the thyme, and discard. Keep the mixture warm.

Meanwhile, separate the eggs and whisk the egg yolks with the water until frothy. In a clean, grease-free bowl, whisk the 8 egg whites until stiff and dry.

Spoon the egg yolk mixture into the egg whites and, using a metal spoon, fold together until well mixed. Take care not to knock out too much of the air.

For each omelet, brush a small omelet pan with 1 teaspoon of the oil and heat until hot. Pour in a quarter of the egg mixture and cook for 4–5 minutes until the mixture has set.

Finish cooking the omelet under a preheated medium broiler for 2–3 minutes.

Transfer the omelet to a warm serving plate. Fill the omelet with a few arugula leaves and a quarter of the mushroom and tomato mixture. Flip over the top of the omelet, garnish with sprigs of thyme, and serve.

home-made turkey burgers

SERVES 4

Cook the rice in a large pan of boiling salted water for about 10 minutes, or until tender. Drain, rinse under cold running water, then drain well again.

Put the cooked rice and all the remaining ingredients in a large bowl and mix well together.

With wet hands, shape the mixture into 8 thick burgers. Pour a little oil into a large, nonstick skillet, add the burgers, and cook for about 10 minutes, turning them over several times, until they are golden brown. Remove from the skillet and serve while hot.

ingredients

¼ cup long grain white rice

salt and pepper

1 lb. lean ground turkey

1 small cooking apple, peeled, cored, and grated

1 small onion, chopped finely

1 garlic clove, chopped finely

1 tsp. ground sage

½ tsp. dried thyme

½ tsp. ground allspice

vegetable oil, for frying

sausages in batter

Preheat the oven to 425°F/220°C.

Grease an 8 x10-inch roasting pan.

Make the batter by sifting the flour and salt into a large bowl.
Make a well in the centre and add the beaten egg and half the
milk. Carefully mix the liquid into the flour until the mixture is
smooth. Gradually beat in the remaining milk. Let stand for
30 minutes.

Prick the sausages and place them in the roasting pan.
Sprinkle over the oil and cook the sausages in the oven for
10 minutes until they are beginning to color and the fat has
begun to run and is sizzling.

Remove from the oven and quickly pour the batter over the
sausages. Return to the oven and cook for 35–45 minutes,
or until the batter is well risen and golden brown.
Serve immediately.

ingredients

butter, for greasing

2/3 cup all-purpose flour

pinch of salt

1 egg, beaten

1¼ cups milk

1 lb. good-quality sausages

1 tbsp. vegetable oil

lamb steaks with herb noodles

APRIL

24

SERVES 4

Start by mixing together the flavorings for the herb noodles. Put the lime juice, Thai fish sauce, sweet chili sauce, brown sugar, and sesame oil in a small bowl and beat together, then set aside.

Heat a large grill pan or skillet over a high heat. Lightly brush the steaks or chops with oil on both sides and season with salt and pepper. Add them to the pan and cook for about 6 minutes for rare, or 10 minutes for well done, turning the meat over once.

Meanwhile, boil the noodles for 3 minutes, until soft. Alternatively, cook according to the packet instructions. Drain well and immediately transfer to a large bowl. Add the lime juice mixture and toss together, then stir in the chopped fresh herbs.

Serve the lamb steaks with the noodles on the side. Garnish with mint or cilantro springs, and serve with lime wedges for squeezing over. This dish is equally good served hot straight from the pan or left to cool for summer eating.

ingredients

4 lamb steaks or boneless
     chump chops
peanut or corn oil
salt and pepper
fresh mint or cilantro sprigs,
     to garnish
lime wedges, to serve

HERB NOODLES
juice of 1 lime
1 tbsp. Thai fish sauce
½ tbsp. sweet chili sauce
1 tsp. brown sugar
½ tbsp. sesame oil
9 oz. dried thick Chinese egg
     noodles
5 tbsp. finely chopped mint leaves
5 tbsp. finely chopped cilantro
     leaves

SERVES 4

1 tbsp. melted butter

12 oz. smoked fish, skinned

2 hard-cooked eggs, chopped

salt and pepper

1 tbsp. butter

1 tbsp. all-purpose flour

1¼ cups milk

½ cup Cheddar cheese, grated

pinch of cayenne pepper

1 tbsp. freshly grated Parmesan
   cheese

brown toast slices, to serve

smoked fish pots

Preheat the oven to 350°F/180°C.

Use the melted butter to grease 4 small soufflé dishes or ramekins.

Flake the fish onto a plate, mix with the chopped egg, and season with a little pepper. Place the mixture into the prepared dishes.

Melt the butter in a pan over a medium heat and stir in the flour. Cook for 1 minute, stirring continuously. Remove from the heat and stir in the milk gradually until smooth. Return to a low heat and stir until the sauce comes to a boil and thickens. Reduce the heat and simmer gently, stirring constantly, until the sauce is creamy and smooth.

Add the grated cheese and stir until melted, then season with salt and pepper to taste and add the cayenne pepper. Pour the sauce over the fish and egg mixture and sprinkle over the Parmesan cheese.

Place the ramekins on a baking sheet and cook in the oven for 10–15 minutes until bubbling and golden. Serve at once with brown toast.

ingredients

6 tbsp. butter

3 lb. waxy potatoes, d

3 garlic cloves, crushed

1 tsp. paprika

2 tomatoes, peeled, seeded,
  and diced

12 eggs

pepper

FILLING

8 oz. baby spinach

1 tsp. fennel seeds

4½ oz. feta cheese, diced
  (drained weight)

4 tbsp. plain yogurt

feta & spinach omelet

Heat 1 tablespoon of the butter in a skillet and cook the potatoes over low heat, stirring, for 7–10 minutes until golden. Transfer to a bowl.

Add the garlic, paprika, and tomatoes to the skillet and cook for a further 2 minutes.

Whisk the eggs together and season with pepper. Pour the eggs into the potatoes and mix well.

Cook the spinach in boiling water for 1 minute until just wilted. Drain and refresh under cold running water. Pat dry with paper towels. Stir in the fennel seeds, feta cheese, and yogurt.

Heat a quarter of the remaining butter in a 6 inch/15 cm omelet pan. Ladle a quarter of the egg and potato mixture into the pan. Cook, turning once, for 2 minutes, until set.

Transfer the omelet to a serving plate. Spoon a quarter of the spinach mixture onto half of the omelet, then fold the omelet in half over the filling. Repeat to make 4 omelets.

cken with vegetables

...arge skillet. Add the garlic
...n-high heat for 1 minute.

...and rice wine, then
... minute, then add the
...d chicken stock and
...bs and cook for
...ok for just

...ed scallions, if
...ed jasmine rice.

SERVES 4

APRIL 26

ingredients

2 tbsp. sesame oil

1 garlic clove, chopped

3 scallions, trimmed and sliced

1 tbsp. cornstarch

2 tbsp. rice wine

4 skinless chicken breasts, cut
    into strips

1 tbsp. Chinese five-spice powder

1 tbsp. grated fresh gingerroot

½ cup chicken stock

3½ oz. baby corncobs, sliced

3 cups bean sprouts

finely chopped scallions, to garnish,
    optional

freshly cooked jasmine rice, to serve

APRIL 28

pasta shells with salmon, sour cream & mustard

Cook the pasta in plenty of boiling salted water until al dente.
Drain and return to the pan. Add the sour cream, mustard,
scallions, smoked salmon, and lemon peel to the pasta. Stir
over a low heat until heated through. Season with pepper.

Transfer to a serving dish. Sprinkle with the chives. Serve
warm or at room temperature.

SERVES 4

ingredients

1 lb. conchiglie or tagliatelle

10 fl oz. sour cream

2 tsp. Dijon mustard

4 large scallions, sliced finely

8 oz. smoked salmon, cut
    into bite-sized pieces

finely grated peel of ½ lemon

pepper

2 tbsp. chopped fresh chives

1 cup baby corn

½ cup whole baby carrots

1¼ cups shelled fava beans

generous 1 cup whole green beans,
   cut into 1 inch pieces

3 cups dried penne

1¼ cups lowfat plain yogurt

1 tbsp. chopped fresh parsley

1 tbsp. chopped fresh chives

salt and pepper

a few fresh chives, to garnish

APRIL

29

SERVES 4

penne primavera

Cook the corn and carrots in boiling salted water for 5 minutes, or until tender, then drain, and rinse under cold running water.

Cook the fava beans and green beans in boiling salted water for 3–4 minutes, or until tender, then drain, and rinse under cold running water. If you like, slip the skins off the fava beans.

Cook the pasta in a large pan of boiling salted water for 10 minutes or as directed on the packet, until tender.

Meanwhile, put the yogurt, parsley, and chopped chives in a bowl and mix together. Season with salt and pepper to taste. Drain the cooked pasta and return to the pan. Add the vegetables and yogurt sauce, heat gently, and toss together, until hot. Serve garnished with a few lengths of chives.

SERVES 4

spicy pork risotto

Cut off and discard the crust from the bread, then soak in the water or milk for 5 minutes to soften. Drain and squeeze well to remove all the liquid. Mix the bread, pork, garlic, onion, crushed peppercorns, and salt together in a bowl. Add the egg and mix well.

Heat the corn oil in a skillet over a medium heat. Form the meat mixture into balls and brown a few at a time in the oil. Remove from the pan, drain, and set aside until all the meatballs are cooked.

Combine the tomatoes, tomato paste, oregano, fennel seeds, and sugar in a heavy-bottom pan. Add the meatballs. Bring the sauce to a boil over a medium heat, then reduce the heat and simmer for 30 minutes or until the meat is thoroughly cooked.

To make the risotto, bring the stock to a boil in a pan, then reduce the heat and keep simmering gently over a low heat while you are cooking the risotto.

Heat the olive oil with 1 tablespoon of the butter in a deep pan over a medium heat until the butter has melted. Stir in the onion and cook, stirring occasionally, for 5 minutes, or until soft and starting to turn golden. Do not brown.

Reduce the heat, add the rice, and mix to coat in oil and butter. Cook, stirring constantly, for 2–3 minutes, or until the grains are translucent.

Add the wine and cook, stirring constantly, for 1 minute until reduced. Gradually add the hot stock, a ladle at a time. Stir constantly and add more liquid as the rice absorbs each addition. Increase the heat to medium so that the liquid bubbles. Cook for 20 minutes, or until all the liquid is absorbed. Season to taste.

Lift out the cooked meatballs and add to the risotto. Remove the risotto from the heat and add the remaining butter. Mix well. Arrange the risotto and a few meatballs on plates. Drizzle with tomato sauce, garnish with basil, and serve.

ingredients

1 thick slice white bread

water or milk, for soaking

1 lb. ground pork

2 garlic cloves, finely minced

1 tbsp. finely chopped onion

1 tsp. black peppercorns, lightly crushed

pinch of salt

1 egg

corn oil, for shallow-frying

14 oz. canned chopped tomatoes

1 tbsp. tomato paste

1 tsp. dried oregano

1 tsp. fennel seeds

pinch of sugar

4 cups beef stock

1 tbsp. olive oil

2 tbsp. butter

1 small onion, finely chopped

10 oz. risotto rice

2/3 cup red wine

salt and pepper

fresh basil leaves, to garnish

COOK'S TIP
For the best quality, it's always best to buy a lean, single piece of meat, trim off any fat and then grind it at home.

CHAPTER

5

May

eggs benedict with quick hollandaise sauce

Fill a wide skillet three-quarters full with water and bring to a boil over a low heat. Reduce the heat to a simmer and add the vinegar. When the water is barely shimmering, carefully break the eggs into the pan. Leave for 1 minute, then, using a large spoon, gently loosen the eggs from the bottom of the pan. Let cook for a further 3 minutes, or until the white is cooked and the yolk is still soft, basting the top of the egg with the water from time to time.

Meanwhile, to make the hollandaise sauce, place the egg yolks in a blender or food processor. Melt the butter in a small pan until bubbling. With the motor running, gradually add the hot butter to the egg in a steady stream until the sauce is thick and creamy. Add the lemon juice, and a little warm water if the sauce is too thick, then season to taste with pepper. Transfer to a dish and keep warm.

Split the muffins and toast them on both sides. To serve, top each muffin with a slice of ham, a poached egg, and a generous spoonful of hollandaise sauce.

ingredients

1 tbsp. white wine vinegar

4 eggs

4 English muffins

4 slices good quality ham

QUICK HOLLANDAISE SAUCE

3 egg yolks

7 oz. butter

1 tbsp. lemon juice

pepper

COOK'S TIP

For best results when poaching eggs, break them into a cup first, then slide them into the hot water. Poach for a little longer than the suggested three minutes if you prefer firmer yolks.

CAUTION

Recipes using raw eggs should be avoided by infants, the elderly, pregnant women, convalescents, and anyone suffering from an illness.

ingredients

½ cup butter, plus extra for greasing

3½ cups all-purpose flour, plus extra
   for dusting

2 tsp. ground ginger

1 tsp. allspice

2 tsp. baking soda

generous ⅓ cup corn syrup

generous ½ cup brown sugar

1 egg, beaten

TO DECORATE

currants

candied cherries

¾ cup confectioners' sugar

3–4 tsp water

MAY

2

MAKES 20

COOK'S TIP

At Christmas, cut out star and bell
shapes. When the biscuits come out
of the oven, pierce a hole in each
with a skewer. Thread through
ribbons and hang on the tree.

gingerbread people

Preheat the oven to 325°F/160°C, then grease 3 large cookie sheets. Sift the flour, ginger, allspice, and baking soda into a large bowl. Place the butter, syrup, and sugar in a pan over low heat and stir until melted. Pour on to the dry ingredients and add the egg. Mix together to make a dough. The dough will be sticky to begin with, but will become firmer as it cools.

On a lightly floured counter, roll out the dough to about ⅛ inch thick and stamp out gingerbread people shapes. Place on the prepared cookie sheets. Re-knead and re-roll the trimmings and cut out more shapes until the dough is used up. Decorate with currants for eyes and pieces of cherry for mouths. Bake in the oven for 15–20 minutes, or until firm and lightly browned. Remove from the oven and let cool on the cookie sheets for a few minutes, then transfer to wire racks to cool completely.

Mix the confectioners' sugar with the water to a thick consistency. Place the frosting in a small plastic bag and cut a tiny hole in one corner. Use the frosting to draw buttons or clothes shapes on to the cooled biscuits.

rösti with roasted vegetables

For the roasted vegetables, mix the oil, vinegar, and honey together in a large, shallow dish. Add the red bell pepper, zucchini, onions, fennel, tomatoes, garlic, and rosemary to the dish and toss in the marinade. Let marinate for at least 1 hour.

Preheat the oven to 400°F/200°C. Cook the potatoes in a pan of lightly salted boiling water for 8–10 minutes, or until partially cooked. Let cool, then coarsely grate.

Transfer the vegetables, except the tomatoes and garlic, and the marinade to a roasting pan. Roast in the preheated oven for 25 minutes, then add the tomatoes and garlic and roast for a further 15 minutes, or until the vegetables are tender and slightly blackened around the edges.

Meanwhile, cook the rösti. Take each quarter of the potato in your hands and form into a roughly shaped cake. Heat just enough oil to cover the base of a skillet over a medium heat. Put the cakes, 2 at a time, into the skillet and flatten with a spatula to form rounds about ¾ inch thick.

Cook the rösti for 6 minutes on each side, or until golden brown and crisp. Mix the dressing ingredients. To serve, top each rösti with the roasted vegetables and drizzle with a little pesto dressing. Season to taste.

ingredients

2 lb. potatoes, halved if large

corn oil, for frying

salt and pepper

ROASTED VEGETABLES

2 tbsp. extra virgin olive oil

1 tbsp. balsamic vinegar

1 tsp. clear honey

1 red bell pepper, seeded and
   quartered

2 zucchini, sliced lengthwise

2 red onions, quartered

1 small fennel bulb, cut into
   thin wedges

16 vine-ripened tomatoes

8 garlic cloves

2 fresh rosemary sprigs

PESTO DRESSING

2 tbsp. pesto

1 tbsp. boiling water

1 tbsp. extra virgin olive oil

chicken livers in red wine & thyme

Rinse the chicken livers under cold running water and pat dry with paper towels. Heat the lemon-flavored oil in a skillet. Add the garlic and cook, stirring, over medium heat for 2 minutes. Add the chicken livers, wine, and thyme. Season with salt and pepper and cook for 3 minutes.

Meanwhile, arrange the arugula leaves on a large serving platter. Remove the pan from the heat and spoon the chicken livers over the bed of arugula. Pour over the cooking juices, then garnish with sprigs of fresh thyme and serve with fresh crusty bread.

ingredients

9 oz. fresh chicken livers

3 tbsp. lemon-flavored oil

2 garlic cloves, finely chopped

4 tbsp. red wine

1 tbsp. chopped fresh thyme

salt and pepper

sprigs of fresh thyme, to garnish

TO SERVE

arugula leaves

fresh crusty bread

MAY
5

SERVES 4

ingredients

8 oz. fresh young spinach leaves

4 oz. cooked ham

4 cups chicken stock

1 tbsp. olive oil

2 tbsp. butter

1 small onion, finely chopped

10 oz. risotto rice

⅔ cup dry white wine

¼ cup light cream

3 oz. freshly grated Parmesan
    cheese

salt and pepper

shredded spinach & ham risotto

Wash the spinach well and slice into thin shreds. Cut the ham into thin strips.

Bring the stock to a boil in a pan, then reduce the heat and keep simmering gently over a low heat while you are cooking the risotto.

Heat the oil with 1 tbsp. of the butter in a deep pan over a medium heat until the butter has melted. Add the onion and cook, stirring occasionally, for 5 minutes, or until soft and starting to turn golden. Do not brown.

Reduce the heat, add the rice, and mix to coat in oil and butter. Cook, stirring constantly, for 2–3 minutes, or until the grains are translucent.

Add the wine and cook, stirring constantly, for 1 minute until reduced.

VARIATION

For a spicier flavor, you could substitute salami for the ham. Make sure that you peel off any rind before cutting the slices into strips.

Gradually add the hot stock, a ladle at a time. Stir constantly and add more liquid as the rice absorbs each addition. Increase the heat to medium so that the liquid bubbles. Cook for 20 minutes, or until all the liquid is absorbed and the rice is creamy. Add the spinach and ham with the last ladleful of stock.

Remove the risotto from the heat and add the remaining butter and the cream. Mix well, then stir in the Parmesan until it melts. Season to taste and serve immediately.

ingredients

1 lb. smoked cod, skinned

2 tbsp. olive oil

1 onion, finely chopped

1 tsp. mild curry paste

6 oz. long-grain rice

salt and pepper

2 tbsp. butter

3 hard-cooked eggs

2 tbsp. chopped fresh parsley, to garnish

VARIATION
This dish can also be
made with salmon.

spicy cod rice

Place the fish in a large pan and cover with water. Bring the water to a boil, then turn down to a simmer and poach the fish for 8–10 minutes until it flakes easily.

Remove the fish and keep warm, reserving the water in a pitcher or bowl.

Add the oil to the pan and gently soften the onion for about 4 minutes. Stir in the curry paste and add the rice.

Measure 2½ cups of the cod water and return to the pan. Bring to a simmer and cover. Cook for 10–12 minutes until the rice is tender and the water has been absorbed. Season to taste with salt and pepper.

Flake the fish and add to the pan with the butter. Stir very gently over a low heat until the butter has melted. Chop 2 of the hard-cooked eggs and add to the pan.

Turn the rice into a serving dish, slice the remaining egg, and use to garnish. Scatter the parsley over and serve at once.

stuffed peppers with cheese

SERVES 4

Preheat the oven to 375°F/190°C. Cut the bell peppers in half lengthwise and seed. Blanch in a large pan of boiling water for 5 minutes. Remove with a slotted spoon and drain upside down.

Pour the stock into a separate pan, add the rice, and bring to a boil. Reduce the heat, cover, and simmer for 15 minutes. Remove from the heat and reserve, covered, for 5 minutes, then drain. Heat the oil in a skillet, add the onion and cook, stirring occasionally, for 5 minutes, or until softened. Add the garlic, mushrooms, tomatoes, and carrot and season to taste. Cover and cook for 5 minutes.

Stir the rice, parsley, goat cheese, and pine nuts into the vegetable mixture. Place the bell pepper halves, cut-side up, in a roasting pan. Divide the rice and vegetable mixture among them. Sprinkle with Parmesan cheese and bake in the preheated oven for 20 minutes, or until the cheese is golden. Serve.

ingredients

4 large green, yellow, or red bell
  peppers
scant 2 cups vegetable stock
1 cup long-grain rice
2 tbsp. olive oil
1 onion, chopped
2 garlic cloves, finely chopped
4 oz. cremini mushrooms, chopped
4 tomatoes, peeled and chopped
1 carrot, diced
salt and pepper
1 tbsp. chopped fresh parsley
3½ oz. goat cheese, crumbled
scant ½ cup pine nuts
¼ cup freshly grated Parmesan
  cheese

COOK'S TIP

The color of bell peppers depends on what stage of development they are at when they are picked. If you prefer a sweeter taste, pick orange and red bell peppers, which are riper than young green bell peppers.

quick mackerel pâté

Remove and discard any remaining bones from the mackerel fillets and put the fish into a small bowl. Mash the fish with a fork and combine with the yogurt, parsley, and lemon juice and rind. Season to taste with pepper.

Divide the pâté among 4 ramekins. Cover and refrigerate until required or serve immediately.

To serve, garnish the pâté with lemon wedges and parsley and serve with the prepared vegetables and toasted bread.

ingredients
9 oz. skinless smoked
    mackerel fillets
2/3 cup lowfat plain yogurt
1 tbsp. chopped fresh parsley
1 tbsp. lemon juice
finely grated rind of 1/2 lemon
freshly ground black pepper

TO GARNISH
4 lemon wedges
few sprigs of fresh parsley

TO SERVE
1 red bell pepper, seeded and cut
    into chunky strips
1 yellow bell pepper, seeded and
    cut into chunky strips
2 carrots, cut into strips
2 celery stalks, cut into strips
slices whole wheat or white bread,
    toasted and cut into triangles

MAY 8

SERVES 4

---

crispy roast asparagus

Preheat the oven to 400°F/200°C. Choose asparagus stalks of similar widths. Trim the base of the stalks so that all the stems are approximately the same length.

Arrange the asparagus in a single layer on a cookie sheet. Drizzle with olive oil and sprinkle with salt. Place the cookie sheet in the oven and bake for 10–15 minutes, turning once.

Remove from the oven, transfer to an attractive dish, and serve immediately, sprinkled with the grated Parmesan.

ingredients
16 asparagus stalks
2 tbsp. extra virgin olive oil
1 tsp. coarse sea salt
1 tbsp. grated Parmesan cheese,
    to serve

COOK'S TIP
As well as there being both green and white varieties of asparagus, there is considerable variation in width, so it is important to try to find stalks of a similar size. Otherwise, some will be tender while others require further cooking. As a general rule, the stalks of green asparagus rarely need peeling, but those of white asparagus do.

MAY 9

SERVES 4

MAY
10

SERVES 4

spaghetti alla carbonara

Bring a large, heavy-bottom pan of lightly salted water to a boil. Add the pasta, return to a boil, and cook for 8–10 minutes, or until tender but still firm to the bite.

Meanwhile, cook the bacon and garlic in a heavy-bottom, dry skillet over a medium heat for 5 minutes, or until crisp-tender. Remove from the skillet and drain on some paper towels.

Drain the pasta and return it to the pan, but do not return to the heat. Add the bacon and garlic and the eggs. Season to taste with salt and pepper. Toss thoroughly with 2 large forks. Add half the Parmesan cheese and toss again. Transfer to a warmed serving dish, sprinkle with the remaining Parmesan cheese and serve immediately.

ingredients
1 lb. dried spaghetti

6 oz. rindless lean bacon, diced

1 garlic clove, finely chopped

3 eggs, lightly beaten

salt and pepper

4 tbsp. fresh Parmesan cheese
    shavings

MAY
11

MAKES 1 X 9-FL OZ
JAR

oven-dried tomatoes

Preheat the oven to 250°F/120°C.

Using a sharp knife, cut each of the tomatoes into quarters.

Using a teaspoon, scoop out the seeds and discard. If the tomatoes are large, cut each quarter in half lengthwise again.

Sprinkle sea salt in a roasting pan and arrange the tomato slices, skin-side down, on top. Roast in the oven for 2½ hours, or until the edges are just starting to look charred and the flesh is dry, but still pliable. The exact roasting time and yield will depend on the size and juiciness of the tomatoes. Check the tomatoes at 30-minute intervals after 1½ hours.

Remove the dried tomatoes from the roasting pan and let cool completely. Put in a 9-fl oz preserving jar and pour over enough oil to cover. Seal the jar tightly and store in the refrigerator, where the tomatoes will keep for up to 2 weeks.

ingredients
2 lb. 4 oz. large, juicy,
    full-flavored tomatoes

extra virgin olive oil

sea salt

bacon with corn salad

Heat 2 teaspoons of the corn oil in a large, heavy-bottom skillet. Add the bacon and cook over medium heat, stirring frequently, for 5 minutes, or until crisp. Remove from the skillet with a slotted spoon and drain on paper towels. Add the garlic and bread to the skillet and cook, stirring and tossing frequently, until crisp and golden on all sides. Remove from the skillet with a slotted spoon and drain on paper towels.

Place the red wine vinegar, balsamic vinegar, mustard, and remaining corn oil in a screw-top jar and shake vigorously, then pour into a bowl. Alternatively, mix the vinegars and mustard together in a bowl and whisk in the oil until the dressing is creamy. Season to taste with salt and pepper. Add the corn salad and bacon to the dressing and toss to coat. Divide the salad among serving plates, sprinkle with the croutons, and serve.

ingredients

6–8 tbsp corn oil

8 oz. rindless lean bacon, diced

2 garlic cloves, finely chopped

4 slices of white bread, crusts
   removed, cut into ½-inch cubes

5 tbsp. red wine vinegar

1 tbsp. balsamic vinegar

2 tsp. whole-grain mustard

salt and pepper

8 oz. corn salad

COOK'S TIP

If you buy corn salad with the root still attached, leave it to stand in a bowl of iced water for 1 hour to refresh (if you have time).

deep-fried green chilies

EACH BAG
OF CHILIES
SERVES 4–6

ingredients

olive oil

sweet or hot green chilies

sea salt

Heat 3 inches of oil in a heavy-bottom pan until it reaches 375°F/190°C, or until a day-old cube of bread turns brown in 30 seconds.

Rinse the chilies and pat them very dry with paper towels. Drop them in the hot oil for no longer than 20 seconds until they turn bright green and the skins blister.

Remove with a slotted spoon and drain well on crumpled paper towels. Sprinkle with sea salt and serve at once.

iced coffee with cream

Use the water and coffee powder to brew some hot coffee, then let cool to room temperature. Transfer to a pitcher, cover with plastic wrap, and chill in the refrigerator for at least 45 minutes.

When the coffee has chilled, pour it into a food processor. Add the sugar, and process until well combined. Add the ice cubes and process until smooth. Pour the mixture into glasses. Float light cream on top, decorate with whole coffee beans, and serve.

ingredients

1¾ cups water

2 tbsp. instant coffee powder

2 tbsp. brown sugar

6 ice cubes

DECORATION

light cream

whole coffee beans

MAY

14

SERVES 2

macaroni & cheese

Put the milk, onion, peppercorns, and bay leaf in a pan and bring to a boil. Remove from the heat and let stand for 15 minutes.

Melt the butter in a pan and stir in the flour until well combined and smooth. Cook over medium heat, stirring constantly, for 1 minute. Remove from the heat. Strain the milk and stir a little into the butter and flour mixture until well incorporated. Return to the heat and gradually add the remaining milk, stirring constantly, until it has all been incorporated. Cook for an additional 3 minutes, or until the sauce is smooth and thickened, then add the nutmeg, cream, and pepper to taste. Add the Cheddar and Roquefort cheeses and stir until melted.

Meanwhile, bring a large pan of water to a boil. Add the macaroni, then return to a boil and cook for 8–10 minutes, or until just tender. Drain well and add to the cheese sauce. Stir well together.

Preheat the broiler to high. Spoon the macaroni and cheese into an flameproof serving dish, then scatter over the Gruyère cheese and cook under the broiler until bubbling and brown.

ingredients

2½ cups milk

1 onion

8 peppercorns

1 bay leaf

scant 4 tbsp. butter

scant ⅓ cup all-purpose flour

½ tsp. ground nutmeg

⅓ cup heavy cream

pepper

3½ oz. sharp Cheddar cheese, grated

3½ oz. Roquefort cheese, crumbled

12 oz. dried macaroni

3½ oz. Gruyère or Emmental cheese, grated

MAY

15

SERVES 4

artichoke heart soufflé

Preheat the oven to 375°F/190°C. Grease a 7-cup soufflé dish with butter, then tie a double strip of waxed paper around the dish so that it protrudes about 2 inches above the rim. Melt the butter in a large, heavy-bottom pan. Add the flour and cook, stirring constantly, for 2 minutes. Remove from the heat and gradually stir in the milk.

Return to the heat and bring to a boil, whisking constantly, for 2 minutes, or until thickened and smooth. Remove from the heat, season with nutmeg, salt, and pepper, then beat in the cream, cheese, and artichoke hearts.

Beat in the egg yolks, 1 at a time. Whisk the egg whites in a grease-free bowl until they form stiff peaks. Fold 2 tablespoons of the egg whites into the artichoke mixture to loosen, then gently fold in the remainder. Carefully pour the mixture into the prepared soufflé dish and bake in the preheated oven for 35 minutes, or until the soufflé is well risen and the top is golden. Serve immediately.

ingredients

¼ cup butter, plus extra for greasing

6 tbsp. all-purpose flour

1¼ cups milk

pinch of freshly grated nutmeg

salt and pepper

2 tbsp. light cream

½ cup grated Emmental cheese

6 canned artichoke hearts, drained
   and mashed

4 egg yolks

5 egg whites

VARIATION

For a spinach soufflé, substitute 8 oz of prepared spinach for the artichoke hearts.

ingredients

1¾ cups all-purpose flour, plus
    extra for dusting

1 tsp. baking powder

pinch of salt

¾ cup golden superfine sugar

2 eggs, beaten

finely grated rind of 1 unwaxed
    orange

⅔ cup whole blanched almonds,
    lightly toasted

MAY

17

MAKES 20

VARIATION

As an alternative to almonds, use
hazelnuts or a mixture of almonds
and pistachio nuts.

almond biscotti

Preheat the oven to 350°F/180°C, then lightly dust a cookie sheet with flour.

Sift the flour, baking powder, and salt into a bowl. Add the sugar, eggs, and orange
rind and mix to a dough, then knead in the toasted almonds.

Roll out the dough into a ball, cut in half, and roll out each portion into a log about
1½ inches in diameter. Place on the floured cookie sheet and bake in the oven for
10 minutes. Remove from the oven and let cool for 5 minutes. Using a serrated knife,
cut the logs into ½-inch/1-cm thick diagonal slices. Arrange the slices on the cookie
sheet and return to the oven for 15 minutes, or until slightly golden. Transfer to a
wire rack to cool and crispen.

mushroom bites with aioli

Preheat the oven to 375°F/190°C. To make the aioli, put the garlic in a bowl, add a pinch of salt, and mash with the back of a spoon. Add the egg yolks and beat with an electric whisk for 30 seconds, or until creamy. Start beating in the oil, one drop at a time. As the mixture begins to thicken, add the oil in a steady stream, beating constantly. Season to taste with salt and pepper, cover the bowl with plastic wrap, and chill in the refrigerator until required.

Line a large cookie sheet with parchment paper. Grate the bread into bread crumbs and place them in a bowl with the Parmesan cheese and paprika. Lightly beat the egg whites in a separate clean bowl, then dip each mushroom first into the egg whites, then into the bread crumbs, and place on the prepared cookie sheet. Bake in the preheated oven for 15 minutes, or until the coating is crisp and golden. Serve immediately with the aioli.

ingredients

4 oz. fresh white bread

2 tbsp. freshly grated Parmesan
    cheese

1 tsp. paprika

2 egg whites

8 oz. white mushrooms

AIOLI

4 garlic cloves, crushed

salt and pepper

2 egg yolks

scant 1 cup extra virgin olive oil

VARIATION

For a herb cream dip, mix 4 tablespoons of chopped herbs with ¾ cup sour cream, 1 chopped garlic clove, lemon juice, and seasoning to taste.

ingredients

4 duck legs, all visible fat trimmed
off

1 lb. 12 oz. canned tomatoes,
chopped

8 garlic cloves, peeled, but left
whole

1 large onion, chopped

1 carrot, peeled and chopped finely

1 celery stalk, peeled and chopped
finely

3 sprigs fresh thyme

generous ½ cup Spanish green
olives stuffed with pimientos
in brine, rinsed

salt and pepper

1 tsp. finely grated orange rind

duck legs with olives

Put the duck legs in the bottom of a flameproof casserole or a large, heavy-bottom skillet
with a tight-fitting lid. Add the tomatoes, garlic, onion, carrot, celery, thyme, and olives,
and stir together. Season with salt and pepper to taste.

Turn the heat to high and cook, uncovered, until the ingredients start to bubble. Reduce
the heat to low, cover tightly, and let simmer for 1¼–1½ hours until the duck is very
tender. Check occasionally and add a little water if the mixture appears to be drying out.

When the duck is tender, transfer it to a serving platter, cover, and keep hot in a
preheated warm oven. Leave the casserole uncovered, increase the heat to medium, and
cook, stirring, for about 10 minutes until the mixture forms a sauce. Stir in the orange
rind, then taste and adjust the seasoning if necessary.

Mash the tender garlic cloves with a fork and spread over the duck legs. Spoon the
sauce over the top. Serve at once.

MAY

20

SERVES 4

sweet chili squid

Place the sesame seeds on a cookie sheet and toast under a hot broiler, then set aside.

Heat 1 tablespoon of oil in a skillet over a medium heat. Add the squid and cook for 2 minutes. Remove from the skillet and set aside. Add the other tablespoon of oil to the skillet and cook the bell peppers and shallots over a medium heat for 1 minute. Add the mushrooms and cook for another 2 minutes.

Return the squid to the skillet and add the sherry, soy sauce, sugar, chili flakes, and garlic, stirring thoroughly. Cook for another 2 minutes. Sprinkle with the sesame seeds, then drizzle over the sesame oil and mix. Serve on a bed of rice.

ingredients

1 tbsp. sesame seeds, toasted

2 tbsp. sesame oil

10 oz. squid, cut into strips

2 red bell peppers, sliced thinly

3 shallots, sliced thinly

1½ cups mushrooms, sliced thinly

1 tbsp. dry sherry

4 tbsp. soy sauce

1 tsp. sugar

1 tsp. hot chili flakes, or to taste

1 clove of garlic, crushed

1 tsp. sesame oil

cooked rice, to serve

MAY

21

SERVES 4

chicken with forty cloves of garlic

Preheat the oven to 350°F/180°C. Season the chicken inside and out with salt and pepper, then truss with fine string or elastic string. Place on a rack in a casserole dish and arrange the garlic and herbs around it.

Pour the wine over the chicken and cover with a tight-fitting lid. Cook in the oven for 1½–1¾ hours, or until tender and the juices run clear when a skewer is inserted into the thickest part of the meat.

Transfer the chicken and garlic to a dish and keep warm. Strain the cooking juices into a bowl. Carve the meat. Skim off any fat on the surface of the cooking juices.

Divide the chicken and garlic among serving plates. Spoon over a little of the cooking juices. Serve immediately with freshly cooked green beans, handing round the remaining cooking juices separately.

ingredients

1 chicken, weighing 3 lb. 8 oz.

salt and pepper

3 garlic bulbs, separated into cloves but unpeeled

6 fresh thyme sprigs

2 fresh tarragon sprigs

2 bay leaves

1¼ cups dry white wine

freshly cooked beans, to serve

chicken tikka

Place the chicken in a large glass bowl. Add the garlic, gingerroot, yogurt, lemon juice, chili powder, turmeric, and cilantro and stir well. Cover with plastic wrap and let marinate in the refrigerator for up to 8 hours.

Preheat the grill. To make the raita, cut the cucumber into thick slices, then chop finely. Place the cucumber and chili in a bowl and beat in the yogurt with a fork. Stir in the cumin and season to taste with salt. Cover and let chill in the refrigerator until required. Thread the chicken cubes onto presoaked wooden skewers and brush with oil.

Cook the chicken, turning and brushing frequently with oil, for 15 minutes, or until thoroughly cooked. Briefly heat the naan bread on the barbecue. Garnish with onion rings, cilantro sprigs, and lemon wedges, and serve with the naan bread and the raita.

ingredients

1 lb. 2 oz. skinless, boneless
   chicken, cut into 2-inch cubes
1 garlic clove, finely chopped
½-inch piece fresh gingerroot, finely
   chopped
⅔ cup plain yogurt
4 tbsp. lemon juice
1 tsp. chili powder
¼ tsp. ground turmeric
1 tbsp. chopped fresh cilantro
vegetable oil, for brushing
naan bread, to serve

RAITA

½ cucumber
1 fresh green chili, seeded and
   finely chopped
1¼ cups plain yogurt
¼ tsp. ground cumin
salt

GARNISH

thinly sliced onion rings
fresh cilantro sprigs
lemon wedges

COOK'S TIP

Fresh chilies can burn the skin several hours after chopping, so it is advisable to wear gloves when handling them. Alternatively, wash your hands thoroughly afterwards.

turkey with bamboo shoots & water chestnuts

Blend the sherry, lemon juice, soy sauce, gingerroot, and garlic in a bowl, then add the turkey and stir. Cover the dish with plastic wrap and refrigerate to marinate for 3–4 hours.

In a wok or skillet, add the sesame oil and vegetable oil and heat slowly. Remove the turkey from the marinade with a slotted spoon (reserving the marinade) and stir-fry a few pieces at a time until browned. Remove the turkey from the wok and set aside.

Add the mushrooms, green bell pepper, and zucchini to the wok and stir-fry for 3 minutes. Add the scallions and stir-fry for 1 minute more. Add the bamboo shoots and water chestnuts, then the turkey along with half of the reserved marinade. Stir over a medium-high heat for another 2–3 minutes, until the ingredients are evenly coated and the marinade has reduced.

Serve immediately over noodles or rice.

ingredients

MARINADE

4 tbsp. sweet sherry

1 tbsp. lemon juice

1 tbsp. soy sauce

2 tsp. grated fresh gingerroot

1 garlic clove, crushed

STIR-FRY

1 lb. turkey breast, cubed

1 tbsp. sesame oil

2 tbsp. vegetable oil

4½ oz. small mushrooms, halved

1 green bell pepper, cut into strips

1 zucchini, sliced thinly

4 scallions, cut into quarters

4 oz. canned bamboo shoots, drained

4 oz. canned sliced water chestnuts, drained

freshly cooked noodles or rice, to serve

double chocolate chip cookies

Preheat the oven to 350°F/180°C, then grease 3 cookie sheets. Place the butter, superfine sugar, and brown sugar in a bowl and beat until light and fluffy. Gradually beat in the egg and vanilla extract.

Sift the flour, cocoa, and baking soda into the mixture and stir in carefully. Stir in the chocolate chips and walnuts.

Drop spoonfuls of the mixture on to the prepared cookie sheets, spaced well apart to allow for spreading. Bake in the oven for 10–15 minutes, or until the mixture has spread and the cookies are beginning to feel firm.

Let cool on the cookie sheets for 2 minutes, then transfer to wire racks to cool completely.

ingredients

½ cup butter, softened,
  plus extra for greasing
¼ cup golden superfine sugar
¼ cup brown sugar
1 egg, beaten
½ tsp. vanilla extract
generous ¾ cup all-purpose flour
2 tbsp. unsweetened cocoa
½ tsp. baking soda
⅔ cup milk chocolate chips
⅓ cup coarsely chopped walnuts

MAY
24

MAKES 24

chili roast potatoes

Cook the potatoes in a pan of boiling water for 10 minutes, then drain them thoroughly.

Pour a little of the oil into a shallow roasting pan to coat the base. Heat the oil in a preheated oven, 400°F/200°C, for 10 minutes. Add the potatoes to the pan and brush them with the hot oil.

In a small bowl, mix together the chili powder, caraway seeds, and salt. Sprinkle the mixture over the potatoes, turning to coat them all over.

Add the remaining oil to the pan and roast in the oven for about 15 minutes, or until the potatoes are cooked through.

Using a slotted spoon, remove the potatoes from the the oil, draining them well, and transfer them to a warmed serving dish. Sprinkle the basil over the top and serve immediately.

ingredients

1 lb. 2 oz. small new potatoes,
  scrubbed
⅔ cup vegetable oil
1 tsp. chili powder
½ tsp. caraway seeds
1 tsp. salt
1 tbsp. chopped basil

MAY
25

SERVES 4

a spoonful of noodles

Drop the noodles in a pan of boiling water and boil for 4 minutes, until soft. Alternatively, cook according to the packet instructions. Drain, rinse well to remove the excess starch, and drain again.

Flake the crabmeat into a bowl. Stir in the parsley and 2 tablespoons of the lemon juice and add the salt, pepper, and paprika. Add a little extra lemon juice, if you like. Toss the noodles with the crab salad.

Use only a small amount of noodles per spoon. Chinese soup spoons are inexpensive to buy from most Chinese food stores – use all one color or a variety of patterns. If you don't have the spoons, serve bite-size mounds of the noodle salad on slices of cucumber or radicchio leaves that are firm enough to pick up.

Using a fork, swirl the noodles and crab into a small mound, then place it in the spoon, with any loose ends tucked underneath. Continue until all the ingredients are used.

You can make the salad and assemble it in the spoons in advance, but be sure to take them out of the refrigerator 15 minutes before you serve, so the flavors aren't dulled.

ingredients

2 oz. dried thin buckwheat noodles, or any other thin noodles, such as Japanese somen

4 oz. canned crabmeat (drained weight), any excess liquid squeezed out

2 tbsp. very finely chopped fresh parsley

about 2 tbsp. fresh lemon juice

salt and pepper

pinch of paprika

VARIATION

For an alternative flavor, toss the noodles with drained, flaked tuna, chopped capers, cilantro, and lime juice to taste.

layered vegetable casserole

Preheat the oven to 350°F/180°C. Brush a large flameproof dish with a little of the olive oil. Prepare all the vegetables. Peel and thinly slice the potatoes, trim and thinly slice the leeks, and slice the tomatoes.

Place a layer of potato slices in the bottom of the dish, sprinkle with half of the basil leaves and cover with a layer of leeks. Top with a layer of tomato slices. Repeat these layers until all the vegetables are used up, ending with a layer of potatoes. Stir the chopped garlic into the vegetable stock and season to taste with salt and pepper. Pour the stock over the vegetables and brush the top with the remaining olive oil.

Bake in the preheated oven for 1½ hours, or until the vegetables are tender and the topping is golden brown. Serve immediately.

ingredients

1 tbsp. olive oil, for brushing

1 lb. 8 oz. potatoes

2 leeks

2 beefsteak tomatoes

8 fresh basil leaves

1 garlic clove, finely chopped

1¼ cups vegetable stock

salt and pepper

chicken kabobs with yogurt sauce

To make the sauce, put the yogurt, garlic, lemon juice, oregano, salt, and pepper in a large bowl and mix well together.

Cut the chicken breasts into chunks measuring about 1½ inches square. Add to the yogurt mixture and toss well together until the chicken pieces are coated. Cover and let marinate in the fridge for about 1 hour. If you are using wooden skewers, soak them in cold water for 30 minutes.

Preheat the broiler. Thread the pieces of chicken onto 8 flat, greased, metal kabob skewers, wooden skewers, or rosemary stems and place on a greased broiler pan.

Cook the kabobs under the broiler for about 15 minutes, turning and basting with the remaining marinade occasionally, until lightly browned and tender.

Pour the remaining marinade into a pan and heat gently but do not boil. Serve the kabobs on a bed of shredded lettuce and garnish with lemon wedges. Accompany with the yogurt sauce.

ingredients

1¼ cups Greek yogurt

2 garlic cloves, crushed

juice of ½ lemon juice

1 tbsp. chopped fresh herbs such as oregano, dill, tarragon, or parsley

salt and pepper

4 large skinned, boned chicken breasts

8 firm stems of fresh rosemary, optional

shredded romaine lettuce, to serve

lemon wedges, to garnish

asparagus with poached eggs & parmesan

Bring 2 pans of water to a boil. Add the asparagus to one of the pans, return to a simmer, and cook for 5 minutes, or until just tender.

Meanwhile, reduce the heat of the second pan to a simmer and carefully crack in the eggs, one at a time. Poach for 3 minutes, or until the whites are just set but the yolks are still soft. Remove with a slotted spoon.

Drain the asparagus and divide among 4 warmed plates. Top each plate of asparagus with an egg and shave over the cheese. Season to taste with pepper and serve immediately.

ingredients

10½ oz. asparagus, trimmed

4 large eggs

3 oz. Parmesan cheese

pepper

zucchini pasta sauce with lemon & rosemary

Heat the olive oil in a large skillet over a medium-low heat. Add the onion and gently fry, stirring occasionally, for about 10 minutes until golden.

Raise the heat to medium-high. Add the garlic, rosemary, and parsley. Cook for a few seconds, stirring.

Add the zucchini and lemon peel. Cook for 5–7 minutes, stirring occasionally, until the zucchini are just tender. Season with salt and pepper. Remove from the heat.

Cook the pasta in plenty of boiling salted water until al dente. Drain and transfer to a warm serving dish.

Briefly reheat the zucchini. Pour over the pasta and toss well to mix. Sprinkle with the Parmesan and serve immediately.

ingredients

6 tbsp. olive oil

1 small onion, sliced very thinly

2 garlic cloves, chopped very finely

2 tbsp. chopped fresh rosemary

1 tbsp. chopped fresh flat-leaf parsley

1 lb. small zucchini, cut into 1½ x ¼ inch strips

finely grated peel of 1 lemon

salt and pepper

1 lb. fusilli

4 tbsp. freshly grated Parmesan

ingredients

2 pork fillets, weighing 12 oz. each

salt and pepper

2 thin slices of cooked ham or
    prosciutto

3 oz. cheese, crumbled

4 prunes, cut in half

4 fresh sage leaves, chopped

1 tbsp. butter

1 cup hard cider or apple juice

1 tsp. mild mustard

½ cup light cream

cheese-stuffed pork fillet

Preheat the oven to 375°F/190°C.

Cut the fillets down the centre, but do not cut right through. Spread them open and flatten out. You can bash the fillets with a rolling pin to flatten them out more if you wish.

Season the fillets well with salt and pepper and place a piece of ham on each one. Crumble over the cheese and arrange the prunes in between. Sprinkle over the sage leaves.

Fold the fillets over into neat sausage shapes and secure with toothpicks or tie with string to make sure they keep their shape.

Place in a small roasting pan, dot with the butter, and pour over the hard cider.

Cover with foil and cook in the oven for 40–45 minutes, removing the foil for the last 10 minutes.

Remove the pan from the oven and place the pork on a warm plate. Remove the toothpicks or string and allow to rest for 10 minutes in a warm place.

Place the roasting pan on the stove over a medium heat and stir the juices well to mix. Add the mustard and bubble away until the sauce is quite thick. Stir in the cream and heat through.

Slice the pork across diagonally and serve the sauce separately.

CHAPTER

6

June

lemon granita

Heat the water in a heavy-bottom pan over low heat. Add the sugar and stir until it has completely dissolved. Bring to a boil, remove the pan from the heat, and set the syrup aside to cool.

Stir the lemon juice and rind into the syrup. Pour the mixture into a freezerproof container and place in the freezer for 3–4 hours.

To serve, remove the container from the freezer and dip the base into hot water. Turn out the ice block and chop coarsely, then place in a food processor and process until it forms small crystals (granita means "granular"). Spoon into sundae glasses and serve immediately.

ingredients

2 cups water

generous ½ cup white granulated sugar

1 cup lemon juice

grated rind of 1 lemon

COOK'S TIP

An ordinary blender may not be sufficiently robust to process the ice as it can damage the blades. A good-quality food processor is recommended.

VARIATION

Many different fruit syrups can be used to flavor granitas—oranges, mandarins, pink grapefruit, or mangoes. Simply substitute the juice in step 2. You can add extra flavor with a splash of liqueur or include herbs, such as lemon balm, or elderflower in the syrup in step 1 (strain before pouring into the freezer container). Coffee granita made with espresso coffee instead of fruit juice, with or without a dash of liqueur, is also delicious.

ingredients

4 boneless chicken breasts

1 bay leaf

1 small onion, sliced

1 carrot, sliced

salt and pepper

4 peppercorns

1 tbsp. olive oil

2 shallots, finely chopped

2 tsp. mild curry paste

2 tsp. tomato paste

juice of ½ lemon

1¼ cups mayonnaise

⅔ cup plain yogurt

3 oz. no-soak dried
  apricots, chopped

2 tbsp. chopped fresh parsley,
  to garnish

coronation chicken

Place the chicken breasts in a large pan with the bay leaf, onion, and carrot. Cover with water and add ½ teaspoon of salt and the peppercorns. Bring to a boil over a medium heat, reduce the heat, and simmer very gently for 20–25 minutes. Remove from the heat and allow to cool in the liquor. Reserve ⅔ cup of the stock for the sauce.

Meanwhile, heat the oil in a skillet and sauté the shallots gently for 2–3 minutes until soft but not colored. Stir in the curry paste and continue to cook for a further minute. Stir in the reserved stock, the tomato paste, and the lemon juice and simmer for 10 minutes until the sauce is quite thick. Cool.

Remove the chicken from the stock, take off the skin and slice into neat pieces.

Mix together the mayonnaise and the yogurt and stir into the sauce. Add the chopped apricots and season to taste with salt and pepper.

Stir the chicken into the sauce until well coated and turn into a serving dish. Allow to stand for at least 1 hour for the flavors to mingle. Serve garnished with the chopped parsley.

tagliatelle with asparagus & gorgonzola

Place the asparagus tips in a single layer in a shallow ovenproof dish. Sprinkle with a little olive oil. Season with salt and pepper. Turn to coat in the oil and seasoning.

Roast in a preheated oven at 450°F/230°C for 10–12 minutes, or until slightly browned and just tender. Set aside and keep warm.

Combine the crumbled cheese with the cream in a bowl. Season with salt and pepper.

Cook the pasta in plenty of boiling salted water until al dente. Drain and transfer to a warm serving dish.

Immediately add the asparagus and the cheese mixture. Toss well until the cheese has melted and the pasta is coated with the sauce. Serve at once.

ingredients

1 lb. asparagus tips

olive oil

salt and pepper

8 oz. Gorgonzola, crumbled

¾ cup heavy cream

12 oz. dried tagliatelle or penne

crispy coated chicken breasts

Preheat the oven to 400°F/200°C. To make the potato wedges, bring a large pan of water to a boil. Add the potatoes and cook over medium heat for 5 minutes. Drain well. Pour 2 tablespoons of the oil into a large bowl and stir in the chili powder. Add the potatoes and turn in the mixture until coated. Transfer to a cookie sheet, drizzle over the remaining oil, and bake for 35–40 minutes, turning frequently, until golden and cooked through.

About 15 minutes before the end of the cooking time, put the hazelnuts, bread crumbs, cheese, and parsley into a bowl, season, and mix. Dip the chicken breasts into the egg, then coat in the bread crumb mixture. Heat the oil in a skillet. Add the chicken and cook over medium heat for 3–4 minutes on each side until golden. Lift out and drain on paper towels. Remove the potatoes from the oven, divide between 4 serving plates, and add a chicken breast to each. Garnish with parsley and serve with lemon wedges.

ingredients

1¾ oz. hazelnuts, toasted
   and ground

3 tbsp. dried white or whole-wheat
   bread crumbs

2 tbsp. freshly grated romano
   cheese

1 tbsp. chopped fresh parsley

salt and pepper

4 skinless chicken breasts

1 egg, beaten

4 tbsp. vegetable oil

sprigs of fresh flat-leaf parsley,
   to garnish

wedges of lemon, to serve

SWEET POTATO WEDGES

4 large sweet potatoes, peeled and
   cut into wedges

4 tbsp. vegetable oil

1 tsp. chili powder

baked fish & chips

Preheat the oven to 400°F/200°C. Line 2 cookie sheets with nonstick liner. Rinse the sliced potatoes under cold running water, then dry well on a clean dish towel. Put in a bowl, spray with oil, and toss together until coated. Spread the fries on a cookie sheet and cook in the oven for 40–45 minutes, turning once, until golden.

Meanwhile, put the flour on a plate, beat the egg in a shallow dish, and spread the seasoned bread crumbs on a large plate. Dip the fish fillets in the flour to coat, then the egg, letting any excess drip off, and finally the bread crumbs, patting them firmly into the fish.

Place the fish in a single layer on a cookie sheet. Fifteen minutes before the fries have cooked, bake the fish fillets in the oven for 10–15 minutes, turning them once during cooking, until the fish is tender. Serve the fish with the fries.

ingredients

1 lb. mealy potatoes, peeled and
    cut into thick, even French fries
vegetable oil spray
½ cup all-purpose white flour
1 egg
1 cup fresh white bread crumbs,
    seasoned with salt and pepper
4 cod or haddock fillets

spaghetti olio e aglio

Bring a large heavy-bottom pan of lightly salted water to a boil. Add the pasta, return to a boil, and cook for 8–10 minutes, or until tender but still firm to the bite.

Meanwhile, heat the olive oil in a heavy-bottom skillet. Add the garlic and a pinch of salt and cook over low heat, stirring constantly, for 3–4 minutes, or until golden. Do not let the garlic brown or it will taste bitter. Remove the skillet from the heat.

Drain the pasta and transfer to a large, warmed serving dish. Pour in the garlic-flavored olive oil, then add the chopped parsley and season to taste with salt and pepper. Toss well and serve immediately.

ingredients

1 lb. dried spaghetti
½ cup extra virgin olive oil
3 garlic cloves, finely chopped
salt and pepper
3 tbsp. chopped fresh flat-leaf
    parsley

strawberry baked alaska

Preheat the oven to 475°F/240°C. Place the sponge cake in a large, shallow, ovenproof dish and sprinkle with the sherry or orange juice.

Whisk the egg whites in a spotlessly clean, greasefree bowl until stiff. Continue to whisk, gradually adding the sugar, until very stiff and glossy.

Working quickly, cover the top of the cake with the ice cream and then top with the strawberry halves. Spread the meringue over the cake, making sure that the ice cream is completely covered. Bake in the preheated oven for 3–5 minutes, or until the meringue is golden brown. Serve immediately, with whole strawberries.

ingredients

9-inch round sponge cake

2 tbsp. sweet sherry or orange juice

5 egg whites

scant ¾ cup superfine sugar

2½ cups strawberry ice cream

generous 1 cup fresh strawberries, halved, plus whole strawberries, to serve

COOK'S TIP

For the perfect meringue, bring the egg whites to room temperature before whisking. It is worth noting that the fresher the eggs, the greater will be the volume of the meringue.

fish roasted with lime

Preheat the oven to 350°F/180°C.

Place the fish fillets in a nonmetallic bowl and season to taste with salt and pepper. Squeeze the juice from the lime halves over the fish.

Heat the oil in a skillet. Add the onion and garlic and cook, stirring frequently, for 2 minutes, or until softened. Remove the skillet from the heat.

Place a third of the onion mixture and a little of the chilies and cilantro in the base of a shallow ovenproof dish or roasting pan. Arrange the fish on top. Top with the remaining onion mixture, chilies, and cilantro.

Roast in the oven for 15–20 minutes, or until the fish has become slightly opaque and firm to the touch. Serve immediately, with lemon and lime wedges for squeezing over the fish.

ingredients

2 lb. 4 oz. white fish fillets,
    such as bass, plaice, or cod
salt and pepper
1 lime, halved
3 tbsp. extra virgin olive oil
1 large onion, finely chopped
3 garlic cloves, finely chopped
2–3 pickled jalapeño chilies
    (jalapeños en escabeche),
    chopped
6–8 tbsp. chopped fresh cilantro
lemon and lime wedges, to serve

ingredients

3½ cups fresh or frozen shelled
   fava beans

olive oil

8 unboned chicken thighs,
   excess fat removed, skin on

1 large onion, sliced finely

1 large garlic clove, crushed

1 lb. 2 oz. cremini mushrooms,
   wiped and sliced thickly

salt and pepper

scant 2½ cups chicken stock

finely chopped fresh parsley,
   to garnish

pan-fried potatoes, to serve

JUNE

9

SERVES 4

chicken thighs with fava beans & mushrooms

To blanch the beans, bring a large pan of salted water to a boil, add the beans, and continue boiling for 5–10 minutes until just tender. Drain and put in a bowl of cold water to stop further cooking. Peel off the outer skins; set aside.

Heat 2 tablespoons of the oil in a large, lidded skillet or flameproof casserole over medium-high heat. Add 4 chicken thighs, skin sides down, and cook for 5 minutes, or until the skins are crisp and golden. Remove from the skillet and keep warm and cook the remaining thighs, adding a little extra oil if necessary.

Drain off all but 2 tablespoons of the fat in the skillet. Add the onion and cook for 3 minutes, then add the garlic and continue cooking for 5 minutes until the onion is golden. Stir in the mushrooms and salt and pepper to taste and continue cooking for 2 minutes, or until the mushrooms absorb all the fat and start to give off their juices.

Return the chicken thighs to the skillet, skin sides up. Pour in the chicken stock and bring to a boil. Reduce the heat to low, cover tightly, and let simmer for 15 minutes.

Add the beans and continue simmering for 5 minutes until the beans are tender and the chicken juices run clear when a thigh is pierced. Taste and adjust the seasoning. Sprinkle with parsley and serve with pan-fried potatoes.

COOK'S TIP
Unblanched fava beans
can take up to 20 minutes
to cook, depending on
their age. Frozen beans
can be added straight from
the freezer.

california smoothie

Put the banana, strawberries, dates, and honey into a blender and blend until smooth.

Add the orange juice and crushed ice cubes and blend again until smooth. Pour into a chilled Collins glass.

ingredients

1 banana, peeled and thinly sliced

½ cup strawberries

½ cup pitted dates

4½ tsp. honey

1 cup orange juice

4–6 crushed ice cubes

shrimp cocktail

Divide the lettuce among 4 small serving dishes (traditionally, stemmed glass ones, but any small dishes will be fine).

Mix together the mayonnaise, cream, and tomato ketchup in a bowl. Add Tabasco and lemon juice to your taste and season well with salt and pepper.

Divide the peeled shrimp equally among the dishes and pour over the dressing. Chill for 30 minutes in the refrigerator.

Sprinkle a little paprika over the cocktails and garnish with a shrimp and a slice of lemon on each dish. Serve with the slices of bread and butter.

ingredients

½ lettuce, finely shredded

⅔ cup mayonnaise

2 tbsp. light cream

2 tbsp. tomato ketchup

few drops of Tabasco sauce

juice of ½ lemon

salt and pepper

6 oz. cooked peeled shrimp

TO GARNISH

dash of ground paprika

4 cooked shrimp in their shells

4 lemon slices

thin buttered whole wheat bread
    slices, to serve

VARIATIONS

Other fish cocktails can be made in the same way. Try using crabmeat, lobster or a mixture of seafood. A more modern approach is to serve the prawns with avocado or mango and to add lime juice and fish sauce as flavorings, omitting the mayonnaise.

ingredients

2 tsp. mirin or sweet sherry

1½ tsp. light soy sauce

1 tsp. toasted sesame oil

½ tsp. salt

4 oz. cooked boneless lamb
  or chicken

2 oz. snow peas

1 small red onion

1 red bell pepper

1 carrot

9 oz. fresh udon or ramen noodles

3½ oz. bean sprouts

2 tbsp. chopped fresh cilantro

1 large egg

1 tsp. oil

pink pickled ginger, sliced or
  shredded, to garnish

toasted sesame seeds, to garnish

hot wok noodles

Combine the mirin, soy sauce, sesame oil, and salt in a large bowl, stirring until the salt dissolves. Set this mixture aside while you prepare the other ingredients, adding each one to the bowl as it is ready.

Remove excess fat from the lamb or any skin from the chicken, then thinly slice the flesh. Cut the snow peas into thin, long strips. Cut the onion in half, then slice into half-moon shapes. Deseed and thinly slice the bell pepper. Peel and coarsely grate the carrot.

Add the noodles and bean sprouts to the bowl, then use your hands to toss and coat all the ingredients. You can now cover and chill the bowl for up to 2 hours, or cook at once.

To make the omelet slices, beat the egg with ½ teaspoon water. Heat 1 teaspoon oil in a skillet over a high heat. Pour in the egg and tilt the pan so it covers the base. Reduce the heat and cook until set. Slide the omelet out, roll up, and slice thinly.

When it's time to cook, heat a wok or large skillet over a high heat. Add the noodle mixture and stir-fry for 3 minutes, or until all the ingredients are hot and the vegetables are just tender. Stir in the cilantro. Divide among 4 plates, then top with omelet slices, pickled ginger, and toasted sesame seeds.

baked herb ricotta

Preheat the oven to 350°F/180°C. Brush a 2-lb. 4 oz. nonstick loaf pan with the oil.

Put the ricotta into a bowl and beat well. Add the eggs and stir until smooth, then stir in the herbs, pepper to taste, and paprika.

Spoon the mixture into the prepared pan and put into a roasting pan half-filled with water. Bake in the preheated oven for 30–40 minutes, or until set. Remove from the oven and let cool.

Meanwhile, cut the crusts off the bread to make Melba toast. Toast each slice and cut widthways in half to create 2 thin slices. Cut each half diagonally into triangles. Arrange in a single layer on a baking sheet and bake in the oven for 10 minutes.

Turn the baked ricotta out on to a serving dish, drizzle with a little oil, and sprinkle with paprika. Serve with the Melba toast and a green salad.

ingredients

1 tbsp. olive oil, plus extra for
    drizzling
2 lb. 4 oz. fresh ricotta cheese,
    drained
3 eggs, lightly beaten
3 tbsp. chopped fresh herbs,
    such as tarragon, parsley, dill,
    and chives
pepper
½ tsp. paprika, plus extra for
    sprinkling
4 slices whole wheat bread
green salad, to serve

blueberry & lemon drizzle cake

Preheat the oven to 350°F/180°C, then grease and line the base of an 8-inch square cake pan. Place the butter and sugar in a bowl and beat together until light and fluffy. Gradually beat in the eggs, adding a little flour towards the end to prevent curdling. Beat in the lemon rind, then fold in the remaining flour and almonds with enough of the lemon juice to give a good dropping consistency.

Fold in three-quarters of the blueberries and turn into the prepared pan. Smooth the surface, then scatter the remaining blueberries on top. Bake in the preheated oven for 1 hour, or until firm to the touch and a skewer inserted into the center comes out clean.

To make the topping, place the lemon juice and sugar in a bowl and mix together. As soon as the cake comes out of the oven, prick it all over with a fine skewer and pour over the lemon mixture. Let cool in the pan until completely cold, then cut into 12 squares to serve.

ingredients

1 cup butter, softened, plus extra
    for greasing
generous 1 cup superfine sugar
4 eggs, beaten
1¾ cups self-rising flour, sifted
finely grated rind and juice of
    1 lemon
generous ¼ cup ground almonds
7 oz. fresh blueberries

TOPPING
juice of 2 lemons
½ cup superfine sugar

COOK'S TIP

If you warm a lemon gently in the microwave for a few seconds on High, it will yield more juice when you squeeze it.

ingredients

1 tbsp. olive oil

4 turkey scallops or steaks

2 red bell peppers

1 red onion

2 garlic cloves, finely chopped

1¼ cups strained canned tomatoes

⅔ cup medium white wine

1 tbsp. chopped fresh marjoram

salt and pepper

14 oz. canned cannellini beans,
    drained and rinsed

3 tbsp. fresh white bread crumbs

fresh basil sprigs, to garnish

VARIATION

*Soak ½ oz. of dried porcini
mushrooms in boiling water to cover
for 20 minutes. Drain and slice, then
add with the onion and bell peppers
in Step 2.*

italian turkey steaks

Heat the oil in a flameproof casserole or skillet. Add the turkey scallops and cook over a medium heat for 5–10 minutes, turning occasionally, until golden. Transfer to a plate.

Seed and slice the red bell peppers. Slice the onion, add to the skillet with the red bell peppers, and cook over a low heat, stirring occasionally, for 5 minutes, or until softened. Add the garlic and cook for a further 2 minutes. Return the turkey to the skillet and add the tomatoes, wine, and marjoram. Season to taste with salt and pepper. Bring to a boil, then reduce the heat, cover and simmer, stirring occasionally, for 25–30 minutes, or until the turkey is cooked through and tender.

Stir in the cannellini beans and simmer for a further 5 minutes. Sprinkle the bread crumbs over the top and place under a preheated medium-hot broiler for 2–3 minutes, or until golden. Serve, garnished with fresh basil sprigs.

hot sesame beef

Mix the beef strips with 1 tablespoon of the sesame seeds in a small bowl. In a separate bowl, whisk together the beef stock, soy sauce, gingerroot, garlic, cornstarch, and chili flakes.

Heat 1 tablespoon of the sesame oil in a wok or large skillet. Stir-fry the beef strips for 2–3 minutes. Remove and set aside. Discard any oil remaining in the wok, then wipe with paper towels to remove any stray sesame seeds.

Heat the remaining oil and add the broccoli, orange bell pepper, chili, and chili oil (if desired), then stir-fry for 2–3 minutes. Stir in the beef stock mixture, then cover and simmer for 2 minutes.

Return the beef to the wok and simmer until the juices thicken, stirring occasionally. Cook for another 1–2 minutes. Sprinkle with the remaining sesame seeds. Serve over cooked wild rice and garnish with fresh cilantro.

ingredients

1 lb. 2 oz. beef fillet, cut into
   thin strips

1½ tbsp. sesame seeds

½ cup beef stock

2 tbsp. soy sauce

2 tbsp. grated fresh gingerroot

2 garlic cloves, chopped finely

1 tsp. cornstarch

½ tsp. chili flakes

3 tbsp. sesame oil

1 large head of broccoli, cut
   into florets

1 orange bell pepper, sliced thinly

1 red chili, seeded and sliced finely

1 tbsp. chili oil, to taste

1 tbsp chopped fresh cilantro,

cooked wild rice, to serve

lemon butterfly cakes

Preheat the oven to 375°F/190°C. Place 12 paper cases in a muffin pan. Sift the flour and baking powder into a bowl. Add the butter, sugar, eggs, lemon rind, and enough milk to give a medium-soft consistency. Beat thoroughly until smooth. Divide the batter between the paper cases and bake in the preheated oven for 15–20 minutes, or until well risen and golden. Transfer to wire racks to cool.

To make the filling, place the butter in a bowl, then strain in the confectioners' sugar and add the lemon juice. Beat well until smooth and creamy. When the cakes are quite cold, use a sharp-pointed vegetable knife to cut a circle from the top of each cake, then cut each circle in half. Spoon a little of the filling into the center of each cake and press the two semi-circular pieces into it to resemble wings. Dust the cakes with strained confectioners' sugar before serving.

ingredients

generous ¾ cup self-rising flour

½ tsp. baking powder

½ cup butter, softened

generous ½ cup golden
   superfine sugar

2 eggs, beaten

finely grated rind of ½ lemon

2–4 tbsp. milk

confectioners' sugar, for dusting

FILLING

¼ cup butter

generous 1 cup confectioners' sugar

1 tbsp. lemon juice

COOK'S TIP

If time is limited and you want to speed things up, then the cake batter could be mixed in a food processor, rather than by hand.

VARIATION

To make these cakes extra special, place a few slices of strawberry on top of each one.

fried puffs with cheese

Sift the flour, paprika, and ½ teaspoon salt together on to a sheet of waxed paper or parchment paper. Place the butter in a large, heavy-bottom pan, pour in the water, and heat gently. The moment the butter has melted and the liquid begins to boil, tip in the flour mixture and beat vigorously with a wooden spoon until the dough comes away from the side of the pan.

Remove the pan from the heat and let cool for 5 minutes. Gradually beat in the eggs to give a stiff, dropping consistency – you may not need all of them. Stir in the Gruyère cheese.

Heat the oil to 350°F–375°F/180°C–190°C, or until a cube of bread browns in 30 seconds. Shape balls of choux dough between 2 teaspoons and drop them into the oil. Cook for 3–4 minutes, or until golden brown. Remove with a slotted spoon, drain on paper towels, and keep warm until all the puffs are cooked. Pile on to a warmed serving dish, sprinkle with grated Parmesan cheese, and serve immediately.

ingredients

⅔ cup all-purpose flour

½ tsp. paprika

salt and pepper

6 tbsp. butter, diced

1 cup water

3 eggs, lightly beaten

¾ cup Gruyère cheese, grated

corn oil, for deep-frying

2 oz. freshly grated Parmesan
   cheese

COOK'S TIP

When deep-frying, either use a deep-fryer or a large, deep, heavy-bottom pan. Do not fill the deep-fryer more than half full with oil nor the pan more than a third full.

shrimp & garlic pasta with cream

Heat the oil and butter in a pan over a medium–low heat. Add the garlic and red bell pepper. Fry for a few seconds until the garlic is just beginning to color. Stir in the tomato paste and wine. Cook for 10 minutes, stirring.

Cook the pasta in plenty of boiling salted water until al dente. Drain and return to the pan.

Add the shrimp to the sauce and raise the heat to medium–high. Cook for 2 minutes, stirring, until the shrimp turn pink. Reduce the heat and stir in the cream. Cook for 1 minute, stirring constantly, until thickened. Season with salt and pepper.

Transfer the pasta to a warm serving dish. Pour the sauce over the pasta. Sprinkle with the parsley. Toss well to mix and serve at once.

ingredients

3 tbsp. olive oil

3 tbsp. butter

4 garlic cloves, chopped very finely

2 tbsp. finely diced red bell pepper

2 tbsp. tomato paste

½ cup dry white wine

1 lb. tagliatelle or spaghetti

12 oz. raw peeled shrimp, cut into
    ½ inch pieces

½ cup heavy cream

salt and pepper

3 tbsp. chopped fresh flat-leaf
    parsley, to garnish

thai-style chicken salad

JUNE

25

SERVES 4

Bring two pans of water to a boil. Put the potatoes into one pan and cook for 15 minutes until tender. Put the corncobs into the other pan and cook for 5 minutes until tender. Drain the potatoes and corncobs well and let cool.

When the vegetables are cool, transfer them into a large serving dish. Add the bean sprouts, scallions, chicken, lemongrass, and cilantro and season with salt and pepper.

To make the dressing, put all the ingredients into a screw-top jar and shake well. Alternatively, put them into a bowl and mix together well.

Drizzle the dressing over the salad and garnish with lime wedges and cilantro leaves. Serve at once.

ingredients

14 oz. small new potatoes, scrubbed and cut in half, lengthwise

7 oz. baby corncobs, sliced

1½ cups bean sprouts

3 scallions, trimmed and sliced

4 cooked, skinless chicken breasts, sliced

1 tbsp. chopped lemongrass

2 tbsp. chopped fresh cilantro

salt and pepper

DRESSING

6 tbsp. chili oil or sesame oil

2 tbsp. lime juice

1 tbsp. light soy sauce

1 tbsp. chopped fresh cilantro

1 small red chile, seeded and finely chopped

GARNISH

wedges of lime

fresh cilantro leaves

eggplant with cucumber & yogurt dip

JUNE

26

SERVES 4

Preheat the grill. To make the cucumber and yogurt dip, finely chop the cucumber. Place the yogurt in a bowl and beat well until smooth. Stir in the cucumber, scallions, garlic, and mint. Season to taste with salt and pepper. Transfer to a serving bowl, cover with plastic wrap and let chill in the refrigerator until required.

Season the olive oil with salt and pepper, then brush the eggplant slices with the oil. Cook the eggplants for 5 minutes on each side, brushing with more oil, if necessary. Transfer to a large serving plate and serve immediately with the cucumber and yogurt dip, garnished with a mint sprig.

ingredients

2 tbsp. olive oil

salt and pepper

2 eggplants, thinly sliced

CUCUMBER & YOGURT DIP

½ cucumber

generous ¾ cup strained plain yogurt

4 scallions, finely chopped

1 garlic clove, finely chopped

3 tbsp. chopped fresh mint

salt and pepper

1 fresh mint sprig, to garnish

bircher muesli

Put the oats and apple juice into a mixing bowl and combine well. Cover and refrigerate overnight.

To serve, stir the apple and yogurt into the soaked oats and divide among 4 serving bowls. Top with the blackberries and plums and drizzle with the honey.

ingredients

1½ cups rolled oats

1 cup apple juice

1 apple, grated

½ cup yogurt

5½ oz. blackberries

2 plums, pitted and sliced

2 tbsp. clear honey

chilled chocolate dessert

Beat the mascarpone with the coffee and confectioners' sugar until thoroughly combined.

Set aside 4 teaspoons of the grated chocolate and stir the remainder into the cheese mixture with 5 tablespoons of the unwhipped cream.

Whisk the remaining cream until it forms soft peaks. Stir 1 tablespoon of the mascarpone mixture into the cream to slacken it, then fold the cream into the remaining mascarpone mixture with a figure-of-eight action.

Spoon the mixture into a freezerproof container and place in the freezer for about 3 hours.

To serve, scoop the chocolate dessert into sundae glasses and drizzle with a little Marsala. Top with whipped cream, if desired, and decorate with the reserved grated chocolate. Serve immediately.

ingredients

1 cup mascarpone cheese

2 tbsp. finely ground coffee beans

¼ cup confectioners' sugar

3 oz. unsweetened chocolate, grated finely

1½ cups heavy cream, plus extra to decorate

Marsala, to serve

COOK'S TIP
Do not freeze the mixture for too long or it will lose its texture.

stuffed zucchini with walnuts & feta

Put the zucchini in a pan of boiling water, return to a boil, and then boil for 3 minutes. Drain, rinse under cold water, and drain again. Let cool.

When the zucchini are cool enough to handle, cut a thin strip off the top side of each one with a sharp knife and gently score around the inside edges to help scoop out the flesh. Using a teaspoon, scoop out the flesh, leaving a shell to hold the stuffing. Chop the zucchini flesh.

SERVES 4

Heat 2 tablespoons of the oil in a pan. Add the onion and garlic and fry for 5 minutes, until softened. Add the zucchini flesh and fry for 5 minutes, until the onion is golden brown. Remove from the heat and let cool slightly. Stir in the cheese then the walnuts, bread crumbs, egg, dill, and salt and pepper. Use the stuffing to fill the zucchini shells and place side by side in an ovenproof dish. Drizzle over the remaining oil.

Cover the dish with foil and bake in a preheated oven, 375°F/190°C, for 30 minutes. Remove the foil and bake for a further 10–15 minutes or until golden brown. Serve hot.

ingredients

4 fat, medium zucchini

3 tbsp. olive oil

1 onion, chopped finely

1 garlic clove, chopped finely

2 oz. feta cheese, crumbled

¼ cup walnut pieces, chopped

1 cup white bread crumbs

1 egg, beaten

1 tsp. chopped fresh dill

salt and pepper

shrimp wrapped in ham

First, make the dressing. Finely chop the prepared tomato flesh and put it in a bowl. Add the onion, parsley, capers, and lemon rind, and gently toss together. Combine the oil and vinegar and add to the other ingredients; set aside until required.

Wrap a slice of ham around each shrimp and rub with a little of the oil. Place the shrimp in a heatproof dish large enough to hold them in a single layer. Bake in a preheated oven, 325°F/170°C, for 10 minutes.

Transfer the shrimp to a serving platter and spoon the tomato-caper dressing over. Serve at once, or let cool to room temperature.

ingredients

TOMATO-CAPER DRESSING

2 tomatoes, peeled and seeded

1 small red onion, chopped very finely

4 tbsp. very finely chopped fresh parsley

1 tbsp. capers in brine, drained, rinsed, and chopped

finely grated rind of 1 large lemon

4 tbsp. extra virgin olive oil

1 tbsp. sherry vinegar

16 thin slices serrano ham or prosciutto

16 uncooked jumbo shrimp, shelled and deveined, tails left on

extra virgin olive oil

COOK'S TIP

To peel and seed tomatoes, remove the stalks and cut a small cross in the top of each one. Put the tomatoes into a heatproof bowl, pour over enough boiling water to cover, and leave for 30 seconds. Use a slotted spoon to transfer to a bowl of iced water. Working with 1 tomato at a time, peel off the skin, then cut in half and use a teaspoon to scoop out the cores and seeds.

MAKES 18 PANCAKES

apple pancakes with maple syrup butter

Mix the flour, sugar, and cinnamon together in a bowl and make a well in the center. Beat the egg and milk together and pour into the well. Using a wooden spoon, gently incorporate the dry ingredients into the liquid until well combined, then stir in the grated apple.

Heat the butter in a large nonstick skillet over low heat until melted and bubbling. Add 3 tablespoons of the pancake mixture to form 3½-inch circles. Cook each pancake for about a minute, until it starts to bubble lightly on the top and looks set, then flip it over and cook the other side for 30 seconds, or until cooked through. The pancakes should be golden brown; if not, increase the heat a little. Remove from the pan and keep warm. Repeat the process until all of the pancake batter has been used up (it is not necessary to add extra butter).

To make the maple syrup butter, melt the butter with the maple syrup in a pan over low heat and stir until combined. To serve, place the pancakes on serving dishes and spoon over the flavored butter. Serve warm.

ingredients

1⅓ cups self-rising flour

⅓ cup superfine sugar

1 tsp. ground cinnamon

1 egg

1 cup milk

2 apples, peeled and grated

1 tsp. butter

MAPLE SYRUP BUTTER

3 tbsp. butter, softened

3 tbsp. maple syrup

berry smoothie

Put the blueberries into a food processor or blender and process for 1 minute. Add the raspberries, honey, and yogurt and process for a further minute.

Add the ice and sesame seeds and process again for a further minute. Pour into a tall glass and serve immediately.

JULY

2

SERVES 1

ingredients

1 oz. blueberries

3 oz. raspberries, thawed if frozen

1 tsp. clear honey

1 cup plain yogurt

about 1 heaped tbsp. crushed ice

1 tbsp. sesame seeds

mixed sushi rolls

Put the rice into a pan and cover with cold water. Bring
to a boil, then reduce the heat, cover, and simmer for
15–20 minutes, or until the rice is tender and the water has
been absorbed. Drain if necessary and transfer to a bowl. Mix
the vinegar, sugar, and salt together, then, using a spatula, stir
well into the rice. Cover with a damp cloth and let cool.

To make the rolls, lay a clean bamboo mat over a cutting
board. Lay a sheet of nori, shiny side-down, on the mat.
Spread a quarter of the rice mixture over the nori, using wet
fingers to press it down evenly, leaving a ½-inch margin at the
top and bottom.

For smoked salmon and cucumber rolls, lay the salmon over
the rice and arrange the cucumber in a line across the center.
For the prawn rolls, lay the prawns and avocado in a line
across the center.

Carefully hold the nearest edge of the mat, then, using the
mat as a guide, roll up the nori tightly to make a neat tube of
rice enclosing the filling. Seal the uncovered edge with a little
water, then roll the sushi off the mat. Repeat to make 3 more
rolls–you need 2 salmon and cucumber and 2 prawn and
avocado in total.

Using a wet knife, cut each roll into 8 pieces and stand upright
on a platter. Wipe and rinse the knife between cuts to prevent
the rice from sticking. Serve the rolls with wasabi, tamari and
pickled ginger.

ingredients

9 oz. sushi rice

2 tbsp. rice vinegar

1 tsp. superfine sugar

½ tsp. salt

4 sheets nori (seaweed) for rolling

FILLINGS

1¾ oz. smoked salmon

1½-inch. piece cucumber, peeled,
   seeded, and cut into short
   thin sticks

1½ oz. cooked peeled shrimp

1 small avocado, pitted, peeled,
   thinly sliced, and tossed in
   lemon juice

TO SERVE

wasabi (Japanese horseradish
   sauce)

tamari (wheat-free soy sauce)

pink pickled ginger

the ultimate cheeseburger

Place the ground steak in a large bowl. Finely grate one onion and add to the ground steak. Add the garlic, horseradish, and pepper to the steak mixture in the bowl. Mix together, then shape into 4 equal-size burgers. Wrap each burger in 2 strips of bacon, then cover and let chill for 30 minutes.

Preheat the broiler to medium-high. Slice the remaining onions. Heat the oil in a skillet. Add the onions and cook over a medium heat for 8–10 minutes, stirring frequently, until the onions are golden brown. Drain on paper towels and keep warm.

SERVES 4

Cook the burgers under the hot broiler for 3–5 minutes on each side or until cooked to personal preference. Lightly toast the sesame seed buns and arrange the shredded lettuce on their bases. Add the burgers, some fried onion, a spoonful of relish, and a cheese slice. Flash broil for 1–2 minutes. Add the lid and serve with extra relish.

ingredients

1 lb. best ground steak

4 onions

2–4 garlic cloves, crushed

2–3 tsp. grated fresh horseradish or
    1–1½ tbsp. creamed horseradish

pepper

8 lean Canadian bacon strips

2 tbsp. corn oil

TO SERVE

4 sesame seed buns

shredded romaine lettuce

4 slices cheese

hamburger relish

VARIATION

For an extra spicy kick to this classic cheeseburger, place a good spoonful of mustard on top of the cooked burger before adding the slice of cheese.

ingredients

2 tbsp. vegetable oil

3 whole cloves

3 cardamom pods, cracked

1 onion, chopped

4 oz. carrots, chopped

2–3 garlic cloves, crushed

1–2 fresh red chilies, seeded
   and chopped

1-inch piece fresh gingerroot, grated

4 oz. cauliflower, broken into
   small florets

6 oz. broccoli, broken into
   small florets

4 oz. green beans, chopped

14 oz. canned chopped tomatoes

2/3 cup vegetable stock

salt and pepper

4 oz. okra, sliced

1 tbsp. chopped fresh cilantro, plus
   extra sprigs to garnish

2/3 cup brown basmati rice

few saffron strands (optional)

zested lime rind, to garnish

vegetable biryani

Heat the oil in a large pan over a low heat, add the spices, onion, carrots, garlic, chilies, and gingerroot and cook, stirring frequently, for 5 minutes.

Add the cauliflower, broccoli, and beans and cook, stirring frequently, for 5 minutes. Stir in the tomatoes, stock, and salt and pepper to taste and bring to a boil. Reduce the heat, cover, and simmer for 10 minutes.

Add the okra and cook for a further 8–10 minutes, or until the vegetables are tender. Stir in the cilantro. Strain off any excess liquid and keep warm.

Meanwhile, cook the rice, with the saffron, if using, in a pan of lightly salted boiling water for 25 minutes, or until tender. Drain and keep warm.

Layer the vegetables and cooked rice in a deep dish or ovenproof bowl, packing the layers down firmly. Leave for about 5 minutes, then invert on to a warmed serving dish and serve, garnished with zested lime rind and cilantro sprigs, with the reserved liquid.

manhattan cheesecake

Preheat the oven to 375°F/190°C. Brush an 8-inch springform pan with oil. Melt the butter in a pan over low heat. Stir in the crackers, then spread in the pan.

Place the cream cheese, eggs, ½ cup of the sugar, and ½ teaspoon of the vanilla extract in a food processor. Process until smooth. Pour over the cracker layer and smooth the top. Place on a baking sheet and bake for 20 minutes, or until set. Remove from the oven and let stand for 20 minutes. Leave the oven switched on. Mix the cream with the remaining sugar and vanilla extract in a bowl. Spoon over the cheesecake. Return it to the oven for 10 minutes, let cool, then chill in the refrigerator for 8 hours, or overnight.

To make the topping, place the sugar in a pan with half of the water over low heat and stir until the sugar has dissolved. Increase the heat, add the blueberries, cover, and cook for a few minutes, or until they begin to soften. Remove from the heat. Mix the arrowroot and remaining water in a bowl, add to the fruit, and stir until smooth. Return to low heat. Cook until the juice thickens and turns translucent. Let cool. Remove the cheesecake from the pan 1 hour before serving. Spoon the fruit on top and chill until ready to serve.

ingredients

sunflower or corn oil, for brushing

6 tbsp. butter

7 oz. graham crackers, crushed

1¾ cups cream cheese

2 large eggs

scant ¾ cup superfine sugar

1½ tsp. vanilla extract

scant 2 cups sour cream

BLUEBERRY TOPPING

¼ cup superfine sugar

4 tbsp. water

9 oz. fresh blueberries

1 tsp. arrowroot

VARIATION

As an alternative to blueberries, try raspberries, black currants, or cranberries for the topping.

pork with basil & lemongrass

Mix the lemongrass, fish sauce (if desired), basil, and lime juice in a bowl. Stir in the pork and toss well to coat. Cover with plastic wrap and refrigerate for 1–2 hours.

Heat 1 tablespoon of the oil in a wok or skillet over a medium heat. Add the meat and the marinade and stir-fry until the pork is browned. Remove from the wok, set aside and keep warm.

Add the remaining 1 tablespoon of oil to the wok and heat. Add all the vegetables and the garlic and stir-fry for about 3 minutes. Return the pork to the wok and add the chicken stock. Cook for 5 minutes, or until the stock is reduced.

Transfer the stir-fry to warm serving dishes and garnish with wedges of lime. Serve on a bed of basmati rice.

ingredients

MARINADE

1 stalk lemongrass, sliced finely

2 tbsp. fish sauce, optional

4 tbsp. fresh basil, shredded

juice of 1 lime

STIR-FRY

12 oz. pork tenderloin, cubed

2 tbsp. sesame oil

5 cups mushrooms, sliced thinly

1 zucchini, sliced thinly

2 carrots, sliced thinly

4 oz. canned bamboo shoots

4 oz. canned water chestnuts, sliced thinly

1 garlic clove, crushed

½ cup chicken stock

wedges of lime, to garnish

cooked basmati rice, to serve

eggplant & garlic dip

Prick the skins of the eggplants with a fork and put on a baking sheet. Bake in a preheated oven, 370°F/190°C, for 45 minutes, or until very soft. Let cool slightly then cut the eggplants in half lengthwise and scoop out the flesh.

Heat the oil in a large, heavy skillet, add the eggplant flesh and fry for 5 minutes. Put the eggplant mixture into a food processor, add the lemon juice, and blend until smooth. Gradually add the yogurt then the garlic and cumin. Season with salt and pepper.

Turn the mixture into a serving bowl and chill in the fridge for at least 1 hour. Garnish with chopped parsley and serve with raw bell pepper strips or sesame crackers.

ingredients

2 large eggplants

¼ cup extra virgin olive oil

juice of ½ lemon

⅔ cup Greek yogurt

2 garlic cloves, crushed

pinch of ground cumin

salt and pepper

chopped fresh flat-leaf parsley, to garnish

strips of red and green bell pepper or sesame crackers, to serve

ingredients

¼ cup olive oil

1 large onion, finely chopped

4 lb. 8 oz. tiny clams, such as
    Venus, well scrubbed

½ cup white wine

4 cups fish stock

3½ cups water

3 garlic cloves, finely chopped

½ tsp. crushed dried chili

14 oz. risotto rice

3 ripe plum tomatoes, peeled
    and roughly chopped

3 tbsp. lemon juice

2 tbsp. chopped fresh chervil
    or parsley

salt and pepper

risotto with clams

Heat 1–2 tablespoons of the oil in a large, heavy-bottom pan over a medium-high heat.
Add the onion and cook, stirring constantly, for 1 minute. Add the clams and wine and
cover tightly. Cook, shaking the pan frequently, for 2–3 minutes until the clams begin
to open. Remove from the heat and discard any clams that do not open.

When cool enough to handle, remove the clams from their shells. Rinse in the cooking
liquid. Cover the clams and set aside. Strain the cooking liquid through a coffee filter or
a sieve lined with paper towels and reserve.

Bring the stock and water to a boil in a pan, then reduce the heat and keep simmering
gently over a low heat while you are cooking the risotto.

Heat the remaining oil in a large, heavy-bottom pan over a medium heat. Add the garlic
and chili and cook gently for 1 minute.

Reduce the heat, add the rice and mix to coat in oil. Cook, stirring constantly, for
2–3 minutes, or until the grains are translucent.

Gradually add the hot stock mixture, a ladle at a time. Stir constantly and add more liquid
as the rice absorbs each addition. Increase the heat to medium so that the liquid bubbles.
Cook for 20 minutes, or until all the liquid is absorbed and the rice is creamy.

Stir in the tomatoes, reserved clams and their cooking liquid, the lemon juice, and chervil.
Heat through gently. Season to taste with salt and pepper. Spoon the risotto onto
warmed plates and serve immediately.

nectarine crunch

Using a sharp knife, cut the nectarines in half, then remove and discard the pits. Chop the flesh into bite-size pieces. Set aside a few pieces for decoration and place a few pieces in the bottom of 4 sundae glasses.

Place a layer of oat cereal in each glass, then drizzle over a little yogurt. Place the jelly and peach nectar in a large pitcher and stir together to mix. Add a few more nectarine pieces to the glasses and drizzle over a little of the jelly mixture. Continue building up the layers in this way, finishing with a layer of yogurt and a sprinkling of oat cereal. Decorate with the reserved nectarine pieces and serve.

ingredients

4 nectarines

6 oz. raisin and nut crunchy
   oat cereal

1¼ cups low fat plain yogurt

2 tbsp. peach jelly

2 tbsp. peach nectar

lemon posset

Mix the lemon rind, lemon juice, wine, and sugar together in a bowl. Stir until the sugar has dissolved. Add the cream and beat with an electric mixer until soft peaks form.

Whisk the egg whites in a separate, spotlessly clean, greasefree bowl until stiff, then carefully fold them into the cream mixture.

Spoon the mixture into tall glasses and let chill in the refrigerator until required. Serve decorated with lemon slices and accompanied by the cats' tongues.

ingredients

grated rind and juice of
   1 large lemon

4 tbsp. dry white wine

generous ¼ cup superfine sugar

1¼ cups heavy cream

2 egg whites

lemon slices, to decorate

cats' tongues, to serve

COOK'S TIP

Use only the very freshest eggs for this dish. It is not advisable to serve any dishes containing raw eggs to the very young or old, pregnant women, the infirm, or anyone whose immune system has been compromised.

cannelloni with ham & ricotta

Preheat the oven to 350°F/180°C. Heat the olive oil in a large heavy-bottom skillet. Add the onions and garlic and cook over low heat, stirring occasionally, for 5 minutes, or until the onion is softened. Add the basil, chopped tomatoes and their can juices, and tomato paste, and season to taste with salt and pepper. Reduce the heat and let simmer for 30 minutes, or until thickened.

Meanwhile, bring a large heavy-bottom pan of lightly salted water to a boil. Add the cannelloni tubes, return to a boil, and cook for 8–10 minutes, or until tender but still firm to the bite. Using a slotted spoon, transfer the cannelloni tubes to a large plate and pat dry with paper towels. Grease a large, shallow ovenproof dish with butter.

Mix the ricotta, ham, and egg together in a bowl and season to taste with salt and pepper. Using a teaspoon, fill the cannelloni tubes with the ricotta mixture and place in a single layer in the dish. Pour the tomato sauce over the cannelloni and sprinkle with the pecorino cheese. Bake in the preheated oven for 30 minutes, or until golden. Serve immediately.

ingredients

2 tbsp. olive oil

2 onions, chopped

2 garlic cloves, finely chopped

1 tbsp. shredded fresh basil

1 lb. 12 oz. canned chopped
    tomatoes

1 tbsp. tomato paste

salt and pepper

12 oz. cannelloni tubes

butter, for greasing

generous 1 cup ricotta cheese

4 oz. cooked ham, diced

1 egg

½ cup freshly grated pecorino
    cheese

VARIATION

Substitute the pecorino cheese with the same amount of freshly grated Parmesan cheese, if you prefer.

basil dumplings

Pour the milk into a pan and bring to just below boiling. Stir in the semolina. Reduce the heat and simmer for 2 minutes until thick and smooth. Remove the pan from the heat. Stir in the basil, tomatoes, eggs, half the butter, and half the Parmesan, and season. Stir well until all the ingredients are incorporated, then pour into a shallow dish or baking sheet and level the surface. Set aside to cool, then let chill for 1 hour until set.

Grease an ovenproof dish with butter. Using a lightly floured cutter, stamp out circles of the set semolina. Place the trimmings in the bottom of the dish and top with the circles. Melt the remaining butter and brush over the circles, then sprinkle with the remaining Parmesan. Bake in a preheated oven, 375°F/190°C, for 30–35 minutes, until golden.

To make the tomato sauce, heat the oil in a heavy-bottom pan. Add the onion, garlic, and bell pepper and cook over a low heat for 5 minutes until soft. Add the tomatoes, tomato paste, sugar, basil, and bay leaf and season with salt and pepper. Cover and simmer, stirring occasionally, for 30 minutes, until thickened. Serve immediately with the dumplings.

ingredients

3 cups milk

1¾ cups semolina

1 tbsp. finely chopped fresh basil leaves

4 sun-dried tomatoes in oil, drained and chopped finely

2 eggs, beaten lightly

2 tbsp. butter, plus extra for greasing

¾ cup freshly grated Parmesan cheese

salt and pepper

TOMATO SAUCE

2 tbsp. olive oil

1 small onion, chopped finely

1 garlic clove, chopped finely

1 red bell pepper, seeded and chopped

8 oz. plum tomatoes, peeled and chopped

1 tbsp. tomato paste

1 tsp. brown sugar

1 tbsp. shredded fresh basil leaves

1 bay leaf

salt and pepper

apricot & yogurt cups

Line a 12-cup muffin pan with small paper cake cases.

Spoon the yogurt into a mixing bowl, add the almond extract and honey, and stir well.

Using a small, sharp knife, cut the almonds into very thin slivers and stir into the yogurt mixture.

Using a pair of kitchen scissors, cut the apricots into small pieces, then stir into the yogurt.

Spoon the mixture into the paper cases and freeze for 1½–2 hours, or until just frozen. Serve immediately.

JULY
14

MAKES 12 CUPS

ingredients

3 cups plain yogurt

few drops of almond extract

2–3 tsp. clear honey, warmed

2 oz. whole blanched almonds

6 oz. no-soak dried apricots

bouillabaisse

Heat the oil in a large pan over medium heat. Add the garlic and onions and cook, stirring, for 3 minutes. Stir in the tomatoes, stock, wine, bay leaf, saffron, and herbs. Bring to a boil, reduce the heat, cover, and simmer for 30 minutes. Meanwhile, soak the mussels in lightly salted water for 10 minutes. Scrub the shells under cold running water and pull off any beards. Discard any with broken shells. Tap the remaining mussels and discard any that refuse to close. Put the rest into a large pan with a little water, bring to a boil and cook over high heat for 4 minutes. Remove from the heat and discard any that remain closed.

When the tomato mixture is cooked, rinse the fish, pat dry, and cut into chunks. Add to the pan and simmer for 5 minutes. Add the mussels, shrimp, and scallops, and season. Cook for 3 minutes, until the fish is cooked through. Remove from the heat, discard the bay leaf, and ladle into serving bowls. Serve with fresh baguettes.

JULY
15

SERVES 4

ingredients

scant ½ cup olive oil

3 garlic cloves, chopped

2 onions, chopped

2 tomatoes, seeded and chopped

generous 2¾ cups fish stock

1¾ cups white wine

1 bay leaf

pinch of saffron threads

2 tbsp. chopped fresh basil

2 tbsp. chopped fresh parsley

7 oz. live mussels

9 oz. snapper or monkfish fillets

9 oz. haddock fillets, skinned

7 oz. shrimp, peeled and deveined

3½ oz. scallops

salt and pepper

fresh baguettes, to serve

JULY
16

SERVES 4

ingredients

9 oz. mixed salad leaves, such as
    red leaf, escarole, and corn salad

6 tbsp. lemon juice

4 globe artichokes

5 tbsp. Calvados

1 shallot, very finely chopped

pinch of salt

1 tbsp. red wine vinegar

3 tbsp. walnut oil

TO GARNISH

½ cup shelled walnuts, chopped

1 tbsp. finely chopped fresh parsley

COOK'S TIP

*This recipe also works well with
good quality canned or bottled
artichoke hearts. Drain and rinse
well before using.*

artichoke hearts
with a warm dressing

Place the salad leaves in a bowl and set aside. Fill a bowl with cold water and add
2 tablespoons of the lemon juice. Working on one artichoke at a time, twist off the
stalks, cut the bases flat, and pull off all the dark outer leaves. Slice the artichokes in half
horizontally and discard the top parts. Trim around the bases to remove the outer dark
green layer and place in the acidulated water.

Bring a pan of water to a boil, add the remaining lemon juice and the artichokes, cover,
and cook for 30–40 minutes, or until tender. Drain, refresh under cold running water, and
drain again. Pull off and discard the remaining leaves, slice off and discard the chokes,
and set the hearts aside.

Pour the Calvados into a small pan, add the shallot and salt and bring to just below boiling
point. Reduce the heat, carefully ignite the Calvados and continue to cook until the
flames have died down. Stir in the vinegar and walnut oil and cook, stirring constantly, for
1 minute. Remove the pan from the heat. Spoon half the dressing over the salad leaves
and toss well to coat. Transfer the salad leaves to a large serving plate and top with the
artichoke hearts. Spoon the remaining dressing over the artichoke hearts, garnish with
the walnuts and parsley, and serve immediately.

strawberry rose meringues

Preheat the oven to 225°F/110°C. Line 2 large cookie sheets with nonstick parchment paper. Place the egg whites in a large, spotlessly clean, greasefree bowl and whisk until stiff peaks form. Whisk in half the sugar, then carefully fold in the remainder. Spoon the meringue into a pastry bag fitted with a large star nozzle. Make 24 x 3-inch lengths on to the cookie sheets. Bake in the oven for 1 hour, or until the meringues are dry and crisp. Cool on wire racks.

To make the filling, place the strawberries in a blender or food processor and process to a purée. Sieve the purée into a bowl and stir in the confectioners' sugar and rose water. Place the cream in a separate bowl and whip until thick. Stir into the strawberry mixture and mix well together. Join the meringues together with the strawberry cream. Cut 6 of the strawberries for the decoration in half and use to decorate the meringues. Scatter rose petals over the top and serve immediately with the remaining whole strawberries.

ingredients

2 egg whites

generous ½ cup superfine sugar

FILLING

⅓ cup strawberries

2 tsp. confectioners' sugar

3 tbsp. rose water

⅔ cup heavy cream

TO DECORATE

12 fresh strawberries

rose petals

COOK'S TIP

When sugar is whisked into egg whites to make a meringue, it should gradually dissolve into the egg whites. Make sure the bowl is very clean, otherwise the meringue will not hold its shape.

VARIATION

You can substitute raspberries for the strawberries, or use a mixture of the 2 fruits, if you like.

angler fish with lime & chili sauce

Toss the fish in the flour, shaking off any excess. Heat the oil in a wok and fry the fish on all sides until browned and cooked through, taking care when turning not to break it up.

Lift the fish out of the wok and keep warm. Add the garlic and chilies and stir-fry for 1–2 minutes, until they have softened.

Add the sugar, the lime juice and rind, and 2–3 tablespoons of water and bring to a boil. Simmer gently for 1–2 minutes, then spoon the mixture over the fish. Serve immediately with rice.

ingredients

4 x 4 oz. angler fish fillets

1 oz. rice flour or cornstarch

6 tbsp. vegetable or peanut oil

4 garlic cloves, crushed

2 large fresh red chilies, seeded and sliced

2 tsp. palm sugar or brown sugar

juice of 2 limes

grated rind of 1 lime

boiled rice, to serve

spaghetti with garlic tomato sauce

Heat the oil in a large pan over a medium heat. Add the onion and fry gently for 5 minutes until soft. Add the tomatoes and garlic. Bring to a boil, then simmer over a medium–low heat for 25–30 minutes until the oil separates from the tomato. Season with salt and pepper.

Cook the pasta in plenty of boiling salted water until al dente. Drain and transfer to a warm serving dish.

Pour the sauce over the pasta. Add the basil and toss well to mix. Serve with Parmesan.

ingredients

5 tbsp. extra-virgin olive oil

1 onion, chopped finely

1 lb. 12 oz. canned chopped
    tomatoes

4 garlic cloves, quartered

salt and pepper

1 lb. dried spaghetti

large handful fresh basil
    leaves, shredded

freshly grated Parmesan, to serve

red snapper cooked in a package

Cut 4 squares of waxed paper large enough to enclose the fish and brush with a little olive oil.

Rinse the fish inside and out under cold running water and pat dry with paper towels. Season. Using a sharp knife, cut 3 diagonal slits in both sides of each fish. Insert the garlic slices into the slits.

Combine the olive oil, tomatoes, and rosemary in a bowl. Spoon a little of the mixture onto each of the waxed paper squares, then place the fish on top. Divide the remaining tomato mixture between the fish.

Fold up the paper round the fish, twisting it into tiny pleats to seal securely. Place the packages on a baking sheet and bake in a preheated oven, 400°F/ 200°C, for 15 minutes.

Transfer the packages to warmed plates and cut off the folded edges of the packages. Serve with bread.

ingredients

4 tbsp. extra virgin olive oil, plus
    extra for brushing

4 x 10 oz. red snapper, cleaned and
    scaled, heads on salt and pepper

4 garlic cloves, sliced thinly
    lengthwise

4 tomatoes, peeled, seeded,
    and diced

2 tsp. finely chopped fresh rosemary

fresh bread, to serve

SERVES 4

fried cheese sandwiches

First, make the tomato sauce. Heat the olive oil in a medium, heavy-bottom pan. Add the onion and garlic and cook over low heat, stirring occasionally, for 5 minutes, until softened. Add the red bell pepper and cook, stirring frequently, for an additional 5 minutes. Stir in the tomatoes, tomato paste, lemon juice, and water, and season to taste with salt and pepper. Cover the pan and let simmer for about 15 minutes, until pulpy.

Meanwhile, slice the mozzarella into 4 thick or 8 medium slices. Spread the bread slices with the butter and place the mozzarella on 4 of them. Top with the salami and sandwich together with the remaining slices of bread. Cut in half to make triangles, wrap in plastic wrap and let chill in the fridge.

Remove the sauce from the heat and set aside to cool slightly in the pan, then process in a food processor or blender until smooth. Return the sauce to a clean pan and reheat gently.

Heat the corn oil in a deep-fryer to 350–375°F/180–190°C or, if using a heavy-bottom pan, until a cube of day-old bread browns in 30 seconds. Meanwhile, beat the eggs with the milk in a shallow dish and season to taste with salt and pepper. Unwrap the sandwiches and dip them, in batches, into the egg mixture, letting them soak briefly. Add the sandwiches, in batches, to the hot oil and cook until golden brown on both sides. Remove with tongs, drain well on paper towels and keep warm while you cook the remaining triangles. Serve the sandwiches hot and hand round the sauce separately.

ingredients

7 oz. mozzarella

8 x ½-inch thick slices day-old white bread, crusts removed

3 oz. unsalted butter

4 medium slices Italian salami

corn oil, for deep-frying

3 eggs

3 tbsp. milk

salt and pepper

TOMATO SAUCE

3 tbsp. olive oil

1 onion, chopped

2 garlic cloves, chopped finely

1 red bell pepper, seeded and chopped

14 oz. canned tomatoes, chopped

2 tbsp. tomato paste

1 tbsp. lemon juice

2 tbsp. water

salt and pepper

walnut & cinnamon blondies

Preheat the oven to 350°F/180°C. Grease and line the bottom of a 7-inch square cake pan. Place the butter and sugar in a pan over low heat and stir until the sugar has dissolved. Cook, stirring, for an additional 1 minute. The mixture will bubble slightly, but do not let it boil. Let cool for 10 minutes.

Stir the egg and egg yolk into the mixture. Sift in the flour and cinnamon, add the nuts, and stir until just blended. Pour the cake batter into the prepared pan, then bake in the preheated oven for 20–25 minutes, or until springy in the center and a skewer inserted into the center of the cake comes out clean.

MAKES 9

Let cool in the pan for a few minutes, then run a knife around the edge of the cake to loosen it. Turn the cake out on to a wire rack and peel off the paper. Let cool completely. When cold, cut into squares.

ingredients

½ cup butter, plus extra for greasing

generous 1 cup brown sugar

1 egg

1 egg yolk

1 cup self-rising flour

1 tsp. ground cinnamon

generous ½ cup coarsely
   chopped walnuts

COOK'S TIP

Do not chop the walnuts too finely, as the blondies should have a good texture and a slight crunch to them.

mustard steaks with tomato relish

To make the tomato relish, place all the ingredients in a heavy-bottom pan, seasoning to taste with salt. Bring to a boil, stirring until the sugar has completely dissolved. Reduce the heat and let simmer, stirring occasionally, for 40 minutes, or until thickened. Transfer to a bowl, cover with plastic wrap and let cool. Preheat the grill.

Using a sharp knife, cut almost completely through each steak horizontally to make a pocket. Spread the mustard inside the pockets and rub the steaks all over with the garlic. Place them on a plate, cover with plastic wrap and let stand for 30 minutes. Cook the steaks for 2½ minutes each side for rare, 4 minutes each side for medium, or 6 minutes each side for well done. Transfer to serving plates, garnish with fresh tarragon sprigs, and serve immediately with the tomato relish.

ingredients

4 sirloin or rump steaks

1 tbsp. tarragon mustard

2 garlic cloves, crushed

fresh tarragon sprigs, to garnish

TOMATO RELISH

2 cups cherry tomatoes

2 tbsp. brown sugar

¼ cup white wine vinegar

1 piece of preserved ginger, chopped

½ lime, thinly sliced

salt

hot cajun seafood fusilli

Heat the cream in a large pan over a medium heat, stirring constantly. When almost boiling, reduce the heat and add the scallions, parsley, thyme, pepper, chili flakes, and salt. Simmer for 7–8 minutes, stirring, until thickened. Remove from the heat.

Cook the pasta in plenty of boiling salted water until al dente. Drain and return to the pan. Add the cream mixture and the cheeses to the pasta. Toss over a low heat until the cheeses have melted. Transfer to a warm serving dish.

Heat the oil in a large skillet over a medium-high heat. Add the shrimp and scallops. Stir-fry for 2–3 minutes, or until the shrimp have just turned pink.

Pour the seafood over the pasta and toss well to mix. Sprinkle with the basil. Serve immediately.

ingredients

generous 2 cups whipping cream

8 scallions, sliced thinly

scant 1 cup fresh parsley, chopped

1 tbsp. chopped fresh thyme

½ tbsp. freshly ground pepper

½–1 tsp. dried chili flakes

1 tsp. salt

1 lb. dried fusilli or tagliatelle

scant ½ cup freshly grated Gruyère

scant ¼ cup freshly grated Parmesan

2 tbsp. olive oil

8 oz. raw shelled shrimp

1 cup scallops, sliced

1 tbsp. shredded fresh basil

crab cakes with salsa verde

SERVES 4

Place the crabmeat, fish, red chili, garlic, gingerroot, lemon grass, cilantro, and egg white in a food processor and process until thoroughly blended, then transfer to a bowl, cover with plastic wrap, and let chill in for 30–60 minutes.

Meanwhile, make the salsa verde. Put the green chilis, scallions, garlic, and parsley in a food processor and process until finely chopped. Transfer to a small bowl and stir in the lime rind, lime and lemon juice, olive oil, and green Tabasco sauce. Season to taste with salt and pepper, cover with plastic wrap, and let chill in the refrigerator until ready to serve.

Heat 2 tablespoons of the peanut oil in a nonstick skillet. Add spoonfuls of the crab mixture, flattening them gently with a spatula and keeping them spaced well apart. Cook for 4 minutes, then turn with a spatula and cook the other side for 3 minutes, or until golden brown. Remove from the skillet and keep warm while you cook the remaining batches, adding more oil if necessary. Transfer the crab cakes to a large serving plate, garnish, and serve with the salsa verde.

ingredients

1¾ cups crabmeat, thawed
   if frozen
9 oz. white fish fillet, such as cod,
   skinned and coarsely chopped
1 fresh red chili, seeded and
   coarsely chopped
1 garlic clove, coarsely chopped
1-inch piece of fresh gingerroot,
   coarsely chopped
1 lemongrass stalk, coarsely
   chopped
3 tbsp. chopped fresh cilantro
1 egg white
peanut or corn oil, for frying

SALSA VERDE

2 fresh green chilies, seeded and
   coarsely chopped
8 scallions, coarsely chopped
2 garlic cloves, coarsely chopped
1 bunch of fresh parsley
grated rind and juice of 1 lime
juice of 1 lemon
4 tbsp. olive oil
1 tbsp. green Tabasco sauce
salt and pepper

VARIATION
Much of the fat in this recipe is contained in the salsa verde dip, so if you would prefer a lower-fat dish, serve only small helpings of the salsa verde. The remainder can be stored in the refrigerator.

ingredients

PASTRY

1½ cups all-purpose flour, plus
   extra for dusting

3 tbsp. superfine sugar

salt

4 oz. unsalted butter, chilled
   and diced

1 egg yolk

FILLING

1 lb. ricotta cheese

½ cup heavy cream

2 eggs, plus 1 egg yolk

⅜ cup superfine sugar

finely grated rind of 1 lemon

finely grated rind of 1 orange

ricotta cheesecake

To make the pastry, sift the flour with the sugar and a pinch of salt on to a counter and make a well in the center. Add the diced butter and egg yolk to the well and, using your fingertips, gradually work in the flour mixture until fully incorporated.

Gather up the dough and knead very lightly. Cut off about one quarter, wrap in plastic wrap, and let chill in the refrigerator. Press the remaining dough into the base of a 9-inch loose-bottom tart pan. Let chill for 30 minutes.

To make the filling, beat the ricotta with the cream, eggs and extra egg yolk, sugar, lemon rind, and orange rind. Cover with plastic wrap and set aside in the fridge until required.

Prick the base of the pastry shell all over with a fork. Line with foil, fill with pie weights, and bake blind in a preheated oven, 375°F/190°C, for 15 minutes.

Remove the pastry shell from the oven and take out the foil and pie weights. Stand the pan on a wire rack and set aside to cool.

Spoon the ricotta mixture into the pastry shell and level the surface. Roll out the reserved pastry on a lightly floured counter and cut it into strips. Arrange the strips over the filling in a lattice pattern, brushing the overlapping ends with water so that they stick.

Bake in the preheated oven, 375°F/190°C, for 30–35 minutes, until the top of the cheesecake is golden and the filling has set. Let cool on a wire rack before lifting off the side of the pan. Cut into wedges to serve.

light bacon & cottage cheese buns

Preheat the broiler to high. Remove any visible fat and rind from the bacon and cut 4 of the tomatoes in half. Place the bacon and tomatoes, cut-side up, under the preheated broiler and cook, turning the bacon over halfway through cooking, for 8–10 minutes, or until the bacon is crisp and the tomatoes are softened. Remove the tomatoes and bacon from the broiler and drain the bacon on paper towels to help remove any excess fat. Keep the bacon and tomatoes warm.

Meanwhile, cut the remaining tomatoes into bite-size pieces and combine with the cottage cheese in a bowl. Cut the bacon into bite-size pieces and stir into the cottage cheese mixture. Season to taste with pepper.

Cut the bread rolls in half and divide the bacon filling evenly over each roll base. Sprinkle the scallions over the filling and cover with the roll tops. Serve immediately with the grilled tomatoes.

ingredients

8 low-salt lean Canadian
    bacon strips
6 tomatoes
9 oz. low-fat natural cottage cheese
freshly ground black pepper
4 large seeded whole wheat or
    white bread rolls
2 scallions, chopped

meringue & strawberries

Preheat the oven to 300°F/150°C.

Whisk the egg whites in a mixing bowl using an electric mixer until thick and in soft peaks. Add the sugar gradually, whisking well with each addition. The meringue mixture should be glossy and firm.

Spoon the meringue onto a baking sheet lined with parchment paper and spread into a rough 12-inch round. Cook for 45–50 minutes until the meringue is firm on the outside but still soft in the centre. Remove from the oven and allow to cool.

Check over the strawberries and hull them.

Place a third of the berries (choose the larger ones) in a blender and purée with the confectioners' sugar. Pour the purée into a bowl, add the liqueur, if using, and the remaining strawberries, and turn in the sauce until well mixed.

Whip together the heavy and light cream until thick but still light and floppy.

Break the meringue into large pieces and place half in a large glass serving bowl. Spoon over half the fruit mixture and half the cream. Layer up the remaining ingredients and lightly fold the mixtures together so you have a streaky appearance.

Serve soon after mixing or the meringues will soften.

ingredients

3 egg whites

¾ cup superfine sugar

1 lb. 9 oz. strawberries

2 tbsp. confectioners' sugar

2 tbsp. crème de fraise (strawberry)
  liqueur (optional)

1¼ cups heavy cream

⅔ cup light cream

ingredients

4 cups chicken or vegetable stock

3 tbsp. butter

3 shallots, chopped finely

4 oz. pancetta or rindless lean
   bacon, diced

scant 1¼ cups risotto rice

⅔ cup dry white wine

1½ cups petits pois, thawed
   if using frozen

salt and pepper

Parmesan cheese shavings,
   to garnish

VARIATION

*You can substitute diced cooked
ham for the pancetta or bacon and
add it toward the end of the cooking
time so that it heats through.*

rice and peas

Pour the stock into a large pan and bring to a boil. Reduce the heat and let simmer gently.

Melt 2 tablespoons of the butter in another large, heavy-bottom pan. Add the shallots and pancetta or bacon and cook over low heat, stirring occasionally, for 5 minutes, until the shallots are softened. Add the rice and cook, stirring constantly, for 2–3 minutes, until all the grains are thoroughly coated and glistening.

Pour in the wine and cook, stirring constantly, until it has almost completely evaporated. Add a ladleful of hot stock and cook, stirring constantly, until all the stock has been absorbed. Continue cooking and adding the stock, a ladleful at a time, for about 10 minutes.

Add the peas, then continue adding the stock, a ladleful at a time, for an additional 10 minutes, or until the rice is tender and the liquid has been absorbed.

Stir in the remaining butter and season to taste with salt and pepper. Transfer the risotto to a warmed serving dish, garnish with Parmesan shavings, and serve immediately.

JULY
30

SERVES 4–6

tomato salad with fried feta

Make the dressing by whisking together the extra virgin olive oil, the lemon juice, oregano, sugar, and pepper in a small bowl. Set aside.

Prepare the salad by arranging the tomatoes, onion, arugula, and olives on 4 individual plates.

Cut the feta cheese into cubes about 1-inch square. Beat the egg in a dish and put the flour on a separate plate. Toss the cheese first in the egg, shake off the excess, and then toss in the flour.

Heat the olive oil in a large skillet, add the cheese and fry over a medium heat, turning over the cubes of cheese until they are golden on all sides.

Scatter the fried feta over the salad. Whisk together the prepared dressing, spoon over the salad, and serve warm.

ingredients

12 plum tomatoes, sliced

1 very small red onion, sliced very thinly

½ oz. arugula leaves

20 Greek black olives

7 oz. feta cheese

1 egg

3 tbsp. all-purpose flour

2 tbsp. olive oil

DRESSING

3 tbsp. extra virgin olive oil

juice of ½ lemon

2 tsp. chopped fresh oregano

pinch of sugar

pepper

JULY
31

SERVES 2

blueberry dazzler

Pour the apple juice into a food processor. Add the yogurt and process until smooth.

Add the banana and half of the frozen blueberries and process well, then add the remaining blueberries and process until smooth.

Pour the mixture into tall glasses and add straws. Decorate with whole fresh blueberries and serve.

ingredients

¾ cup apple juice

½ cup plain yogurt

1 banana, sliced and frozen

6 oz. frozen blueberries

whole fresh blueberries, to decorate

August

prosciutto with arugula

Separate the arugula leaves, wash in cold water, and pat dry on paper towels. Place the leaves in a bowl.

Pour the lemon juice into a small bowl and season to taste with salt and pepper. Whisk in the olive oil, then pour the dressing over the arugula leaves and toss lightly so they are evenly coated.

Carefully drape the prosciutto in folds on 4 individual serving plates, then add the arugula. Serve at room temperature.

ingredients

4 oz. arugula

1 tbsp. lemon juice

salt and pepper

3 tbsp. extra virgin olive oil

8 oz. prosciutto, sliced thinly

VARIATION

For a more substantial salad, add 1 thinly sliced fennel bulb and 2 thinly sliced oranges to the arugula before dressing. Substitute orange juice or balsamic vinegar for the lemon juice.

jerk chicken

Seed and finely chop the red chilies, then place them in a small glass bowl with the oil, garlic, onion, scallion, vinegar, lime juice, raw brown sugar, thyme, cinnamon, allspice, and nutmeg. Season to taste with salt and pepper and crush thoroughly with a fork.

Using a sharp knife, make a series of diagonal slashes in the chicken pieces and place them in a large, shallow, nonmetallic dish. Spoon the jerk seasoning over the chicken, rubbing it well into the slashes. Cover and let marinate in the refrigerator for up to 8 hours.

Preheat the grill. Remove the chicken from the marinade, discarding the marinade, brush with oil and cook over medium heat, turning frequently, for 30–35 minutes. Transfer to plates and serve.

ingredients

2 fresh red chilies

2 tbsp. corn oil, plus extra for brushing

2 garlic cloves, finely chopped

1 tbsp. finely chopped onion

1 tbsp. finely chopped scallion

1 tbsp. white wine vinegar

1 tbsp. lime juice

2 tsp. raw brown sugar

1 tsp. dried thyme

1 tsp. ground cinnamon

1 tsp. ground allspice

¼ tsp. freshly grated nutmeg

salt and pepper

4 chicken quarters

chilled pea soup

Bring the stock to a boil in a large pan over a medium heat. Reduce the heat, add the peas and scallions, and simmer for 5 minutes.

Let cool slightly, then sieve twice, making sure that you remove and discard any pieces of skin. Pour into a large bowl, season to taste with salt and pepper, and stir in the yogurt. Cover the bowl with plastic wrap and chill in the refrigerator for several hours.

To serve, mix the soup well and ladle into large soup bowls or mugs. Garnish with chopped mint or snipped chives, scallions, and grated lemon rind.

ingredients

2 cups vegetable stock or water

1 lb. frozen peas

2 oz. scallions, chopped, plus extra
   to garnish

salt and pepper

1¼ cups plain yogurt or light cream

TO GARNISH

2 tbsp. chopped fresh mint or
   snipped fresh chives

grated lemon rind

easy mango ice cream

Mix the custard, cream, and mango purée together in a bowl.

Taste for sweetness and, if desired, add confectioners' sugar to taste, remembering that when frozen the mixture will taste less sweet.

Transfer to an ice-cream maker and process for 15 minutes. Alternatively, transfer the mixture to a freezerproof container. Cover and freeze for 2–3 hours until just frozen. Spoon into a bowl and beat with a fork or whisk to break down any ice crystals. Return the mixture to the container and freeze for a further 2 hours. Beat the ice cream once more, then freeze for 2–3 hours until firm.

Transfer from the freezer to the refrigerator 20–30 minutes before serving, to soften. Serve with the passion fruit pulp.

ingredients

2½ cups ready-made traditional
   custard, such as Bird's

⅔ cup whipping cream,
   lightly whipped

flesh of 2 ripe mangoes, puréed

confectioners' sugar (optional)

passion fruit pulp, to serve

tomato, zucchini & basil tartlets

Preheat the oven to 375°F/190°C. Lightly oil 4 x 4½-inch individual loose-bottom tart pans.

Working quickly so that the phyllo pastry does not dry out, cut each sheet into 6 equal-size pieces measuring about 6¼ x 5½ inches. Layer 3 pieces of pastry at a time in the 4 tart pans, lightly brushing between each layer with oil. Carefully press the pastry into the sides of the pans so that the corners of the pastry squares point upwards. Arrange the pans on a large baking sheet.

Sprinkle two-thirds of the torn basil leaves over the pastry bases and cover with overlapping slices of tomato and zucchini. Beat the eggs with the milk in a bowl and season well with pepper. Divide the egg mixture evenly among the tins and sprinkle the remaining torn basil leaves over it.

Bake in the preheated oven for 20–25 minutes, or until the egg mixture has set and the pastry is crisp and golden. Serve warm or cold, garnished with basil leaves, and with a selection of salads and boiled new potatoes.

ingredients

olive oil, for oiling and brushing

19 x 11-inch sheets phyllo pastry

1 tbsp. torn fresh basil leaves, plus
    extra leaves to garnish

7–8 cherry tomatoes, thinly sliced

1 zucchini, thinly sliced

2 eggs, beaten

⅔ cup skim or lowfat milk

freshly ground black pepper

TO SERVE

selection of salads

boiled new potatoes

skate in mustard & caper sauce

Cut each skate wing in half and place in a large skillet. Cover with salted water, bring to a boil then simmer for 10–15 minutes, until tender.

Meanwhile, make the mustard and caper sauce. Heat the oil in a saucepan, add the onion and garlic, and cook for 5 minutes, until softened. Add the yogurt, lemon juice, parsley, and capers and cook for 1–2 minutes, until heated through. (Do not boil or the sauce will curdle.) Stir in the mustard and season with salt and pepper.

Drain the skate and put on 4 warmed serving plates. Pour over the mustard and caper sauce and sprinkle with chopped parsley. Serve hot, with lemon wedges.

ingredients

2 skate wings

2 tbsp. olive oil

1 onion, chopped finely

1 garlic clove, chopped finely

2/3 cup Greek yogurt

1 tsp. lemon juice

1 tbsp. chopped fresh flat-leaf parsley

1 tbsp. capers, chopped coarsely

1 tbsp. whole-grain mustard

salt and pepper

chopped fresh flat-leaf parsley, to garnish

lemon wedges, to serve

peach cobbler

Preheat the oven to 425°F/220°C. Put the peaches in a 9-inch square ovenproof dish that is also suitable for serving. Add the sugar, lemon juice, cornstarch, and almond extract and toss together. Bake the peaches in the oven for 20 minutes.

Meanwhile, to make the topping, sift the flour, all but 2 tablespoons of the sugar, the baking powder, and salt into a bowl. Rub in the butter with the fingertips until the mixture resembles bread crumbs. Mix the egg and 5 tablespoons of the milk in a bowl, then mix into the dry ingredients with a fork until a soft, sticky dough forms. If the dough seems too dry, stir in the extra tablespoon of milk.

Reduce the oven temperature to 400°F/200°C. Remove the peaches from the oven and drop spoonfuls of the topping over the surface, without smoothing. Sprinkle with the remaining sugar, return to the oven, and bake for a further 15 minutes, or until the topping is golden brown and firm (the topping will spread as it cooks). Serve hot or at room temperature with ice cream.

ingredients

FILLING

6 peaches, peeled and sliced

4 tbsp. superfine sugar

1/2 tbsp. lemon juice

1 1/2 tsp. cornstarch

1/2 tsp. almond or vanilla extract

vanilla or pecan ice cream, to serve

PIE TOPPING

1 1/4 cups all-purpose flour

1/2 cup superfine sugar

1 1/2 tsp. baking powder

1/2 tsp. salt

3 tbsp. butter, diced

1 egg

5–6 tbsp. milk

speedy vegetable pilau

Rinse the basmati rice thoroughly in 2–3 changes of water, drain well, and reserve until required.

Heat the oil in a large, heavy-bottom pan or flameproof casserole. Add the garlic, cinnamon stick, cardamom, and cumin and cook, stirring constantly, for 1 minute. Add the tomato and mushrooms and cook, stirring constantly, for 3 minutes.

Stir in the rice and peas and cook for 1 minute, stirring to coat the grains, then add the vegetable stock and bring to a boil. Reduce the heat, cover, and simmer for 10–15 minutes, or until the rice is tender and the liquid has been absorbed. Remove the cinnamon stick and serve the pilau immediately.

ingredients

1 lb. basmati rice

2 tbsp. corn oil

2 garlic cloves, finely chopped

½ cinnamon stick

2 cardamom pods

½ tsp. black cumin seeds

1 tomato, sliced

2 oz. baby white mushrooms

3 oz. shelled peas

3 cups vegetable stock

COOK'S TIP

If you have time, soak the rice in a large bowl of cold water for 10 minutes before cooking to lighten the grain.

VARIATION

Use the same amount of sliced cremini mushrooms instead of the white ones, and if shelled peas are not available, use frozen instead.

minted green risotto

Bring the stock to a boil in a pan, then reduce the heat and keep simmering over a low heat while you are cooking the risotto.

Heat half the butter in a skillet over a medium-high heat until sizzling. Add the peas, spinach, mint leaves, basil, and oregano and season with the nutmeg. Cook, stirring frequently, for 3 minutes, or until the spinach and mint leaves are wilted. Cool slightly.

Pour the spinach mixture into a food processor and process for 15 seconds. Add the mascarpone (or cream) and process again for 1 minute. Transfer to a bowl and set aside.

Heat the oil and remaining butter in a large, heavy-bottom pan over a medium heat. Add the onion, celery, garlic, and thyme and cook, stirring occasionally, for 2 minutes, or until the vegetables are softened.

Reduce the heat, add the rice, and mix to coat in oil and butter. Cook, stirring constantly, for 2–3 minutes, or until the grains are translucent.

Add the vermouth and cook, stirring constantly, until it has reduced. Gradually add the hot stock, a ladle at a time. Stir constantly and add more liquid as the rice absorbs each addition. Increase the heat to medium so that the liquid bubbles. Cook for 20 minutes, or until the liquid is absorbed and the rice is creamy.

Stir in the spinach-mascarpone mixture and the Parmesan. Transfer to warmed plates and serve immediately.

ingredients

4 cups chicken or vegetable stock

1 tbsp. butter

8 oz. shelled fresh peas or thawed frozen peas

9 oz. fresh young spinach leaves, washed and drained

1 bunch of fresh mint, leaves stripped from stalks

2 tbsp. chopped fresh basil

2 tbsp. chopped fresh oregano

pinch of freshly grated nutmeg

4 tbsp. mascarpone cheese or heavy cream

2 tbsp. vegetable oil

1 onion, finely chopped

2 celery stalks, including leaves, finely chopped

2 garlic cloves, finely chopped

½ tsp. dried thyme

10½ oz. risotto rice

¼ cup dry white vermouth

3 oz. freshly grated Parmesan cheese

broiled steak with tomatoes & garlic

Place the oil, tomatoes, red bell pepper, onion, garlic, parsley, oregano, and sugar in a heavy-bottom pan and season to taste with salt and pepper. Bring to a boil, reduce the heat, and let simmer for 15 minutes.

Meanwhile, snip any fat round the outsides of the steaks. Season each generously with pepper (but no salt) and brush with oil. Cook on a griddle pan for 1 minute on each side. Reduce the heat to medium and cook according to taste: 1½–2 minutes each side for rare; 2½–3 minutes each side for medium; 3–4 minutes each side for well done.

Transfer the steaks to warmed individual plates and spoon the sauce over them. Serve immediately.

ingredients

3 tbsp. olive oil, plus extra for
   brushing
1 lb. 9 oz. tomatoes, peeled
   and chopped
1 red bell pepper, seeded and
   chopped
1 onion, chopped
2 garlic cloves, chopped finely
1 tbsp. chopped fresh flat-leaf
   parsley
1 tsp. dried oregano
1 tsp. sugar
salt and pepper
4 x 6 oz. entrecôte or rump steaks

shrimp, peas & pasta

Place the saffron in a small bowl, add the wine, and let soak.

Heat the olive oil and butter in a large heavy-bottom skillet. Add the shallot and cook over low heat, stirring occasionally, for 5 minutes, or until softened. Add the peas and cooked shrimp and cook, stirring occasionally, for 2–3 minutes.

Bring a large heavy-bottom pan of lightly salted water to a boil. Add the pasta, return to a boil, and cook for 8–10 minutes, or until tender but still firm to the bite.

Meanwhile, stir the saffron and wine mixture into the skillet. Increase the heat and cook until the liquid is reduced by about half. Season to taste with salt and pepper. Drain the pasta and add to the skillet. Cook for 1–2 minutes, or until it is well coated with the sauce. Transfer to a warmed serving dish, sprinkle with dill, and serve.

ingredients

pinch of saffron threads

1 cup dry white wine

3 tbsp. olive oil

2 tbsp. unsalted butter

1 shallot, chopped

2 cups peas

12 oz. cooked shelled shrimp

12 oz. dried fusilli bucati or ditali

salt and pepper

2 tbsp. chopped fresh dill, to garnish

COOK'S TIP

If you are using frozen peas, make sure that they are thoroughly thawed before you start.

hot & spicy ribs

Preheat the grill. Put the onion, garlic, gingerroot, chili, and soy sauce into a food processor and process to a paste. Transfer to a measuring cup and stir in the lime juice, sugar, and oil. Season with salt and pepper.

Place the spareribs in a preheated wok or large, heavy-bottom pan and pour in the soy sauce mixture. Place on the stove and bring to a boil, then let simmer over low heat, stirring frequently, for 30 minutes. If the mixture appears to be drying out, add a little water. Remove the spareribs, reserving the sauce.

Cook the ribs over medium heat, turning and basting frequently with the sauce, for 20–30 minutes. Transfer to a large serving plate and serve immediately.

ingredients

1 onion, chopped

2 garlic cloves, chopped

1-inch piece fresh gingerroot, sliced

1 fresh red chili, seeded
and chopped

5 tbsp. dark soy sauce

3 tbsp. lime juice

1 tbsp. jaggery or brown sugar

2 tbsp. peanut oil

salt and pepper

2 lb. 4 oz. pork spareribs, separated

COOK'S TIP
Peanut oil is used extensively in
South-east Asian supermarkets,
but if you cannot find it, then use
sunflower-seed oil instead.

AUGUST

13

SERVES 4

italian pesto chicken

Preheat the oven to 350°F/180°C.

To make the pesto, put all the ingredients into a food processor, seasoning to taste with salt and pepper. Blend for a few seconds until smooth. Halve each chicken breast and pound lightly to flatten each piece. Spread on one side only with pesto, then top with the prosciutto. Add a tablespoon of sun-dried tomatoes to each one, then roll them up and secure with toothpicks.

Pour the olive oil into a large roasting pan. Arrange the chicken in the pan, then pour over the wine. Add the chopped tomatoes and bake in the preheated oven for 30 minutes. Stir any remaining pesto into the cooked pasta and arrange on 4 serving plates.

Remove the chicken from the oven, discard the toothpicks and slice in half, widthwise. Divide among the plates. Pour over some of the cooking sauce, garnish with black olives and sprigs of basil, and serve.

ingredients

4 skinless chicken breasts

8 slices prosciutto

2¾ oz. sun-dried tomatoes in olive oil, drained and chopped

2 tbsp. extra-virgin olive oil

½ cup white wine

7 oz. canned chopped tomatoes

PESTO

1 oz fresh basil, thick stems removed

generous 1¼ cups pine nuts

3 garlic cloves, coarsely chopped

scant ½ cup extra-virgin olive oil

¾ cup freshly grated Parmesan cheese

salt and pepper

GARNISH

black olives, pitted and halved

sprigs of fresh basil

freshly cooked linguine, to serve

AUGUST

14

SERVES 4

blueberry frozen yogurt

Put the blueberries and orange juice into a food processor or blender and process to a purée. Strain through a sieve into a bowl.

Stir the maple syrup and yogurt together in a large mixing bowl, then fold in the fruit purée.

Churn the mixture in an ice-cream maker, following the manufacturer's instructions, then freeze for 5–6 hours. If you don't have an ice-cream maker, transfer the mixture to a freezerproof container and freeze for 2 hours. Remove from the freezer, turn out into a bowl, and beat until smooth. Return to the freezer and freeze until firm.

ingredients

6 oz. fresh blueberries

finely grated rind and juice of 1 orange

3 tbsp. maple syrup

1 lb. 2 oz. plain lowfat yogurt

eggplant tagine with polenta

Preheat the broiler to medium. Toss the eggplant in
1 tablespoon of the oil and arrange in the grill pan. Cook under
the preheated broiler for 20 minutes, turning occasionally, until
softened and beginning to blacken around the edges – brush
with more oil if the eggplant becomes too dry.

Heat the remaining oil in a large skillet over a medium heat.
Add the onion and fry, stirring occasionally, for 8 minutes, or
until soft and golden. Add the carrot, garlic, and mushrooms
and cook for 5 minutes. Add the spices and cook, stirring
constantly, for a further minute.

Add the tomatoes and stock, stir well, then add the tomato
paste. Bring to a boil, then reduce the heat and simmer for
10 minutes, or until the sauce begins to thicken and reduce.

Add the eggplant, apricots, and chickpeas, partially cover,
and cook for a further 10 minutes, stirring occasionally.
Season to taste.

Meanwhile, to make the polenta, pour the hot stock into
a nonstick pan and bring to a boil. Pour in the polenta in a
steady stream, stirring constantly with a wooden spoon.
Reduce the heat to low and cook for 1–2 minutes, or until the
polenta thickens to a creamed potato-like consistency. Serve
the tagine with the polenta, sprinkled with the fresh cilantro.

ingredients

1 eggplant, cut into ½-inch cubes

3 tbsp. olive oil

1 large onion, thinly sliced

1 carrot, diced

2 garlic cloves, chopped

4 oz. mushrooms, sliced

2 tsp. ground coriander

2 tsp. cumin seeds

1 tsp. chili powder

1 tsp. ground turmeric

3½ cups canned chopped tomatoes

1¼ cups vegetable stock

1 tbsp. tomato paste

2¾ oz. no-soak dried apricots,
    roughly chopped

14 oz. canned chickpeas, drained
    and rinsed

salt and pepper

2 tbsp. fresh cilantro, to garnish

POLENTA

5 cups hot vegetable stock

7 oz. instant polenta

pasta with sun-dried tomato sauce

Put the tomatoes and boiling water in a bowl and let stand for 5 minutes. Using a slotted spoon, remove one-third of the tomatoes from the bowl. Cut into bite-size pieces. Put the remaining tomatoes and water into a blender and purée.

Heat the oil in a large skillet over a medium heat. Add the onion and gently fry for 5 minutes until soft. Add the garlic and fry until just beginning to color. Add the puréed tomato and the reserved tomato pieces to the pan. Bring to a boil, then simmer over a medium–low heat for 10 minutes. Stir in the herbs and season with salt and pepper. Simmer for 1 minute, then remove from the heat.

Cook the pasta in plenty of boiling salted water until al dente. Drain and transfer to a warm serving dish. Briefly reheat the sauce. Pour over the pasta, add the basil, and toss well to mix. Sprinkle with the Parmesan and serve immediately.

ingredients

3 oz. sun-dried tomatoes
  (not in oil)

3 cups boiling water

2 tbsp. olive oil

1 onion, chopped finely

2 large garlic cloves, sliced finely

2 tbsp. chopped fresh
  flat-leaf parsley

2 tsp. chopped fresh oregano

1 tsp, chopped fresh rosemary

salt and pepper

12 oz. dried spaghetti or fusilli

10 fresh basil leaves, shredded

3 tbsp. freshly grated Parmesan,
  to serve

lime-drizzled shrimp

Grate the rind and squeeze out the juice from 2 of the limes. Cut the remaining 2 limes into wedges and reserve for later.

To prepare the shrimp, remove the legs, leaving the shells and tails intact. Using a sharp knife, make a shallow slit along the underside of each shrimp, then pull out the dark vein and discard. Rinse the shrimp under cold water and dry well on paper towels.

Heat the olive oil in a large skillet, then add the garlic and fry for 30 seconds. Add the shrimp and fry for 5 minutes, stirring from time to time, or until they turn pink and begin to curl. Mix in the lime rind, juice, and a splash of sherry to moisten, then stir well together.

Transfer the cooked shrimp to a serving dish, season to taste with salt and pepper, and sprinkle over the parsley. Serve hot, accompanied by the reserved lime wedges for squeezing over the shrimp.

ingredients

4 limes

12 raw jumbo shrimp, in their shells

3 tbsp. olive oil

2 garlic cloves, finely chopped

splash of dry sherry

salt and pepper

4 tbsp. chopped fresh
    flat-leaf parsley

AUGUST
17

SERVES 4

gazpacho

Reserve some of the tomatoes, cucumber, and bell pepper for a garnish. Place the bread in a food processor and process until crumbs form. Add the remaining tomatoes, cucumber, and bell pepper. Add the onion, garlic, vinegar, and oil and process until smooth.

The tomatoes should have sufficient juice in them to make enough liquid but add a little water if the soup is too thick. Season to taste with salt.

Divide the soup among 4 serving bowls and add a few ice cubes to make sure that the soup is served chilled. Garnish with the reserved tomatoes, cucumber, and bell pepper. Add a few sprigs of basil and serve with fresh crusty bread.

ingredients

2lb. 4 oz. ripe tomatoes, peeled,
    seeded, and roughly chopped

½ cucumber, peeled, seeded, and
    roughly chopped

1 green bell pepper, seeded and
    roughly chopped

4 oz. fresh bread, crusts removed

1 small onion, roughly chopped

1 garlic clove, chopped

1 tbsp. white wine vinegar

½ cup olive oil

salt, to taste

ice cubes

few fresh basil sprigs, to garnish

fresh crusty bread, to serve

AUGUST
18

SERVES 4

AUGUST
19

MAKES 20

ingredients

7 oz. ready-made puff pastry

all-purpose flour, for dusting

3 tbsp. pesto

20 cherry tomatoes, each cut
    into 3 slices

4 oz. goat cheese

salt and pepper

fresh basil sprigs, to garnish

COOK'S TIP

*These tartlets are quicker to make
if you use the ready-rolled variety
of ready-made puff pastry, which is
available in most large food stores.*

instant pesto & goat cheese tartlets

Preheat the oven to 400°F/200°C, then lightly flour a cookie sheet. Roll out the pastry on a floured counter to ⅛ inch thick. Cut out 20 circles with a 2-inch plain cutter and arrange the pastry circles on the floured cookie sheet. Spread a little pesto on each circle, leaving a margin around the edges, then arrange 3 tomato slices on top of each one.

Crumble the goat cheese over and season to taste with salt and pepper. Bake in the preheated oven for 10 minutes, or until the pastry is puffed up, crisp, and golden. Garnish with basil sprigs and serve warm.

cajun chicken salad

Make 3 diagonal slashes across each chicken breast. Put the chicken into a shallow dish and sprinkle all over with the Cajun seasoning. Cover and refrigerate for at least 30 minutes.

When ready to cook, brush a grill pan with the oil, if using. Heat over a high heat until very hot and a few drops of water sprinkled on to it sizzle immediately. Add the chicken and cook for 7–8 minutes on each side, or until thoroughly cooked. If still slightly pink in the center, cook a little longer. Remove the chicken and reserve.

Add the mango slices to the pan and cook for 2 minutes on each side. Remove and reserve.

Meanwhile, arrange the salad greens in a salad bowl and scatter over the onion, beetroot, radishes, and walnut halves.

Put the walnut oil, mustard, lemon juice, and salt and pepper to taste in a screw-top jar and shake until well blended. Pour over the salad and sprinkle with the sesame seeds.

Arrange the mango and the salad on a serving plate and top with the chicken breast and a few of the salad leaves.

ingredients

4 skinless, boneless chicken
    breasts, about 5 oz. each

4 tsp. Cajun seasoning

2 tsp. corn oil (optional)

1 ripe mango, peeled, pitted,
    and cut into thick slices

7 oz. salad greens

1 red onion, thinly sliced and
    cut in half

6 oz. cooked beetroot, diced

3 oz. radishes, sliced

2 oz. walnut halves

4 tbsp. walnut oil

1–2 tsp. Dijon mustard

1 tbsp. lemon juice

salt and pepper

2 tbsp. sesame seeds

lemonade

Put the pared lemon rind, the sugar, water, and cinnamon in a saucepan. Bring to a boil, stirring until the sugar has dissolved, and then simmer for 5 minutes, without allowing the syrup to color. Let cool.

When cool, strain the syrup then strain in the lemon juice. Pour into a clean bottle and seal. Label and store in the fridge for up to 2 weeks.

To serve, pour the lemonade into a glass, add ice cubes and dilute with still or sparkling water, allowing 1 part lemonade to 3 parts water or according to taste.

ingredients

pared rind and juice of
    3 large lemons

2 cups white granulated sugar

2/3 cup water

1 cinnamon stick

TO SERVE

still or sparkling water

ice cubes

good coleslaw

Finely shred the cabbage. Grate the carrots and core and slice the apples. Finely chop the celery and scallions. Put in a large bowl.

Mix the mayonnaise and yogurt together in a small bowl. Whisk in the mustard and lemon juice and season well with salt and pepper.

Add the raisins and walnuts to the salad vegetables, if using. Pour over the dressing and mix well. Serve at once.

ingredients

1/2 hard white cabbage

2 carrots

2 eating apples

2 celery stalks

3 scallions

2/3 cup mayonnaise

2/3 cup plain yogurt

1 tsp. French mustard

2 tbsp. lemon juice

1 1/2 oz. raisins (optional)

1 1/2 oz. walnuts (optional)

chargrilled devils

Preheat the grill. Open the oysters, catching the juice from the shells in a bowl. Cut the oysters from the bottom shells, set aside, and tip any remaining juice into the bowl.

To make the sauce, add the red chili, garlic, shallot, parsley, and lemon juice to the bowl, then season to taste with salt and pepper and mix well. Cover the bowl with plastic wrap and let chill in the refrigerator until required.

Using a sharp knife, cut each bacon strip in half across the center. Season the oysters with paprika and cayenne, then roll each oyster up inside ½ a bacon strip. Thread 9 wrapped oysters onto 4 presoaked wooden skewers or toothpicks. Cook, turning frequently, for 5 minutes, or until the bacon is well browned and crispy. Transfer to a large serving plate and serve immediately with the sauce.

ingredients

36 fresh oysters

1 fresh red chili, seeded and finely chopped

1 garlic clove, finely chopped

1 shallot, finely chopped

2 tbsp. finely chopped fresh parsley

2 tbsp. lemon juice

salt and pepper

18 lean bacon strips, rinded

1 tbsp. mild paprika

1 tsp. cayenne pepper

COOK'S TIP

To shuck an oyster, wrap a dish towel round one hand and grasp the oyster, flat shell uppermost. Prise open with a strong knife, then run the blade around the inside of the shell to sever the muscle.

VARIATION

You can replace the shallot with a small, finely chopped onion and the fresh parsley with the same amount of snipped fresh chives, if you prefer.

spicy indian vegetarian stir-fry

In a wok or large skillet, heat 2 tablespoons of the oil and add the turmeric and a pinch of salt. Carefully add the potatoes, stirring continuously to coat in the turmeric. Stir-fry for 5 minutes, then remove from the wok and set aside.

Heat the remaining tablespoon of oil and stir-fry the shallots for 1–2 minutes. Mix in the bay leaf, cumin, gingerroot, and chili powder, then add the tomatoes and stir-fry for two minutes. Add the spinach, mixing well to combine all the flavors. Cover and simmer for 2–3 minutes.

Return the potatoes to the wok and add the peas and lemon juice. Cook for 5 minutes, or until the potatoes are tender. Remove the wok from the heat and discard the bay leaf, then season with salt and pepper. Serve with the cooked basmati rice.

ingredients

3 tbsp. vegetable oil

½ tsp. turmeric

8 oz. potatoes, cut into
    ½ inch cubes

3 shallots, chopped finely

1 bay leaf

½ tsp. ground cumin

1 tsp. finely grated fresh gingerroot

¼ tsp. chili powder

4 tomatoes, chopped coarsely

10½ oz. spinach (de-stalked),
    chopped coarsely

1¼ cups fresh or frozen peas

1 tbsp. lemon juice

salt and pepper

cooked basmati rice, to serve

stuffed eggplant

Preheat the oven to 400°F/200°C. Put the eggplant on a roasting pan and cook in the preheated oven for 8–10 minutes until just softened. Cut in half and scoop out the flesh, reserving the shells.

Heat the oil in a preheated wok or large skillet, add the shallots, garlic, and chilies and stir-fry for 2–3 minutes. Add the zucchini, eggplant flesh, coconut, herbs, and soy sauce and simmer, stirring frequently, for 3–4 minutes.

Divide the mixture among the eggplant shells. Return to the oven for 5–10 minutes until heated through and serve at once, accompanied by rice with scallions and sweet chili sauce.

ingredients

8 small eggplant

2 tbsp. vegetable or peanut oil

4 shallots, finely chopped

2 garlic cloves, crushed

2 fresh red chilies, seeded and chopped

1 zucchini, roughly chopped

4 oz. creamed coconut, chopped

few fresh Thai basil leaves, chopped

small handful of fresh cilantro, chopped

4 tbsp. soy sauce

TO SERVE

rice with chopped scallions

sweet chili sauce

COOK'S TIP

If you can only find large eggplants, 1 half per person would probably be enough.

smooth nectarine shake

Pour the milk into a food processor, add half of the lemon sherbet, and process until combined. Add the remaining sherbet and process until smooth.

When the mixture is thoroughly blended, gradually add the mango and nectarines and process until smooth. Pour the mixture into glasses, add straws, and serve.

ingredients

1 cup milk

12 oz. lemon sherbet

1 ripe mango, pitted and diced

2 ripe nectarines, pitted and diced

pasta salad with bell peppers

Put the whole bell peppers on a baking sheet and place under a preheated broiler, turning frequently, for 15 minutes, until charred all over. Remove with tongs and place in a bowl. Cover with crumpled paper towels and set aside.

Meanwhile, bring a large pan of lightly salted water to a boil. Add the pasta, bring back to a boil, and cook for 8–10 minutes, until tender, but still firm to the bite.

Combine the olive oil, lemon juice, pesto, and garlic in a bowl, whisking well to mix. Drain the pasta, add it to the pesto mixture while still hot, and toss well. Set aside.

When the bell peppers are cool enough to handle, peel off the skins, then cut open and remove the seeds. Chop the flesh coarsely and add to the pasta with the basil. Season to taste with salt and pepper and toss well. Serve at room temperature.

ingredients

1 red bell pepper

1 orange bell pepper

10 oz. dried conchiglie

5 tbsp extra virgin olive oil

2 tbsp. lemon juice

2 tbsp. pesto

1 garlic clove

3 tbsp. shredded fresh basil leaves

salt and pepper

VARIATION

A more traditional salad, without the pasta, can be made in the same way. When the bell peppers have been under the broiler for 10 minutes, add 4 tomatoes, and broil for an additional 5 minutes. Cover the bell peppers with paper towels, then peel and chop. Peel and coarsely chop the tomatoes. Combine them with the dressing and garnish with black olives.

turkish kabobs

Place the lamb cubes in a large, shallow, nonmetallic dish. Mix the olive oil, wine, mint, garlic, orange rind, paprika, and sugar together in a measuring cup and season to taste with salt and pepper. Pour the mixture over the lamb, turning to coat, then cover and let marinate in the refrigerator for 2 hours, turning occasionally.

Preheat the grill. To make the sesame seed cream, put the sesame seed paste, garlic, oil, and lemon juice into a food processor and process briefly to mix. With the motor still running, gradually add the water through the feeder tube until smooth. Transfer to a bowl, cover, and let chill in the refrigerator until required.

Drain the lamb, reserving the marinade, and thread it onto several long metal skewers. Cook over medium heat, turning and brushing frequently with the reserved marinade, for 10–15 minutes. Serve with the sesame seed cream.

ingredients

1 lb. 2 oz. boned shoulder of lamb,
 cut into 1-inch cubes

1 tbsp. olive oil

2 tbsp. dry white wine

2 tbsp. finely chopped fresh mint

4 garlic cloves, finely chopped

2 tsp. grated orange rind

1 tbsp. paprika

1 tsp. sugar

salt and pepper

SESAME SEED CREAM

8 oz. sesame seed paste

2 garlic cloves, finely chopped

2 tbsp. extra virgin olive oil

2 tbsp. lemon juice

½ cup water

COOK'S TIP

Sesame seed paste or tahini is available from most supermarkets and specialist food stores. It is made from ground, pulped sesame seeds.

carrot & ginger energizer

Put the carrot juice, tomatoes, and lemon juice into a food processor and process gently until combined. Add the parsley to the food processor along with the gingerroot and ice cubes.

Process until well combined, then pour in the water and process until smooth.

Pour the mixture into glasses and garnish with chopped fresh parsley. Serve at once.

ingredients

1 cup carrot juice

4 tomatoes, skinned, seeded, and coarsely chopped

1 tbsp. lemon juice

1 oz. fresh parsley

1 tbsp. grated fresh gingerroot

6 ice cubes

½ cup water

GARNISH

chopped fresh parsley

raspberry shortcake

Lightly grease 2 cookie sheets with a little butter.

To make the shortcake, sift the self-rising flour into a bowl. Add the butter and rub it into the flour with your fingertips until the mixture resembles fine bread crumbs.

Stir the sugar, egg yolk, and rose water into the mixture and bring together with your fingers to form a soft dough. Divide the dough in half.

Roll out each piece of dough to an 8-inch round on a lightly floured counter. Carefully lift each of them with the rolling pin onto the prepared cookie sheets. Gently crimp the edges of the dough with your finger.

Bake in a preheated oven, 375°F/190°C, for 15 minutes until lightly golden. Transfer the shortcakes to a wire rack and set aside to cool completely.

Mix the whipped cream with the raspberries and spoon the mixture on top of one of the shortcakes, spreading it out evenly. Top with the other shortcake round, dust with a little confectioners' sugar, and decorate with the extra raspberries and mint leaves.

ingredients

7 tbsp. butter, cut into cubes, plus
  extra for greasing

1½ cups self-rising flour

scant ½ cup superfine sugar

1 egg yolk

1 tbsp. rose water

2½ cups whipping cream, lightly
  whipped

1⅓ cups raspberries, plus a few
  extra for decoration

TO DECORATE

confectioners' sugar

mint leaves

teriyaki chicken with sesame noodles

Using a sharp knife, score each chicken breast diagonally across 3 times and rub all over with some of the teriyaki sauce. Set aside to marinate for at least 10 minutes, or cover and chill all day.

When you are ready to cook the chicken, preheat the broiler to high. Bring a pan of water to a boil, add the buckwheat noodles, and boil for 3 minutes, until soft. Alternatively, cook according to packet instructions. Drain and rinse well in cold water to stop the cooking and remove excess starch, then drain again.

Lightly brush the broiler rack with oil. Add the chicken breasts, skin-side up, and brush again with a little extra teriyaki sauce. Grill the chicken breasts about 4 inches from the heat, brushing occasionally with extra teriyaki sauce, for 15 minutes, or until cooked through and the juices run clear.

Meanwhile, heat a wok or large skillet over a high heat. Add the sesame oil and heat until it shimmers. Add the noodles and stir around to heat through, then stir in the sesame seeds and parsley. Finally, add salt and pepper to taste.

Transfer the chicken breasts to plates and serve with a portion of noodles each.

COOK'S TIP

These noodles also go well with broiled cod, salmon, tuna, or mackerel, but leave the fish to marinate for 30 minutes at the most. Broil the fish, brushing with the sauce, until the flesh flakes easily.

ingredients

4 boneless chicken breasts, about
    6 oz. each, with or without skin,
    as you wish
about 4 tbsp. teriyaki sauce
peanut or sunflower oil

SESAME NOODLES
9 oz. dried thin buckwheat noodles
1 tbsp. toasted sesame oil
2 tbsp. toasted sesame seeds
2 tbsp. finely chopped fresh parsley
salt and pepper

CHAPTER

9

September

tabasco steaks with watercress butter

Preheat the grill. Using a sharp knife, finely chop enough watercress to fill 4 tablespoons. Set aside a few watercress leaves for the garnish. Place the butter in a small bowl and beat in the chopped watercress with a fork until fully incorporated. Cover with plastic wrap and let chill in the refrigerator until required.

Sprinkle each steak with 1 teaspoon of the Tabasco sauce, rubbing it in well. Season to taste with salt and pepper. Cook the steaks for 2½ minutes each side for rare, 4 minutes each side for medium, and 6 minutes each side for well done.

Transfer to serving plates, garnish with the reserved watercress leaves, and serve immediately, topped with the watercress butter.

ingredients

1 bunch of watercress

3 tbsp. unsalted butter, softened

4 sirloin steaks, about 8 oz. each

4 tsp. Tabasco sauce

salt and pepper

VARIATION

If you like, substitute the same amount of fresh parsley for the watercress. Alternatively, serve the steaks with some pesto.

traditional greek salad

Make the dressing by whisking together the oil, lemon juice, garlic, sugar, salt, and pepper in a small bowl. Set aside.

Cut the feta cheese into cubes about 1-inch square. Put the lettuce, tomatoes, and cucumber in a salad bowl. Scatter over the cheese and toss together.

ingredients

6 tbsp. extra virgin olive oil

2 tbsp. fresh lemon juice

1 garlic clove, crushed

pinch of sugar

salt and pepper

7 oz. feta cheese

½ head of iceberg lettuce or
    1 lettuce such as romaine or
    escarole, shredded or sliced

4 tomatoes, quartered

½ cucumber, sliced

12 Greek black olives

2 tbsp. chopped fresh herbs
    such as oregano, flat-leaf
    parsley, mint, or basil

Just before serving, whisk the dressing, pour over the salad leaves, and toss together. Scatter over the olives and chopped herbs and serve.

corncobs with creamy bleu cheese dressing

Preheat the grill. Crumble the Danablu cheese, then place in a bowl. Beat with a wooden spoon until creamy. Beat in the curd cheese until thoroughly blended. Gradually beat in the yogurt and season to taste with salt and pepper. Cover with plastic wrap and let chill in the refrigerator until required.

ingredients

5 oz. Danablu cheese

5 oz. curd cheese

½ cup strained plain yogurt

salt and pepper

6 corncobs in their husks

Fold back the husks on each corncob and remove the silks. Smooth the husks back into place. Cut out 6 rectangles of foil, each large enough to enclose a corncob. Wrap the corncobs in the foil.

Cook the corncobs, turning frequently, for 15–20 minutes. Unwrap the corncobs and discard the foil. Peel back the husk on one side of each and trim off with a sharp knife or kitchen scissors. Serve immediately with the bleu cheese dressing.

traditional apple pie

To make the pastry, sift the flour and salt into a mixing bowl. Add the butter and shortening and rub in with the fingertips until the mixture resembles fine bread crumbs. Add the water and gather the mixture together into a dough. Wrap the dough and chill in the refrigerator for 30 minutes.

Preheat the oven to 425°F/220°C. Roll out almost two-thirds of the pastry thinly and use to line a deep 9-inch pie plate or pie pan.

Mix the apples with the sugar and spice and pack into the pastry case; the filling can come up above the rim. Add the water if needed, particularly if the apples are not very juicy.

Roll out the remaining pastry to form a lid. Dampen the edges of the pie rim with water and position the lid, pressing the edges firmly together. Trim and crimp the edges.

Use the trimmings to cut out leaves or other shapes to decorate the top of the pie, dampen, and attach. Glaze the top of the pie with beaten egg or milk, make 1 to 2 slits in the top and place the pie on a baking sheet.

Bake in the preheated oven for 20 minutes, then reduce the temperature to 350°F/180°C and bake for a further 30 minutes, or until the pastry is a light golden brown. Serve hot or cold, sprinkled with sugar.

ingredients

PASTRY

2⅓ cups all-purpose flour

pinch of salt

3 tbsp. butter, cut into small pieces

3 oz. shortening, cut into
    small pieces

about 6 tbsp. cold water

beaten egg or milk, for glazing

FILLING

1 lb. 10 oz.–2 lb. 4 oz. cooking
    apples, peeled, cored, and sliced

⅔ cup brown or superfine sugar,
    plus extra for sprinkling

½–1 tsp. ground cinnamon, allspice,
    or ground ginger

1–2 tbsp. water (optional)

macaroni with roasted vegetables

Preheat the oven to 475°F/240°C. Spread out the onions, zucchinis, red and yellow bell peppers, eggplant, and tomatoes in a single layer in a large roasting pan. Sprinkle with the garlic, drizzle with the olive oil, and season to taste with salt and pepper. Stir well until all the vegetables are coated.

Roast in the preheated oven for 15 minutes, then remove from the oven and stir well. Return to the oven for an additional 15 minutes. Bring a large heavy-bottom pan of lightly salted water to a boil. Add the pasta, return to a boil, and cook for 8–10 minutes, or until tender but still firm to the bite.

Meanwhile, transfer the roasted vegetables to a large heavy-bottom pan and add the strained tomatoes and olives. Heat through gently, stirring occasionally. Drain the pasta and transfer to a warmed serving dish. Add the roasted vegetable sauce and toss well. Garnish with the fresh basil and parsley and serve immediately.

ingredients

2 red onions, cut into wedges

2 zucchinis, cut into chunks

1 red bell pepper, seeded and cut
   into chunks

1 yellow bell pepper, seeded and
   cut into chunks

1 eggplant, cut into chunks

1 lb. plum tomatoes, quartered
   and seeded

3 garlic cloves, chopped

4 tbsp. olive oil

salt and pepper

12 oz. dried short-cut macaroni

1¼ cups strained tomatoes

½ cup black olives, pitted and
   halved

TO GARNISH

fresh basil sprigs

fresh flat-leaf parsley sprigs

COOK'S TIP

When buying fresh tomatoes, always choose ones that are firm and bright red. Ripe tomatoes can be stored in the refrigerator for up to 2 days, and underripe ones should be kept at room temperature.

VARIATION

Other vegetables would work well in this dish, such as bite-size pieces of butternut squash, and cherry tomato halves.

COOK'S TIP

Fresh dill goes particularly well with fish, especially salmon, as it has a delicate aniseed flavor. It cannot withstand high temperatures, so is best used at the end of cooking or as a garnish.

VARIATION

If watercress is unavailable, then replace with the same amount of arugula or baby spinach leaves.

salmon with watercress cream

Pour the sour cream into a large, heavy-bottom pan and heat gently to simmering point. Remove the pan from the heat, stir in the dill, and set aside.

Melt the butter with the corn oil in a heavy-bottom skillet. Add the salmon fillets and cook over medium heat for 4–5 minutes on each side, or until cooked through. Remove the fish from the skillet, cover, and keep warm. Add the garlic to the skillet and cook, stirring, for 1 minute. Pour in the white wine, bring to a boil and cook until reduced. Stir the sour cream mixture into the skillet and cook for 2–3 minutes, or until thickened. Stir in the watercress and cook until just wilted. Season to taste with salt and pepper. Place the salmon fillets on warmed serving plates, spoon the watercress sauce over them, and serve immediately.

ingredients

1¼ cups sour cream

2 tbsp. chopped fresh dill

2 tbsp. unsalted butter

1 tbsp. corn oil

4 salmon fillets, about 6 oz.
   each, skinned

1 garlic clove, finely chopped

generous ⅓ cup dry white wine

1 bunch of watercress,
   finely chopped

salt and pepper

individual chocolate desserts

To make the desserts, put the sugar and eggs into a heatproof bowl and place over a pan of simmering water. Whisk for about 10 minutes until frothy. Remove the bowl from the heat and fold in the flour and cocoa. Fold in the butter, then the chocolate. Mix well.

Grease 4 small heatproof bowls with butter. Spoon the mixture into the bowls and cover with waxed paper. Top with foil and secure with string. Place the desserts in a large pan filled with enough simmering water to reach halfway up the sides of the bowls. Steam for about 40 minutes, or until cooked through.

About 2–3 minutes before the end of the cooking time, make the sauce. Put the butter, chocolate, water, and sugar into a small pan and warm over low heat, stirring constantly, until melted together. Stir in the liqueur.

Remove the desserts from the heat, turn out into serving dishes, and pour over the sauce. Decorate with coffee beans and serve.

ingredients

DESSERTS

½ cup superfine sugar

3 eggs

½ cup all-purpose flour

½ cup unsweetened cocoa

scant ½ cup unsalted butter, melted, plus extra for greasing

3½ oz. semisweet chocolate, melted

CHOCOLATE SAUCE

2 tbsp. unsalted butter

3½ oz. semisweet chocolate

5 tbsp. water

1 tbsp. superfine sugar

1 tbsp. coffee-flavored liqueur, such as Kahlua

coffee beans, to decorate

chicken, cheese & arugula salad

Wash the arugula leaves, pat dry with paper towels, and put them into a large salad bowl. Add the celery, cucumber, scallions, parsley, and walnuts and mix together well. Transfer onto a large serving platter. Arrange the chicken slices over the salad, then scatter over the cheese. Add the red grapes, if using. Season well with the salt and pepper.

To make the dressing, put all the ingredients into a screw-top jar and shake well. Alternatively, put them into a bowl and mix together well. Drizzle the dressing over the salad and serve.

ingredients

½ oz. arugula leaves

2 celery stalks, trimmed and sliced

½ cucumber, sliced

2 scallions, trimmed and sliced

2 tbsp. chopped fresh parsley

1 oz. walnut pieces

12 oz. boneless roast chicken, sliced

4½ oz. Stilton cheese, cubed

handful of seedless red grapes, cut in half (optional)

salt and pepper

DRESSING

2 tbsp. olive oil

1 tbsp. sherry vinegar

1 tsp. Dijon mustard

1 tbsp. chopped mixed herbs

sage & onion drumsticks

Preheat the oven to 400°F/200°C. Melt the butter in a skillet over medium heat. Add the onion and garlic and cook, stirring, for 3 minutes. Remove from the heat and stir in the bread crumbs, sage, and lemon juice. Season well with salt and pepper. Transfer to a large bowl.

Rinse the drumsticks and pat dry with paper towels. Turn the drumsticks in the beaten egg, then coat them in the sage and onion mixture by pressing it around them. Arrange them in a shallow roasting pan, drizzle over the oil, then roast them in the preheated oven for about 50 minutes until golden and crispy and cooked right through. If they start to brown too quickly, cover the roasting pan with foil. Remove from the oven and pile onto a serving platter. Garnish with lemon wedges and sprigs of fresh flatleaf parsley and serve with salad. Alternatively, to serve cold, let cool, cover with plastic wrap, and refrigerate until required.

ingredients

6 tbsp. butter

1 onion, finely chopped

1 garlic clove, finely chopped

2½ cups fresh white or whole wheat bread crumbs

2 tbsp. finely chopped fresh sage

1 tbsp. lemon juice

salt and pepper

8 large chicken drumsticks

2 eggs, beaten

3 tbsp. vegetable oil

GARNISH

wedges of lemon

sprigs of fresh flatleaf parsley

fresh salad greens, to serve

sausage & rosemary risotto

Strip the long, thin leaves from the rosemary sprigs and chop finely, then set aside.

Bring the stock to a boil in a pan, then reduce the heat and keep simmering gently over a low heat while you are cooking the risotto.

Heat the oil and half the butter in a deep pan over a medium heat. Add the onion and celery and cook, stirring occasionally, for 2 minutes. Stir in the garlic, thyme, sausage, and rosemary. Cook, stirring frequently, for 5 minutes, or until the sausage begins to brown. Transfer the sausage to a plate.

Reduce the heat, add the rice, and mix to coat in oil and butter. Cook, stirring constantly, for 2–3 minutes, or until the grains are translucent.

Add the wine and cook, stirring constantly, for 1 minute until it has reduced.

ingredients

2 long fresh rosemary sprigs, plus extra to garnish

6 cups chicken stock

2 tbsp. olive oil

2 tbsp. butter

1 large onion, finely chopped

1 celery stalk, finely chopped

2 garlic cloves, finely chopped

½ tsp. dried thyme leaves

1 lb. pork sausage, such as Italian luganega, cut into ½-inch pieces

12 oz. risotto rice

½ cup fruity red wine

salt and pepper

3 oz. freshly grated Parmesan cheese

Gradually add the hot stock, a ladle at a time. Stir constantly and add more liquid as the rice absorbs each addition. Increase the heat to medium so that the liquid bubbles. Cook for 20 minutes, or until all the liquid is absorbed and the rice is creamy.

Towards the end of cooking, return the sausage pieces to the risotto and heat through. Season to taste with salt and pepper.

Remove from the heat and add the remaining butter. Mix well, then stir in the Parmesan until it melts. Spoon the risotto onto warmed plates, garnish with rosemary sprigs, and serve.

lemon meringue pie

Grease a 10-inch fluted tart pan. On a lightly floured counter, roll out the pastry into a circle 2 inches larger than the tart pan. Ease the pastry into the pan without stretching and press down lightly into the corners. Roll off the excess pastry to neaten the pastry case. Prick the base of the tart and chill, uncovered, in the refrigerator for 20–30 minutes.

Preheat the oven to 400°F/200°C. Line the pastry case with parchment paper and fill with dried beans. Bake on a heated baking sheet for 15 minutes. Remove the beans and paper and return to the oven for 10 minutes until the pastry is dry and just coloring. Remove from the oven and reduce the temperature to 300°F/150°C.

Put the cornstarch, sugar, and lemon rind into a pan. Pour in a little of the water and blend to a smooth paste. Gradually add the remaining water and the lemon juice. Place the pan over a medium heat and bring the mixture to a boil, stirring continuously. Simmer gently for 1 minute until smooth and glossy. Remove the pan from the heat and beat in the egg yolks, one at a time, then beat in the butter. Place the pan in a bowl of cold water to cool the filling. When cool, spoon the mixture into the pastry case.

To make the meringue, whisk the egg whites using an electric mixer until thick and in soft peaks. Add the superfine sugar gradually, whisking well with each addition. The mixture should be glossy and firm. Spoon the meringue over the filling to cover it completely and make a seal with the pastry shell. Swirl the meringue into peaks and sprinkle with the granulated sugar.

Bake for 20–30 minutes until the meringue is crispy and pale gold (the center should still be soft). Allow to cool slightly before serving.

ingredients

butter, for greasing

all-purpose flour, for dusting

9 oz. ready-rolled pastry, thawed if frozen

3 tbsp. cornstarch

⅓ cup superfine sugar

grated rind of 3 lemons

1¼ cups cold water

⅔ cup lemon juice

3 egg yolks

2 tbsp. unsalted butter, cut into small cubes

MERINGUE

3 egg whites

¾ cup caster sugar

1 tsp. golden granulated sugar

ingredients

1 lb. 5 oz. new potatoes

3 red onions, cut into wedges

2 zucchini, cut into chunks

8 garlic cloves, peeled but left whole

2 lemons, cut into wedges

4 fresh rosemary sprigs

4 tbsp. olive oil

12 oz. unpeeled raw shrimp

2 small raw squid, cut into rings

4 tomatoes, quartered

SERVES 4

COOK'S TIP

Most vegetables are suitable for roasting in the oven. Try adding 1 lb. pumpkin, squash, or eggplant, if you like.

roasted seafood

Preheat the oven to 400°F/200°C.

Scrub the potatoes to remove any dirt. Cut any large potatoes in half. Parboil the potatoes in a pan of boiling water for 10–15 minutes. Place the potatoes in a large roasting pan together with the onions, zucchini, garlic, lemons, and rosemary sprigs.

Pour over the oil and toss to coat all the vegetables in it. Roast in the oven for 30 minutes, turning occasionally, until the potatoes are tender.

Once the potatoes are tender, add the shrimp, squid, and tomatoes, tossing to coat them in the oil, and roast for 10 minutes. All the vegetables should be cooked through and slightly charred for full flavor.

Transfer the roasted seafood and vegetables to warmed serving plates and serve hot.

charred bell pepper salad

Preheat the broiler. Broil the bell peppers, turning frequently, until the skins are charred all over. Put the bell peppers in a bowl, cover with a damp dish towel and leave until cold.

When the bell peppers are cold, hold them over a clean bowl to collect the juices and peel off the skin. Remove the stem, core, and seeds and cut the peppers into thin strips. Arrange the bell pepper strips on a flat serving plate.

If using cumin seeds, dry-toast them in a dry skillet until they turn brown and begin to pop. Shake the skillet continuously to prevent them from burning and do not allow them to smoke. Lightly crush the toasted seeds with a pestle and mortar.

Add the cumin or marjoram, the oil, lemon juice, garlic, sugar, salt, and pepper to the bell pepper juices and whisk together.

Pour the dressing over the bell peppers and chill in the fridge for 3–4 hours or overnight. Serve at room temperature, garnished with olives.

ingredients

2 green bell peppers

2 red bell peppers

2 yellow bell peppers

½ tsp. cumin seeds or 2 tbsp. chopped fresh marjoram

5 tbsp. extra virgin olive oil

2 tbsp. lemon juice

2 garlic cloves, crushed

pinch of sugar

salt and pepper

olives, to garnish

warm fruit nests

Preheat the oven to 350°F/180°C. Brush 4 small muffin pans with oil. Cut the pastry into 16 squares measuring about 4½ inches across. Brush each square with oil and use to line the muffin pans. Place 4 sheets in each pan, staggering them so that the overhanging corners make a decorative star shape. Transfer to a cookie sheet and bake for 7–8 minutes, until golden. Remove from the oven and set aside.

Meanwhile, warm the fruit in a pan with the superfine sugar and allspice over medium heat until simmering. Lower the heat and continue simmering, stirring, for 10 minutes. Remove from the heat and drain.

Using a perforated spoon, divide the warm fruit between the tartlet shells. Garnish with sprigs of fresh mint and serve warm with heavy cream.

ingredients

2–3 tbsp. lemon oil

8 sheets of frozen phyllo pastry, thawed

9 oz. blueberries

9 oz. raspberries

9 oz. blackberries

3 tbsp. superfine sugar

1 tsp. ground allspice

sprigs of fresh mint, to decorate

heavy cream, to serve

chicken with smoked ham & parmesan

Cut each chicken breast through the thickness to open them out, then place the pieces between 2 sheets of plastic wrap and pound with the flat end of a meat mallet or the side of a rolling pin until they are as thin as possible. Spread out the flour on a shallow plate and season with salt and pepper. Coat the chicken pieces in the seasoned flour, shaking off any excess.

Melt half the butter in a large, heavy-bottom skillet. Add the chicken pieces, in batches if necessary, and cook over medium heat, turning frequently, for 10–15 minutes, until golden brown all over and cooked through.

Meanwhile, melt the remaining butter in a small pan. Remove the skillet containing the chicken from the heat. Place a slice of ham on each piece of chicken and sprinkle with the cheese. Pour the melted butter over the chicken and return the skillet to the heat for 3–4 minutes, until the cheese has melted. Serve immediately, garnished with basil sprigs.

ingredients

4 skinned, boneless chicken breasts

2 tbsp. all-purpose flour

salt and pepper

2 tbsp. unsalted butter

8 thin slices smoked ham, trimmed

2 oz. freshly grated Parmesan cheese

fresh basil sprigs, to garnish

VARIATION

A similar dish is made in the Valle d'Aosta, but instead of the chicken breasts being cut and opened out, they are slit to make a pocket. The pockets are then filled with slices of smoked ham or prosciutto and fontina cheese before cooking.

basque scrambled eggs

Heat 2 tablespoons of oil in a large, heavy-bottom skillet over medium-high heat. Add the onion and bell peppers and cook for about 5 minutes, or until the vegetables are soft, but not brown. Add the tomatoes and heat through. Transfer to a plate and keep warm in a preheated low oven.

Add another tablespoon of oil to the skillet. Add the chorizo and cook for 30 seconds, just enough to warm through and flavor the oil. Add the sausage to the reserved vegetables.

Make the oil remaining in the skillet up to 2 tablespoons. Add the butter and let melt. Season the eggs with salt and pepper, then add them to the skillet. Scramble the eggs until they are cooked to the desired degree of firmness. Add extra seasoning to taste. Return the vegetables and sausage to the skillet and stir through. Serve at once with hot toast.

ingredients

olive oil

1 large onion, chopped finely

1 large red bell pepper, cored, seeded, and chopped

1 large green bell pepper, cored, seeded, and chopped

2 large tomatoes, peeled, seeded, and chopped

2 oz. chorizo sausage, sliced thinly, casings removed, if preferred

3 tbsp. butter

10 large eggs, beaten lightly

salt and pepper

4–6 thick slices country-style bread, toasted, to serve

ingredients

1 large head radicchio, outer
   damaged leaves removed

3 pints chicken or vegetable stock

2 tbsp. vegetable oil

1 tbsp. butter

4 oz. pancetta or thick-cut smoked
   bacon, diced

1 large onion, finely chopped

1 garlic clove, finely chopped

14 oz. risotto rice

¼ cup heavy cream

2 oz. freshly grated Parmesan
   cheese

3–4 tbsp. chopped fresh
   flat-leaf parsley

salt and pepper

radicchio risotto

Cut the radicchio head in half lengthwise and remove the triangular core. Place the halves cut-side down and shred finely. Set aside.

Bring the stock to a boil in a pan, then reduce the heat and keep simmering gently over a low heat while you are cooking the risotto.

Heat the oil and butter in a large, heavy-bottom pan over a medium heat. Add the pancetta and cook, stirring occasionally, for 3–4 minutes until it begins to color. Add the onion and garlic and cook for 1 minute.

Reduce the heat, add the rice, and mix to coat in oil and butter. Cook, stirring constantly, for 2–3 minutes or until the grains are translucent. Add the radicchio and cook, stirring for 1 minute until it just begins to wilt.

Gradually add the hot stock, a ladle at a time. Stir constantly and add more liquid as the rice absorbs each addition. Increase the heat to medium so that the liquid bubbles. Cook for 20 minutes, or until all the liquid is absorbed and the rice is creamy.

Stir in the cream, Parmesan, and parsley and season to taste with salt and pepper. Remove the pan from the heat and spoon the risotto onto warmed plates. Serve immediately.

corn & smoked chili soup

Heat the oil in a large, heavy-bottom pan. Add the onion and cook over a low heat, stirring occasionally, for 5 minutes, or until softened. Stir in the corn, cover, and cook for a further 3 minutes.

Add the stock, half the milk, the chilies, and garlic and season with salt. Bring to a boil, reduce the heat, then cover and simmer for 15–20 minutes.

Stir in the remaining milk. Reserve about ¾ cup of the soup solids, draining off as much liquid as possible. Transfer the remaining soup to a food processor or blender and process to a coarse purée.

Return the soup to the pan and stir in the reserved soup solids, the chorizo, lime juice, and cilantro. Reheat to simmering point, stirring constantly. Ladle into warmed bowls and serve immediately.

ingredients

1 tbsp. corn oil

2 onions, chopped

1 lb. 4 oz. frozen corn kernels, thawed

3½ cups chicken stock

2 cups milk

4 chipotle chilies, seeded and finely chopped

2 garlic cloves, finely chopped

salt

2 oz. thinly sliced chorizo sausage

2 tbsp. lime juice

2 tbsp. chopped fresh cilantro

fruit & nut squares

Preheat the oven to 350°F/180°C. Lightly grease a 7-inch shallow, square baking pan with butter. Beat the remaining butter with the honey in a bowl until creamy, then beat in the egg with the almonds.

Add the remaining ingredients and mix together. Press into the prepared pan, ensuring that the mixture is firmly packed. Smooth the top.

Bake in the preheated oven for 20–25 minutes, or until firm to the touch and golden brown.

Remove from the oven and leave for 10 minutes before marking into squares. Leave until cold before removing from the pan. Store in an airtight container.

MAKES 9 SQUARES

ingredients

4 tbsp. unsalted butter, plus
    extra for greasing

2 tbsp. clear honey

1 egg, beaten

3 oz. ground almonds

4 oz. no-soak dried apricots,
    finely chopped

2 oz. dried cherries

2 oz. toasted chopped hazelnuts

1 oz. sesame seeds

3 oz. large oatmeal

SEPTEMBER
20

SERVES 4

ingredients

4 tbsp. olive oil

5 tbsp. butter

3 garlic cloves, chopped very finely

1 lb. boneless, skinless chicken
 breasts, diced

1/4 tsp. dried chili flakes

salt and pepper

1 lb. small broccoli florets

2 2/3 cups dried farfalle or fusilli

6 oz. bottled roasted red bell
 peppers, drained and diced

generous 1 cup chicken stock

freshly grated Parmesan, to serve

farfalle with chicken, broccoli & roasted red bell pepper

Bring a large pan of salted water to a boil. Meanwhile, heat the olive oil, butter, and garlic in a large skillet over a medium-low heat. Cook the garlic until just beginning to color. Add the diced chicken, then raise the heat to medium and stir-fry for 4-5 minutes, or until the chicken is no longer pink. Add the chili flakes and season with salt and pepper. Remove from the heat.

Plunge the broccoli into the boiling water and cook for 2 minutes, or until tender-crisp. Remove with a perforated spoon and set aside.

Bring the water back to a boil. Add the pasta and cook until al dente. Drain and add to the chicken mixture in the pan. Add the broccoli and roasted bell peppers. Pour in the stock. Simmer briskly over a medium-high heat, stirring frequently, until most of the liquid has been absorbed. Sprinkle with the Parmesan and serve.

lamb with eggplant and black olive sauce

SERVES 4

Cut the eggplant into ¾-inch cubes, put in a colander standing over a large plate, and sprinkle each layer with some salt. Cover with a plate and place a heavy weight on top. Leave for 30 minutes.

Preheat the broiler. Rinse the eggplant slices under cold running water, then pat dry with paper towels. Season the lamb chops with pepper.

Place the lamb chops on the broiler pan and cook under medium heat for 10–15 minutes until tender, turning once during the cooking time.

Meanwhile, heat the oil in a pan, add the eggplant, onion, and garlic, and fry for 10 minutes, until softened and starting to brown. Add the tomatoes and their juice, the sugar, olives, herbs, salt, and pepper and simmer for 5–10 minutes.

To serve, spoon the sauce onto 4 warmed serving plates and top with the lamb chops.

ingredients

1 eggplant

salt and pepper

4-8 lamb chops

3 tbsp. olive oil

1 onion, chopped coarsely

1 garlic clove, chopped finely

14 oz. canned chopped tomatoes
   in juice

pinch of sugar

16 black olives, pitted and
   chopped coarsely

1 tsp. chopped fresh herbs such
   as basil, flat-leaf parsley, or
   oregano

MAKES 4

steak & potato pies

To make the pastry, sift the flour and salt into a bowl and gently rub in the shortening and butter until the mixture resembles bread crumbs. Add the water, a spoonful at a time, and stir the mixture with a knife until it holds together.

Turn out onto a lightly floured counter and gently press together until smooth. Wrap in plastic wrap and allow to chill for 1 hour.

Meanwhile, to prepare the filling, mix the meat and vegetables together and season well with salt and pepper.

Divide the pastry into 4 even-size pieces and roll one out until just larger than the size of an 8-inch plate. Place the plate on top of the pastry and cut round it to give a neat edge. Repeat with the other pieces.

Arrange the meat and vegetable mixture across the 4 rounds of pastry, making sure the filling goes to the edge.

Brush the edges of the pastry with water, then bring the edges up over the filling and press together to form a ridge. You can flute the edges of the pies with your fingers or fold over the pastry to form a cord-like seal. Tuck in the ends.

Allow to chill for 1 hour, then glaze with the egg.

Preheat the oven to 375°F/190°C.

Place on a greased baking sheet and cook in the center of the oven for 50–60 minutes. The pies should be crisp and golden in color. Cover with foil and reduce the temperature if the pastry is getting too brown.

ingredients

9 oz. chuck steak, trimmed
and cut into ½-inch dice

6 oz. rutabaga, peeled and
cut into ½-inch dice

12 oz. potatoes, peeled and
cut into ½-inch dice

1 onion, finely chopped

salt and pepper

1 egg, beaten

UNSWEETENED PASTRY

3 cups all-purpose flour, plus
extra for dusting

pinch of salt

4 oz. shortening

4 oz. butter

¾ cup cold water

spaghetti with anchovies, olives, capers & tomatoes

Heat the oil with the anchovies in a large skillet over a low heat. Stir until the anchovies dissolve. Add the garlic and cook for a few seconds, or until just beginning to color. Add the tomatoes, oregano, and chili flakes, then season with salt and pepper. Bring to a boil, then simmer over a medium-low heat for 30 minutes, or until the oil begins to separate from the tomatoes.

Cook the pasta in plenty of boiling salted water until al dente. Drain and transfer to a warm serving dish. Add the olives and capers to the sauce. Pour over the pasta and toss well to mix. Serve immediately.

ingredients

6 tbsp. olive oil

4 anchovy fillets, chopped

2 garlic cloves, chopped very finely

1 lb. 12 oz. canned chopped
   tomatoes

1 tsp. dried oregano

¼ tsp. dried chili flakes

salt and pepper

12 oz. dried spaghetti

10–12 black olives, pitted and sliced

2 tbsp. capers, drained

ingredients

1 lb. green cabbage

1 onion, thinly sliced

4 tbsp. olive oil

salt and pepper

CREAMED POTATO

1 lb. mealy potatoes, peeled
and cut into chunks

salt and pepper

2 tbsp. butter

3 tbsp. hot milk

potato & cabbage cake

To make the creamed potato, cook the potatoes in a large pan of boiling salted water for 15–20 minutes. Drain well and cream with a potato creamer until smooth. Season with salt and pepper, add the butter and milk, and stir well.

Cut the cabbage into fourths, remove the center stalk, and shred finely.

In a large skillet, fry the onion in half the oil until soft. Add the cabbage to the pan and stir-fry for 2–3 minutes until softened. Season with salt and pepper, add the creamed potato, and mix together well.

Press the mixture firmly into the skillet and allow to cook over a high heat for 4–5 minutes so that the base is crispy. Place a plate over the skillet and invert the skillet so that the potato cake falls onto the plate. Add the remaining oil to the skillet, reheat, and slip the cake back into the skillet with the uncooked side down.

Continue to cook for a further 5 minutes until the bottom is crispy too. Turn out onto a hot plate and cut into wedges for serving. Serve at once.

VARIATIONS

This dish can be made with kale or Brussels sprouts instead of the cabbage. The potato and cabbage mix can also be formed into small cakes and fried separately like fish cakes. This is a good way for children to be encouraged to eat cabbage. The cakes can also be fried with bacon to accompany bacon and eggs for breakfast.

orange & fennel salad

Finely grate the rind of the oranges into a bowl and set aside. Working over a bowl to catch the juice, use a small serrated knife to remove all the white pith from the oranges. Cut the oranges horizontally into thin slices.

Toss the orange slices with the fennel and onion slices in a large bowl. Whisk the oil into the reserved orange juice, then spoon over the oranges. Scatter the olive slices over the top, add the chili, if using, then sprinkle with the orange rind and parsley. Serve with French bread.

ingredients

4 large, juicy oranges

1 large fennel bulb, very thinly sliced

1 mild white onion, finely sliced

2 tbsp. extra virgin olive oil

12 plump black olives, pitted and
    thinly sliced

1 fresh red chili, seeded and very
    thinly sliced (optional)

finely chopped fresh parsley

French bread, to serve

stir-fried japanese noodles

Place the Japanese egg noodles in a large bowl. Pour over enough boiling water to cover and let the noodles soak for 10 minutes.

Heat the corn oil in a large preheated wok. Add the red onion and garlic to the wok and cook for 2–3 minutes, or until softened. Add the mushrooms to the wok and cook for about

5 minutes, or until the mushrooms have softened.

Drain the egg noodles thoroughly. Add the the bok choy, noodles, sherry, and oyster sauce to the wok. Toss the ingredients together and cook for just 2–3 minutes or until the liquid is just bubbling.

Transfer the noodles to warm bowls and scatter with scallions and sesame seeds. Serve immediately.

ingredients

8 oz. Japanese egg noodles

2 tbsp. corn oil

1 red onion, sliced

1 clove garlic, crushed

1 lb. mixed mushrooms (shiitake,
    oyster, brown cap)

12 oz. bok choy

2 tbsp. sweet sherry

6 tbsp. oyster sauce

4 scallions, sliced

1 tbsp. toasted sesame seeds

chocolate brownie roulade

Grease a 12 x 8 inch jelly roll pan, line with baking parchment, and grease the parchment.

Melt the chocolate with the water in a small pan over a low heat until the chocolate has just melted. Let cool.

In a bowl, whisk the sugar and egg yolks for 2–3 minutes with a hand-held electric whisk until thick and pale. Fold in the cooled chocolate, raisins, and pecan nuts.

In a separate bowl, whisk the egg whites with the salt. Fold one quarter of the egg whites into the chocolate mixture, then fold in the rest of the whites, working lightly and quickly.

Transfer the mixture to the prepared pan and bake in a preheated oven, 350°F/180°C, for 25 minutes, until risen and just firm to the touch. Let the cake cool before covering with a sheet of non-stick baking parchment and a damp clean dish towel. Set aside until completely cold.

Turn the roulade out on to another piece of baking parchment dusted with confectioners' sugar and remove the lining paper.

Spread the cream over the roulade. Starting from a short end, roll the sponge away from you using the parchment to guide you. Trim the ends of the roulade to make a neat finish and transfer to a serving plate. Chill in the refrigerator until ready to serve. Dust with a little confectioners' sugar before serving.

ingredients

5½ oz. dark chocolate, broken into pieces

3 tbsp. water

¾ cup superfine sugar

5 eggs, separated

2 tbsp. raisins, chopped

2 tbsp. chopped pecan nuts

pinch of salt

1¼ cups heavy cream, lightly whipped

confectioners' sugar, for dusting

crisp noodle & vegetable stir-fry

Half-fill a preheated wok or deep, heavy-bottom skillet with oil. Heat to 350–375°F/180–190°C, or until a cube of bread browns in 30 seconds. Add the noodles, in batches, and cook for 1½–2 minutes, or until crisp and puffed up. Drain on paper towels. Pour off all but 2 tablespoons of oil from the wok.

ingredients

peanut or corn oil, for deep-frying

4 oz. rice vermicelli, broken into 3-inch lengths

4 oz. green beans, cut into short lengths

2 carrots, cut into thin sticks

2 zucchini, cut into thin sticks

4 oz. shiitake mushrooms, sliced

1-inch piece fresh gingerroot, shredded

½ small head Napa cabbage, shredded

4 scallions, shredded

generous ¾ cup bean sprouts

2 tbsp. dark soy sauce

2 tbsp. Chinese rice wine

large pinch of sugar

2 tbsp. coarsely chopped fresh cilantro

Heat the remaining oil over high heat, then add the green beans and stir-fry for 2 minutes. Add the carrot and zucchini sticks, mushrooms, and gingerroot and stir-fry for an additional 2 minutes. Add the cabbage and scallions with the bean sprouts and stir-fry for an additional 1 minute. Add the soy sauce, Chinese rice wine, and sugar and cook, stirring constantly, for 1 minute. Add the noodles and cilantro and toss well. Serve immediately.

pork chops with bell peppers & corn

Heat the oil in a large, flameproof casserole. Add the pork chops in batches and cook over medium heat, turning occasionally, for 5 minutes, or until browned. Transfer the chops to a plate with a perforated spoon.

Add the chopped onion to the casserole and cook, stirring occasionally, for 5 minutes, or until softened. Add the garlic and bell peppers and cook, stirring occasionally for an additional 5 minutes. Stir in the corn kernels and their juices and the parsley, and season to taste with salt and pepper. Return the chops to the casserole, spooning the vegetable mixture over them. Cover and simmer for 30 minutes, or until tender. Serve immediately with creamed potato.

ingredients

1 tbsp. corn oil

4 pork chops, trimmed of visible fat

1 onion, chopped

1 garlic clove, finely chopped

1 green bell pepper, seeded and sliced

1 red bell pepper, seeded and sliced

11½ oz. canned corn kernels

1 tbsp. chopped fresh parsley

salt and pepper

creamed potato, to serve

ingredients

4 tbsp. butter

2 garlic cloves, chopped

3 onions, sliced

1 lb. mixed white and chestnut
    mushrooms, sliced

3½ oz. fresh cèpes or porcini
    mushrooms, sliced

3 tbsp. chopped fresh parsley

generous 2 cups vegetable stock

salt and pepper

3 tbsp. all-purpose flour

½ cup milk

2 tbsp. sherry

½ cup sour cream

GARNISH

sour cream

chopped fresh parsley

fresh crusty rolls, to serve

mushroom & sherry soup

Melt the butter in a large pan over low heat. Add the garlic and onions and cook, stirring, for 3 minutes, until slightly softened. Add the mushrooms and cook for another 5 minutes, stirring. Add the chopped parsley, pour in the stock, and season with salt and pepper. Bring to a boil, then reduce the heat, cover the pan, and simmer for 20 minutes.

Put the flour into a bowl, mix in enough milk to make a smooth paste, then stir it into the soup. Cook, stirring, for 5 minutes. Stir in the remaining milk and the sherry and cook for another 5 minutes. Remove from the heat and stir in the sour cream.

Return the pan to the heat and warm gently. Remove from the heat and ladle into serving bowls. Garnish with sour cream and chopped fresh parsley, and serve the soup with crusty rolls.

October

mixed vegetable curry with chickpea pancakes

SERVES 4

To make the pancakes, sift the flour, salt, and baking soda into a large mixing bowl. Make a well in the center and add the water. Using a whisk, gradually mix the flour into the water until you have a smooth batter. Let stand for 15 minutes.

Heat enough oil to cover the bottom of a skillet over a medium heat. To make small pancakes, pour a small quantity of batter into the skillet, or, if you prefer to make larger pancakes, swirl the skillet to spread the batter mixture. Cook one side for 3 minutes, then, using a spatula, turn over and cook the other side until golden. Keep warm while you repeat with the remaining batter to make 8 pancakes.

Meanwhile, to make the curry, put the carrots and potatoes into a steamer and steam until just tender but still retaining some bite.

Heat the oil in a large, heavy-bottom pan over a medium heat and add the cumin seeds, cardamom seeds, and mustard seeds. When they begin to darken and sizzle, add the onions, partially cover and cook over a medium-low heat, stirring frequently, for 10 minutes, or until soft and golden.

Add the turmeric, coriander, bay leaf, chili powder, gingerroot, and garlic and cook, stirring constantly, for 1 minute. Add the tomatoes, stock, potatoes, and carrots, partially cover, and cook for 10–15 minutes, or until the vegetables are tender. Add the peas and spinach, then cook for just a further 2–3 minutes. Season to taste with salt before serving with the warm chickpea pancakes.

ingredients

VEGETABLE CURRY

7 oz. carrots, cut into chunks

10½ oz. potatoes, quartered

2 tbsp. vegetable oil

1½ tsp. cumin seeds

seeds from 5 green cardamom pods

1½ tsp. mustard seeds

2 onions, grated

1 tsp. ground turmeric

1 tsp. ground coriander

1 bay leaf

1½ tsp. chili powder

1 tbsp. grated fresh gingerroot

2 large garlic cloves, crushed

1¼ cups strained canned tomatoes

1 cup vegetable stock

4 oz. frozen peas

4 oz. frozen spinach leaves

salt

CHICKPEA PANCAKES

8 oz. gram or chickpea flour

1 tsp. salt

½ tsp. baking soda

1¾ cups water

vegetable oil, for frying

exotic mushroom omelets

To make the exotic mushroom filling, heat the butter in a large, heavy-bottom skillet. Add the mushrooms and cook over low heat, stirring occasionally, for 5 minutes. Stir in the sour cream and season with salt and pepper. Keep warm.

To make the omelets, melt half the butter in an omelet pan or small skillet over medium-high heat. Season the eggs to taste with salt and pepper, add half to the omelet pan and stir with a fork. As the egg sets, draw it toward the center and tilt the omelet pan so that the uncooked egg runs underneath. Cook until the underside of the omelet is golden and set, but the top is still moist. Remove the omelet pan from the heat.

Spoon half the mushroom mixture along a line just to one side of the center of the omelet. Flip the other side over and slide the omelet onto a plate. Keep warm. Melt the remaining butter and cook a second omelet in the same way. Serve the omelets immediately.

ingredients

2 tbsp. butter

6 eggs, lightly beaten

salt and pepper

EXOTIC MUSHROOM FILLING

1 tbsp. butter

5½ oz. exotic mushrooms, sliced

2 tbsp. sour cream

salt and pepper

COOK'S TIP

Use whatever mushrooms are available, such as morels, chanterelles, and portobello mushrooms. To clean, rinse morels and chanterelles and shake dry. Wipe portobello mushrooms with a damp cloth.

OCTOBER

3

SERVES 4

ingredients

4 skinless chicken breasts

salt and pepper

½ cup all-purpose flour

2 tbsp. olive oil

2 large garlic cloves, chopped

1 bay leaf

1 tbsp. grated fresh gingerroot

1 tbsp. chopped fresh lemongrass

4 tbsp. sherry vinegar

5 tbsp. rice wine or sherry

1 tbsp. clear honey

1 tsp. chili powder

½ cup orange juice

4 tbsp. lime juice

toasted slivered almonds and
  wedges of lime, to garnish

freshly cooked noodles, to serve

sweet & sour chicken

Season the chicken breasts on both sides with salt and pepper, then roll them in the flour until coated. Heat the olive oil in a large skillet. Add the garlic and cook, stirring, over a medium heat for 1 minute. Add the chicken, bay leaf, gingerroot, and lemongrass and cook for 2 minutes on each side.

Add the vinegar, rice wine, and honey, bring to a boil, then lower the heat and simmer, stirring occasionally, for 10 minutes. Add the chili powder, then stir in the orange juice and lime juice. Simmer for a further 10 minutes. Using a slotted spoon, lift out the chicken and reserve. Strain and reserve the liquid and discard the bay leaf, then return the liquid to the pan with the chicken. Simmer for a further 15–20 minutes.

Remove from the heat and transfer to individual serving plates. Garnish with toasted slivered almonds and lime wedges and serve with noodles.

watercress soup

Remove the leaves from the stalks of the watercress and set aside. Roughly chop the stalks.

Melt the butter in a large pan over a medium heat, add the onion, and cook for 4–5 minutes until soft. Do not brown.

Add the potato to the pan and mix well with the onion. Add the watercress stalks and the stock.

Bring to a boil, then reduce the heat, cover, and simmer for 15–20 minutes until the potato is soft.

Add the watercress leaves and stir in to heat through. Remove from the heat and use a hand-held stick blender to process the soup until smooth. Alternatively, liquidize the soup in a blender and return to the rinsed-out pan. Reheat and season with salt and pepper to taste, adding a good grating of nutmeg, if using.

Serve in warm bowls with the sour cream spooned on top.

ingredients

2 bunches of watercress (approx. 7 oz.), thoroughly cleaned
2 tbsp. butter
2 onions, chopped
8 oz. potatoes, peeled and roughly chopped
5 cups vegetable stock or water
salt and pepper
whole nutmeg, for grating (optional)
½ cup sour cream

OCTOBER
4

SERVES 4

creamy buttered cabbage & potato

To make the creamed potato, cook the potatoes in a large pan of boiling salted water for 15–20 minutes. Drain well and cream with a potato creamer until smooth. Season with salt and pepper, add the butter and cream and stir well. The potato should be very soft.

Cut the cabbage into fourths, remove the centre stalk, and shred finely.

Cook the cabbage in a large pan of boiling salted water for just 1–2 minutes until it is soft. Drain thoroughly.

Mix the potato and cabbage together and stir in the scallions. Season well with salt and pepper.

Serve in individual bowls and top with a good piece of butter.

ingredients

8 oz. green or white cabbage
6 scallions, cut into ¼-inch pieces
salt and pepper
2 tbsp. butter, cut into 4 pieces, to serve

CREAMED POTATO

1 lb. mealy potatoes, peeled and cut into chunks
salt and pepper
2 tbsp. butter
⅔ cup light cream

OCTOBER
5

SERVES 4

fettuccine with scallops & porcini

Put the porcini and hot water in a bowl. Let soak for 20 minutes. Strain the mushrooms, reserving the soaking water, and chop coarsely. Line a strainer with paper towels and strain the mushroom water into a bowl.

Heat the oil and butter in a large skillet over a medium heat. Add the scallops and cook for 2 minutes, or until just golden.

Add the garlic and mushrooms, then stir-fry for another minute. Stir in the lemon juice, cream, and ½ cup of the mushroom water. Bring to a boil, then simmer over a medium heat for 2–3 minutes, stirring constantly, until the liquid is reduced by half. Season with salt and pepper. Remove from the heat.

Cook the pasta in plenty of boiling salted water until al dente. Drain and transfer to a warm serving dish. Briefly reheat the sauce and pour over the pasta. Sprinkle with the parsley and toss well to mix. Serve immediately.

ingredients

1 oz. dried porcini mushrooms

generous 2 cups hot water

3 tbsp. olive oil

3 tbsp. butter

1½ cups scallops, sliced

2 garlic cloves, chopped very finely

2 tbsp. lemon juice

1 cup heavy cream

salt and pepper

12 oz. dried fettuccine or pappardelle

2 tbsp. chopped fresh flat-leaf parsley, to serve

ingredients

1²/₃ cup vegetable stock

1-inch piece fresh galangal, sliced

2 garlic cloves, chopped

1 lemongrass stalk (white part only),
   chopped finely

2 fresh red chilies, seeded
   and chopped

4 carrots, peeled and cut
   into chunks

8 oz. pumpkin, peeled, seeded, and
   cut into cubes

2 tbsp. vegetable or peanut oil

2 shallots, chopped finely

1¾ cups coconut milk

4–6 sprigs fresh Thai basil

⅛ cup toasted pumpkin seeds,
   to garnish

YELLOW CURRY PASTE

3 small fresh orange or yellow
   chilies, chopped coarsely

3 large garlic cloves, chopped
   coarsely

4 shallots, chopped coarsely

3 tsp. ground turmeric

1 tsp. salt

12–15 black peppercorns

1 lemon grass stalk (white part
   only), chopped coarsely

1-inch piece fresh gingerroot,
   chopped

carrot & pumpkin curry

Pour the stock into a large pan and bring to a boil. Add the galangal, half the garlic, the lemongrass, and chilies, and let simmer for 5 minutes. Add the carrots and pumpkin and let simmer for 5–6 minutes, until tender.

To make the yellow curry paste, put all the ingredients into a food processor or blender and process to a thick paste, scraping down the sides occasionally and making sure they are well combined.

Meanwhile, heat the oil in a wok or skillet and stir-fry the shallots and the remaining garlic for 2–3 minutes. Add 3 tablespoons of the curry paste and stir-fry for 1–2 minutes.

Stir the shallot mixture into the pan and add the coconut milk and basil. Let simmer for 2–3 minutes. Serve hot, sprinkled with the toasted pumpkin seeds.

braised pork with fennel

Crush the fennel seeds and mix with the lemon rind, salt, and pepper. Spread the mixture over both sides of the pork chops and let marinate for about 1 hour.

Dust the pork chops with the flour. Heat the oil in a flameproof casserole or Dutch oven, add the pork, and fry until browned. Remove from the casserole. Add the scallions, garlic, and fennel to the casserole and fry for 5–10 minutes until softened and beginning to brown. Return the chops to the casserole.

Pour in the wine, stirring in any glazed bits from the bottom of the casserole, and bring to a boil. Reduce the heat and add the bay leaf. Cover the casserole with a lid and simmer for 45 minutes, until the pork chops are tender. Serve sprinkled with the reserved snipped fennel fronds.

ingredients

1 tsp. fennel seeds

grated rind of 1 lemon

salt and pepper

4 pork chops

1 tbsp. all-purpose flour

2 tbsp. olive oil

2 bunches scallions, sliced thinly

1 garlic clove, chopped finely

2 fennel bulbs, sliced thinly with
   fronds reserved

1 cup dry white wine

1 bay leaf

cinnamon lamb casserole

Put the flour and pepper in a plastic bag, add the lamb, and shake well to coat each piece. Heat the oil in a large, flameproof casserole or Dutch oven. Add the onions and garlic and fry for 5 minutes, until softened. Add the lamb to the casserole and fry for about 5 minutes, stirring frequently, until browned on all sides.

Pour in the wine, vinegar, and tomatoes, stirring in any glazed bits from the bottom of the casserole, and bring to a boil. Reduce the heat and add the raisins, cinnamon, sugar, and bay leaf. Season with salt and pepper.

Cover the casserole with a lid and simmer gently for 2 hours, until the lamb is tender.

Meanwhile, make the topping. Put the yogurt into a small serving bowl, stir in the garlic, and season with salt and pepper. Chill in the fridge until ready to serve.

Serve the casserole hot, topped with a spoonful of the garlic yogurt, and dust with paprika.

ingredients

2 tbsp. all-purpose flour

pepper

2 lb. 4 oz. lean boned lamb, cubed

2 tbsp. olive oil

2 large onions, sliced

1 garlic clove, chopped finely

1¼ cups full-bodied red wine

2 tbsp. red wine vinegar

14 oz. canned chopped tomatoes
   in juice

⅓ cup seedless raisins

1 tbsp. ground cinnamon

pinch of sugar

1 bay leaf

salt

paprika, to garnish

TOPPING

⅔ cup Greek yogurt

2 garlic cloves, crushed

salt and pepper

ingredients

4 large eggs

2 tbsp. water

1 tbsp. Thai soy sauce

6 scallions, chopped finely

1 fresh red chili, seeded and
   chopped finely

1 tbsp. vegetable or peanut oil

1 tbsp. green curry paste

bunch of fresh cilantro, chopped

OCTOBER

10

SERVES 4

omelet rolls

Put the eggs, water, and Thai soy sauce in a bowl. Set aside. Mix together the scallions and chopped chili to form a paste.

Heat half the oil in an 8-inch skillet and pour in half the egg mixture. Tilt to coat the bottom of the skillet evenly and cook until set. Lift out and set aside. Heat the remaining oil and make a second omelet in the same way.

Spread the scallions, chili paste, and curry paste in a thin layer over each omelet and sprinkle the cilantro on top. Roll up tightly. Cut each one in half and then cut each piece on the diagonal in half again. Serve immediately, while still warm.

pappardelle with pumpkin sauce

Melt the butter in a large heavy-bottom pan. Add the shallots, sprinkle with a little salt, cover, and cook over very low heat, stirring occasionally, for 30 minutes. Add the pumpkin pieces and season to taste with nutmeg. Cover and cook over very low heat, stirring occasionally, for 40 minutes, or until the pumpkin is pulpy. Stir in the cream, Parmesan cheese, and parsley, and remove the pan from the heat.

SERVES 4

Meanwhile, bring a large heavy-bottom pan of lightly salted water to a boil. Add the pasta, return to a boil, and cook for 8–10 minutes, or until tender but still firm to the bite. Drain, reserving 2–3 tablespoons of the cooking water.

Add the pasta to the pumpkin mixture and stir in the reserved cooking water if the mixture seems too thick. Cook, stirring constantly, for 1 minute, then transfer to a large, warmed serving dish and serve immediately with extra grated Parmesan cheese.

ingredients

4 tbsp. butter

6 shallots, very finely chopped

salt

1 lb. 12 oz. pumpkin, peeled,
    seeded, and cut into pieces

pinch of freshly grated nutmeg

generous ¾ cup light cream

4 tbsp. freshly grated Parmesan
    cheese, plus extra to serve

2 tbsp. chopped fresh
    flat-leaf parsley

12 oz. dried pappardelle

ingredients

2 tbsp. butter, plus extra for
  greasing
4 oz. semisweet chocolate, broken
  into pieces
¾ cup dark brown sugar
2 eggs
2 tbsp. strong coffee, cooled
generous ½ cup all-purpose flour
½ tsp. baking powder
pinch of salt
¼ cup shelled walnuts, chopped

FROSTING

4 oz. semisweet chocolate, broken
  into pieces
⅔ cup sour cream

COOK'S TIP

*Do not leave the brownies to set in
the refrigerator but leave them in
the cake pan in a cool place. Store
any unfrosted brownies in an airtight
container for up to 3 days.*

mocha brownies with sour cream frosting

Preheat the oven to 350°F/180°C. Grease an 8-inch square cake pan with butter and line with parchment paper. Place the chocolate and butter in a small heatproof bowl and set over a pan of gently simmering water until melted. Stir until smooth. Remove from the heat and let cool.

Beat the sugar and eggs together until pale and thick. Fold in the chocolate mixture and coffee. Mix well. Sift the flour, baking powder, and salt into the cake batter and fold in. Fold in the walnuts.

Pour the cake batter into the pan and bake in the oven for 20–25 minutes, or until set. Let cool in the pan. To make the frosting, melt the chocolate in a glass bowl over a pan of simmering water. Stir in the sour cream and beat until evenly blended. Spoon the topping over the brownies and make a swirling pattern with a spatula. Let set in a cool place. Cut into squares, then remove from the pan and serve.

smoked cheddar & hard cider fondue

Put the lime juice and all but 2 tablespoons of the hard cider into a large pan and bring to a gentle simmer over low heat. Add a handful of the cheese and stir until melted. Add the remaining cheese gradually, stirring constantly after each addition.

In a bowl, mix the cornstarch with the remaining hard cider, then stir into the pan. Continue to stir for 3–4 minutes, or until thickened and bubbling. Stir in the allspice and add salt and pepper to taste.

Pour the mixture into a fondue pot and, using protective mitts, transfer to a lit tabletop burner. To serve, allow your guests to spear pieces of apple, bread, pineapple, and ham on to fondue forks and dip them into the fondue.

ingredients

2 tbsp. lime juice

2 cups dry hard cider

1 lb. 9 oz. smoked Cheddar
   cheese, grated

2 tbsp. cornstarch

pinch of ground allspice

salt and pepper

DIPPERS

4 apples, cored and cut into
   bite-size cubes, then brushed
   with lemon juice

fresh crusty bread, cut into
   bite-size cubes

canned pineapple chunks, drained

lean cooked ham, cut into
   bite-size cubes

bacon-wrapped trout

Preheat the grill. Rinse the trout inside and out under cold running water and pat dry with paper towels.

Stretch the bacon using the back of a heavy, flat-bladed knife. Season the flour with salt and pepper and spread it out on a large, flat plate.

ingredients

4 trout, cleaned

4 smoked lean bacon strips, rinded

4 tbsp. all-purpose flour

salt and pepper

2 tbsp. olive oil

2 tbsp. lemon juice

corn salad, to serve

TO GARNISH

fresh parsley sprigs

lemon wedges

Gently roll each trout in the seasoned flour until thoroughly coated. Starting just below the head, wrap a strip of bacon in a spiral along the length of each fish.

Brush the trout with olive oil and cook for 5–8 minutes on each side. Transfer to 4 large serving plates and drizzle with the lemon juice. Garnish with parsley and lemon wedges, and serve with corn salad.

ingredients

¾ cup unsalted peanuts

11½ oz. canned corn, drained

1 onion, finely chopped

¾ cup all-purpose flour

1 tsp. ground coriander

½ tsp. sambal ulek or chili sauce

salt

1–2 tbsp. warm water (optional)

peanut oil, for deep-frying

COOK'S TIP

Sambal ulek is a fiery hot chili sauce available from Asian food stores and supermarkets. If you cannot find it, then use chili sauce instead.

indonesian corn balls

Place the peanuts in a food processor and process briefly until coarsely ground. Alternatively, grind them in a mortar with a pestle. Transfer to a bowl and stir in the corn, onion, flour, coriander, and sambal ulek. Season to taste with salt. Knead to a dough, adding a little warm water, if necessary, to make the dough workable.

Heat the oil in a deep-fryer or large, heavy-bottom pan. Using your hands, form tablespoonfuls of the dough into balls, then drop the corn balls into the hot oil, in batches, and cook until golden and crisp. Remove the corn balls with a slotted spoon, drain on paper towels and keep warm while you cook the remaining batches. Serve immediately or let cool first.

ingredients

2½ tbsp. all-purpose flour

1 tsp. salt

¼ tsp. pepper

1 rolled brisket joint, weighing
  3 lb. 8 oz.

2 tbsp. vegetable oil

2 tbsp. butter

1 onion, finely chopped

2 celery stalks, diced

2 carrots, peeled and diced

1 tsp. dill seed

1 tsp. dried thyme or oregano

1½ cups red wine

²/₃–1 cup beef stock

4–5 potatoes, cut into large chunks
  and boiled until just tender

2 tbsp. chopped fresh dill, to serve

beef pot roast with potatoes & dill

Preheat the oven to 275°F/140°C.

Mix 2 tablespoons of the flour with the salt and pepper in a shallow dish. Dip the meat to coat. Heat the oil in a flameproof casserole and brown the meat all over. Transfer to a plate.

Add half the butter to the casserole and cook the onion, celery, carrots, dill seed, and thyme for 5 minutes. Return the meat and juices to the casserole.

Pour in the wine and enough stock to reach one-third of the way up the meat. Bring to a boil, cover, and cook in the oven for 3 hours, turning the meat every 30 minutes. After it has been cooking for 2 hours, add the potatoes and more stock if necessary.

When ready, transfer the meat and vegetables to a warmed serving dish. Strain the cooking liquid into a pan.

Mix the remaining butter and flour to a paste. Bring the cooking liquid to a boil. Whisk in small pieces of the flour and butter paste, whisking constantly until the sauce is smooth. Pour the sauce over the meat and vegetables. Sprinkle with the fresh dill to serve.

COOK'S TIP
When using a flour and butter paste, also known as beurre manié, to thicken a sauce or gravy, whisk it into the sauce in small pieces, making sure each piece has been blended in before adding the next.

white fish with spiced noodles

Preheat the broiler to high. While the broiler is heating, put the noodles in a pan of boiling water and boil for 3 minutes, until soft. Alternatively, cook according to the packet instructions. Drain, rinse with cold water to stop the cooking, and drain again, then set aside. (If you want to cook the noodles in advance, toss them with a teaspoon or so of sesame oil and set aside).

To cook the fish, mix 1 tablespoon of the oil with the lemon juice and brush over one side of each fish steak. Sprinkle with the lemon rind and a dusting of paprika and add a little salt and pepper. Lightly brush the broiler rack with oil, then broil the fish, about 4 inches from the heat, for 8–10 minutes until the flesh flakes easily.

Meanwhile, heat a wok or large skillet over a high heat. Add 1 tablespoon oil and heat until it shimmers. Add the garlic and gingerroot and stir-fry for about 30 seconds. Add the cilantro and kecap manis and stir around. Add the noodles and give a good stir so they are coated in the kecap manis. Stir in the chopped chili and nam pla.

Serve each grilled fish steak on top of a bed of noodles.

ingredients

1 tbsp. peanut or corn oil

finely grated rind and juice of
   1 large lemon

4 white fish steaks, about
   5 oz. each, skinned

paprika, to taste

salt and pepper

SPICED NOODLES

9 oz. dried medium Chinese
   egg noodles

1 tbsp. peanut or corn oil

2 garlic cloves, chopped

1-inch piece fresh gingerroot,
   peeled and finely chopped

2 tbsp. very finely chopped fresh
   cilantro roots

1 tbsp. kecap manis (sweet soy
   sauce)

1 Thai chili, seeded and
   finely chopped

1 tbsp. nam pla (Thai fish sauce)

broiled chicken with lemon

Prick the skin of the chicken quarters all over with a fork. Put the chicken pieces in a dish, add the lemon juice, oil, garlic, thyme, salt, and pepper, and mix well. Cover and let marinate in the fridge for at least 2 hours.

To cook the chicken, preheat the broiler. Put the chicken in a broiler pan and baste with the marinade. Cook for about 30–40 minutes, basting and turning occasionally, until the chicken is tender. (To test if the chicken is cooked, pierce the thickest part of the chicken pieces with a skewer. If the juices run clear, they are ready).

Serve hot, with any remaining marinade spooned over, and garnished with the grated lemon rind.

ingredients

4 chicken quarters

grated rind and juice of 2 lemons

4 tbsp. olive oil

2 garlic cloves, crushed

2 sprigs fresh thyme

salt and pepper

onion soup with croûtons

Melt the butter in a large pan over medium heat. Add the garlic, onions, and sugar and cook, stirring, for about 25 minutes, until the onions have caramelized.

In a bowl, mix the flour with enough wine to make a smooth paste, then stir it into the onion mixture. Cook for 2 minutes, then stir in the remaining wine and the stock. Season with salt and pepper. Bring to a boil, then reduce the heat, cover the pan, and simmer for 30 minutes.

Meanwhile, to make the croûtons, heat the oil in a skillet until hot. Cut the bread into small cubes and cook over high heat, stirring, for about 2 minutes, until crisp and golden. Remove from the heat, drain the croûtons on paper towels, and set them aside. When the soup is cooked, remove from the heat and ladle into serving bowls. Scatter over some fried croûtons and serve with slices of wholewheat and white bread.

ingredients

scant ½ cup butter

2 garlic cloves, crushed

3 large onions, thinly sliced

1 tsp. sugar

2 tbsp. all-purpose flour

scant 1 cup dry white wine

6¼ cups vegetable stock

salt and pepper

CROÛTONS

2 tbsp. olive oil

2 slices day-old white bread,
   crusts removed

slices of fresh wholewheat and
   white bread, to serve

ingredients

generous 1 cup blanched almonds

1¼ cups heavy cream

¼ tsp. almond extract

⅔ cup light cream

½ cup confectioners' sugar

HOT CHOCOLATE SAUCE

3½ oz. semisweet chocolate,
    broken into pieces

3 tbsp. golden syrup

4 tbsp. water

2 tbsp. unsalted butter, diced

¼ tsp. vanilla extract

OCTOBER

20

SERVES 4–6

frozen almond cream with hot chocolate sauce

Place the almonds on a baking sheet and toast in a preheated oven, 400°F/200°C, for 8–10 minutes, stirring occasionally, until golden and giving off a "toasted" aroma: watch carefully after 7 minutes because they burn quickly. Immediately pour onto a cutting board and let cool. Coarsely chop scant ½ cup by hand, and finely grind the remainder; set both aside.

Whip the heavy cream with the almond extract until soft peaks form. Stir in the light cream and continue whipping, sifting in the confectioners' sugar in three batches. Transfer to an ice-cream maker and freeze following the manufacturer's instructions. When the cream is almost frozen, transfer it to a bowl, and stir in the chopped almonds so they are evenly distributed. Put the cream mixture in a 1-lb. loaf pan and smooth the top. Wrap tightly in foil and put in the freezer for at least 3 hours.

To make the hot chocolate sauce, place a heatproof bowl over a pan of simmering water. Add the chocolate, syrup, and water and stir until the chocolate melts. Stir in the butter and vanilla extract until smooth.

To serve, unwrap the pan and dip the bottom in a sink of boiling water for just a couple of seconds. Invert onto a freezerproof tray, giving a sharp shake until the frozen cream drops out. Using a spatula, coat the top and sides with the finely chopped almonds; return to the freezer unless serving at once. Use a warm knife to slice into 8 to 12 slices. Arrange 2 slices on each plate and spoon the hot chocolate sauce over.

COOK'S TIP
If you don't have an ice-cream maker, put the mixture in a freezerproof container and freeze for 2 hours, or until it is starting to thicken and set around the edge. Beat well and return to the freezer until almost frozen. Stir in the chopped almonds.

almost instant toffee pudding

Using a fork, beat the eggs with 6 tablespoons of the milk and the cinnamon in a large, shallow dish.

Cut the bread into triangles and place in the dish, in batches if necessary, to soak for 2–3 minutes. Melt half the butter with half the oil in a heavy-bottom skillet. Add the bread triangles, in batches, and cook for 2 minutes on each side, or until golden brown, adding a little more butter and oil as necessary Remove with a spatula, drain on paper towels, transfer to serving plates, and keep warm.

Add the remaining butter and milk to the skillet with the sugar and golden syrup and cook, stirring constantly, until hot and bubbling. Pour the toffee sauce over the bread triangles and serve.

ingredients

2 eggs

generous ⅓ cup milk

pinch of ground cinnamon

6 slices of white bread,
    crusts removed

4 oz. unsalted butter

1 tbsp. corn oil

generous ¼ cup brown sugar

4 tbsp. golden syrup

creamy chicken & shiitake pasta

Put the dried mushrooms in a bowl with the hot water. Let soak for 30 minutes until softened. Remove, squeezing excess water back into the bowl. Strain the liquid in a fine-meshed strainer and reserve. Slice the soaked mushrooms, discarding the stalks.

Heat the oil in a large skillet over a medium heat. Add the bacon and chicken, then stir-fry for about 3 minutes. Add the dried and fresh mushrooms, the onion, and oregano. Stir-fry for 5–7 minutes until soft. Pour in the stock and the mushroom liquid. Bring to a boil, stirring. Simmer briskly for about 10 minutes, continuing to stir, until reduced. Add the cream and simmer for 5 minutes, stirring, until beginning to thicken. Season with salt and pepper. Remove the skillet from the heat and set aside.

Cook the pasta until al dente. Drain and transfer to a serving dish. Pour the sauce over the pasta. Add half the Parmesan and mix together well. Sprinkle with parsley and serve with the remaining Parmesan.

ingredients

1 oz. dried shiitake mushrooms

1½ cups hot water

1 tbsp. olive oil

6 bacon strips, chopped

3 boneless, skinless chicken
    breasts, sliced into strips

4 oz. fresh shiitake
    mushrooms, sliced

1 small onion, chopped finely

1 tsp. fresh oregano or marjoram,
    chopped finely

1¼ cups chicken stock

1¼ cups whipping cream

salt and pepper

1 lb. dried tagliatelle

2 oz. freshly grated Parmesan

chopped fresh flat-leaf parsley,
    to garnish

ingredients

2 tbsp. all-purpose flour

salt and pepper

4 x 8 oz. swordfish steaks

generous ⅓ cup olive oil

2 garlic cloves, halved

1 onion, chopped

4 anchovy fillets, drained
   and chopped

4 tomatoes, peeled, seeded,
   and chopped

12 green olives, pitted and sliced

1 tbsp. capers, rinsed

fresh rosemary leaves, to garnish

OCTOBER

23

SERVES 4

swordfish with olives & capers

Spread out the flour on a plate and season with salt and pepper. Coat the fish in the seasoned flour, shaking off any excess.

Gently heat the olive oil in a large, heavy-bottom skillet. Add the garlic and cook over low heat for 2–3 minutes, until just golden. Do not let it turn brown or burn. Remove the garlic and discard.

Add the fish to the skillet and cook over medium heat for about 4 minutes on each side, until cooked through and golden brown. Remove the steaks from the skillet and set aside.

Add the onion and anchovies to the skillet and cook, crushing the anchovies with a wooden spoon until they have turned to a purée and the onion is golden. Add the tomatoes and cook over low heat, stirring occasionally, for about 20 minutes, until the mixture has thickened.

Stir in the olives and capers and taste and adjust the seasoning. Return the steaks to the skillet and heat through gently. Serve garnished with rosemary.

ingredients

12 ripe figs

12 oz. bleu cheese, crumbled

extra virgin olive oil

CARAMELIZED ALMONDS

½ cup superfine sugar

generous ¾ cup whole almonds,
blanched or unblanched

COOK'S TIP

Store the nuts in an airtight jar for up to 3 days until required; any longer and they become soft.

VARIATION

Walnut halves can also be caramelized and used in this recipe.

figs with bleu cheese

First make the caramelized almonds. Put the sugar in a pan over medium-high heat and stir until the sugar melts and turns golden brown and bubbles: do not stir once the mixture starts to bubble. Remove from the heat and add the almonds one at a time and quickly turn with a fork until coated; if the caramel hardens, return the pan to the heat. Transfer each almond to a lightly buttered baking sheet once it is coated. Let stand until cool and firm.

To serve, slice the figs in half and arrange four halves on each plate. Coarsely chop the almonds by hand. Place a mound of bleu cheese on each plate and sprinkle with chopped almonds. Drizzle the figs very lightly with the oil.

risotto with broiled chicken

Place the chicken breasts in a shallow, nonmetallic dish and season. Mix the lemon rind and juice, 4 tablespoons of the olive oil, the garlic, and thyme together in a bowl. Spoon the mixture over the chicken and rub in. Cover with plastic wrap and marinate in the refrigerator for 4–6 hours.

Remove the chicken from the refrigerator and return to room temperature. Preheat a broiler over a high heat. Put the chicken, skin-side down, on the broiler and cook for 10 minutes, or until the skin is crisp and starting to brown. Turn over and brown the underside. Reduce the heat and cook for a further 10–15 minutes, or until the juices run clear when pierced with a skewer.

Meanwhile, bring the stock to a boil in a pan, then reduce the heat and keep simmering gently over a low heat while you are cooking the risotto.

Heat the remaining oil with 1 tablespoon of the butter in a deep pan over a medium heat until the butter has melted. Add the onion and cook, stirring occasionally, for 5 minutes, or until soft and starting to turn golden. Do not brown.

Reduce the heat, add the rice, and mix to coat in oil and butter. Cook, stirring constantly, for 2–3 minutes, or until the grains are translucent.

Add the wine and cook, stirring constantly, for 1 minute until reduced. Gradually add the hot stock, a ladle at a time. Stir constantly and add more liquid as the rice absorbs each addition. Increase the heat to medium so that the liquid bubbles. Cook for 20 minutes, or until all the liquid is absorbed and the rice is creamy. Season to taste.

Transfer the cooked chicken to a carving board. Let rest for 5 minutes, then cut into thick slices. Remove the risotto from the heat and add the remaining butter. Mix well, then stir in the Parmesan until it melts. Put a scoop of risotto on each plate and add the chicken slices. Garnish with lemon wedges and thyme sprigs and serve immediately.

ingredients

4 boneless chicken breasts, about
  4 oz. each

grated rind and juice of 1 lemon

5 tbsp. olive oil

1 garlic clove, crushed

8 fresh thyme sprigs, finely chopped

4 cups chicken stock

2 tbsp. butter

1 small onion, finely chopped

10 oz. risotto rice

2/3 cup dry white wine

salt and pepper

3 oz. freshly grated Parmesan or
  Grana Padano cheese

TO GARNISH

lemon wedges

fresh thyme sprigs

leek & sausage tortilla

Slice the sausage. Heat the oil in a large skillet. Add the leeks and cook over medium heat, stirring occasionally, for 5 minutes, or until softened. Add the bell pepper and sausage slices and cook for 5 minutes.

Beat the eggs in a bowl and season to taste with salt and pepper. Pour the eggs into the skillet and cook for a few seconds. Loosen any egg that has set at the edge of the pan with a spatula and tilt the pan to let the uncooked egg run underneath. Continue cooking until the underside has set.

Remove the skillet from the heat, place an upside-down plate on top and, holding the 2 together, invert the tortilla on to the plate. Slide it back into the skillet and cook for an additional 2 minutes, until the second side has set. Slide the tortilla out of the skillet and cut into wedges to serve.

ingredients

4 oz. chorizo sausage

2 tbsp. olive oil

4 leeks, thinly sliced

½ red bell pepper, seeded and chopped

6 eggs

salt and pepper

chicken with vegetables & cilantro rice

Heat the oil in a wok or large skillet and sauté the onion, garlic, and gingerroot together for 1–2 minutes.

Add the chicken and mushrooms and cook over high heat until browned. Add the coconut milk, sugar snap peas, and sauces, and bring to a boil. Let simmer gently for 4–5 minutes until tender.

Heat the oil for the rice in a separate wok or large skillet and cook the onion until softened but not browned. Add the cooked rice, bok choy, and fresh cilantro, and heat gently until the leaves have wilted and the rice is hot. Sprinkle over the soy sauce and serve immediately with the chicken.

ingredients

2 tbsp. vegetable or peanut oil

1 red onion, chopped

2 garlic cloves, chopped

1-inch piece fresh gingerroot, peeled and chopped

2 skinless, boneless chicken breasts, cut into strips

4 oz. white mushrooms

14 oz. canned coconut milk

2 oz. sugar snap peas, trimmed and halved lengthwise

2 tbsp. soy sauce

1 tbsp. fish sauce

CILANTRO RICE

1 tbsp. vegetable or peanut oil

1 red onion, sliced

3 cups rice, cooked and cooled

8 oz. bok choy, torn into large pieces

handful of fresh cilantro, chopped

2 tbsp. Thai soy sauce

apple fritters

SERVES 4

Pour the corn oil into a deep fryer or large, heavy-bottom pan and heat to 350–375°F/ 180–190°C, or until a cube of bread browns in 30 seconds. Meanwhile, using an electric mixer, beat the egg and salt together until frothy, then quickly whisk in the water and flour. Do not overbeat the batter. It doesn't matter if it isn't completely smooth.

Mix the cinnamon and sugar together in a shallow dish and set aside. Slice the apples into ¼-inch thick rings. Spear with a fork, one slice at a time, and dip in the batter to coat. Add to the hot oil, in batches, and cook for 1 minute on each side, or until golden and puffed up. Remove with a slotted spoon and drain on paper towels.

Keep warm while you cook the remaining batches. Transfer to a large serving plate, sprinkle with the cinnamon sugar, and serve.

ingredients

corn oil, for deep-frying

1 large egg

pinch of salt

¾ cup water

⅜ cup all-purpose flour

2 tsp. ground cinnamon

generous ¼ cup superfine sugar

4 eating apples, peeled and cored

VARIATION

Replace the apple with 1 small pineapple, peeled and cut into rings. Banana fritters would also be delicious. Use 4 bananas instead of apples.

COOK'S TIP

The best and easiest way to core an apple is to use an apple corer. Push the corer into the stalk end of the apple and twist to cut round the core, then pull it out and discard.

pork with sweet bell peppers

Place the pork in a nonmetallic bowl. Pour over the wine and add 4 of the garlic cloves. Cover with plastic wrap and let marinate in the refrigerator for at least 8 hours.

Put the chilies in a flameproof bowl and pour over enough boiling water to cover. Let soften for 20 minutes, then seed and chop. Set them aside.

Preheat the oven to 325°F/160°C.

Heat the oil in a large, heavy-bottom flameproof casserole over a medium-high heat. Add the onions and fry for 3 minutes, then add the remaining garlic, chopped chilies, bell pepper slices, and paprika and fry for a further 2 minutes until the onions are soft, but not brown. Use a slotted spoon to transfer the mixture to a plate, leaving as much oil as possible in the base of the casserole.

Drain the pork, reserving the marinade, and pat dry. Add the pork to the casserole, and fry until brown on both sides.

Return the onion mixture to the casserole with the pork and stir in the reserved marinade, tomatoes and their can juices, the herbs, and salt and pepper to taste. Bring to a boil, scraping any glazed bits from the base of the pan. Cover, transfer the casserole to the oven and cook for 1 hour, or until the pork is tender. If the juices are too thin, remove the pork from the casserole and keep warm. Put the casserole over a high heat and let the juices bubble until reduced.

Taste and adjust the seasoning. Cut the pork into pieces and serve with the peppers and sauce from the casserole.

ingredients

1 piece of pork shoulder, weighing 2 lb., boned and trimmed, but left in 1 piece

1 cup dry white wine

6 garlic cloves, crushed

2 dried ancho or pasilla chilies

about 4 tbsp. olive oil

2 large onions, chopped

4 red or green bell peppers, or a mixture, broiled, peeled, seeded, and sliced

½ tsp. hot paprika

1 lb. 12 oz. canned chopped tomatoes

2 fresh thyme sprigs

2 fresh parsley sprigs

salt and pepper

ingredients

8 tbsp. olive oil

12 garlic cloves, very finely chopped

12 oz. chickpeas, soaked overnight
    in cold water and drained

6 pints water

1 tsp. ground cumin

1 tsp. ground coriander

2 carrots, very finely chopped

2 onions, very finely chopped

6 celery stalks, very finely chopped

juice of 1 lemon

salt and pepper

4 tbsp. chopped fresh cilantro

OCTOBER

30

SERVES 4

tunisian garlic & chickpea soup

Heat half the oil in a large, heavy-bottom pan. Add the garlic and cook over a low heat, stirring frequently, for 2 minutes. Add the chickpeas to the pan with the measured water, cumin, and ground coriander. Bring to a boil, then reduce the heat, and simmer for 2½ hours, or until tender.

Meanwhile, heat the remaining oil in a separate pan. Add the carrots, onions, and celery, cover and cook over a medium-low heat, stirring occasionally, for 20 minutes.

Stir the vegetable mixture into the pan of chickpeas. Transfer about half the soup to a food processor or blender and process until smooth. Return the purée to the pan, add about half the lemon juice, and stir. Taste and add more lemon juice as required. Season to taste with salt and pepper. Ladle into warmed bowls, sprinkle with the fresh cilantro and serve.

pumpkin chestnut risotto

Bring the stock to a boil, then reduce the heat and keep simmering gently over a low heat while you are cooking the risotto.

Heat the oil with 1 tablespoon of the butter in a deep pan over a medium heat until the butter has melted. Stir in the onion and pumpkin and cook, stirring occasionally, for 5 minutes, or until the onion is soft and starting to turn golden and the pumpkin begins to color. Roughly chop the chestnuts and add to the mixture. Stir thoroughly to coat.

Reduce the heat, add the rice, and mix to coat in oil and butter. Cook, stirring constantly, for 2–3 minutes, or until the grains are translucent. Add the wine and cook, stirring constantly, for 1 minute until it has reduced.

If using the saffron threads, dissolve them in 4 tablespoons of the hot stock and add the liquid to the rice after the wine has been absorbed. Cook, stirring constantly, until the liquid has been absorbed.

Gradually add the hot stock, a ladle at a time. Stir constantly and add more liquid as the rice absorbs each addition. Increase the heat to medium so that the liquid bubbles. Cook for 20 minutes, or until all the liquid is absorbed and the rice is creamy. Season to taste.

Remove the risotto from the heat and add the remaining butter. Mix well, then stir in the Parmesan until it melts. Adjust the seasoning if necessary, spoon the risotto onto 4 warmed plates and serve immediately.

ingredients

4 cups vegetable or chicken stock

1 tbsp. olive oil

2 tbsp. butter

1 small onion, finely chopped

8 oz. pumpkin, diced

8 oz. chestnuts, cooked and shelled

10 oz. risotto rice

2/3 cup dry white wine

1 tsp. crumbled saffron threads (optional)

salt and pepper

3 oz. freshly grated Parmesan or Grana Padano cheese

November

NOVEMBER

1

SERVES 4

ingredients

4 tbsp. butter, slightly softened

1 tbsp. chopped fresh thyme

1 tbsp. chopped fresh parsley

2 oven-ready young pheasants

salt and pepper

4 tbsp. vegetable oil

½ cup red wine

TO SERVE

honey-glazed parsnips

sautéed potatoes

freshly cooked Brussels sprouts

COOK'S TIP

Only young birds are suitable for roasting, as older pheasants are fairly tough and need a slower cooking method. Even so, the meat on the legs tends to be quite tough and sinewy, whereas the lighter breasts are more delicate and tender. It is quite usual to serve only the breasts. Keep the leg meat for making a ground pasta sauce or using in a pie. You can also make delicious stock with the carcasses.

roast pheasant with red wine & herbs

Preheat the oven to 375°F/190°C.

Put the butter in a small bowl and mix in the chopped herbs. Lift the skins away from the breasts, taking care not to tear them, and push the herb butter under the skins. Season to taste with salt and pepper. Pour the oil into a roasting pan, add the pheasants, and cook in the oven for 45 minutes, basting occasionally.

Remove from the oven, pour over the wine, then return to the oven and cook for a further 15 minutes, or until cooked through. Check that each bird is cooked by inserting a knife between the legs and body. If the juices run clear, they are cooked.

Remove the pheasants from the oven, cover with foil, and let stand for 15 minutes. Divide among individual serving plates, and serve with honey-glazed parsnips, sautéed potatoes, and freshly cooked Brussels sprouts.

steamed syrup sponge dessert

Butter a 2½-pint ovenproof bowl and put the syrup into the bottom.

Beat together the butter and sugar until soft and creamy, then beat in the eggs, a little at a time.

Fold in the flour and stir in the milk to make a soft dropping consistency. Add the lemon rind. Turn the mixture into the ovenproof bowl.

Cover the surface with a circle of waxed or parchment paper and top with a pleated sheet of foil. Secure with some string or crimp the edges of the foil to ensure a tight fit around the bowl.

Place the dessert in a large pan half-filled with boiling water. Cover the pan and bring back to a boil over a medium heat. Reduce the heat to a slow simmer and steam for 1½ hours until risen and firm. Keep checking the water level and top up with boiling water as necessary.

Remove the pan from the heat and lift out the ovenproof bowl. Remove the cover and loosen the dessert from the sides of the bowl using a knife.

Turn out into a warmed dish and heat a little more syrup to serve with the dessert.

ingredients

butter, for greasing

2 tbsp. corn syrup, plus extra
   to serve

4 tbsp. butter

½ cup superfine sugar

2 eggs, lightly beaten

1¼ cups self-rising flour

2 tbsp. milk

grated rind of 1 lemon

chicken fried rice

ingredients

½ tbsp. sesame oil

6 shallots, peeled and cut
  into fourths

1 lb. cooked, cubed chicken meat

3 tbsp. soy sauce

2 carrots, diced

1 celery stalk, diced

1 yellow bell pepper, diced

1½ cups fresh peas

3½ oz. canned corn

3⅔ cups cooked long-grain rice

2 large eggs, scrambled

Heat the oil in a large skillet over a medium heat. Add the shallots and cook until soft, then add the chicken and 2 tablespoons of the soy sauce and stir-fry for just 5–6 minutes.

Stir in the carrots, celery, yellow bell pepper, peas, and corn and stir-fry for another 5 minutes. Add the rice and stir thoroughly.

Finally, stir in the scrambled eggs and the remaining tablespoon of soy sauce. Serve immediately.

toffee bananas

Sift the flour into a bowl. Make a well in the center, add the egg and 5 tablespoons of the iced water, and beat from the center outwards, until combined into a smooth batter. Peel the bananas and cut into 2-inch pieces. Gently shape them into balls with your hands. Brush with lemon juice to prevent discoloration, then roll them in rice flour until coated.

Pour oil into a pan to a depth of 2½ inches and preheat to 375°F/190°C. Coat the balls in the batter, and cook in batches in the hot oil for about 2 minutes each, until golden. Lift them out and drain on paper towels.

To make the caramel, put the sugar into a pan over low heat. Add 4 tablespoons of iced water and heat, stirring, until the sugar dissolves. Simmer for 5 minutes, remove from the heat, and stir in the sesame seeds. Toss the banana balls in the caramel, scoop them out, and drop into the bowl of iced water to set. Lift out and divide among serving bowls. Serve hot.

ingredients

½ cup self-rising flour

1 egg, beaten

5 tbsp. iced water

4 large, ripe bananas

3 tbsp. lemon juice

2 tbsp. rice flour

vegetable oil, for deep-frying

CARAMEL

generous ½ cup superfine sugar

4 tbsp. iced water, plus an extra
  bowl of iced water for setting

2 tbsp. sesame seeds

ingredients

4 x 12 oz. lamb shanks

6 garlic cloves

2 tbsp. virgin olive oil

1 tbsp. very finely chopped
   fresh rosemary

salt and pepper

4 red onions

12 oz. carrots, cut into thin sticks

4 tbsp. water

NOVEMBER

5

SERVES 4

lamb shanks with roasted onions

Trim off any excess fat from the lamb. Using a small, sharp knife, make 6 incisions in each shank. Cut the garlic cloves lengthwise into 4 slices. Insert 6 garlic slices in the incisions in each lamb shank.

Place the lamb in a single layer in a roasting pan, drizzle with the olive oil, sprinkle with the rosemary, and season with pepper. Roast in a preheated oven, 350°F/180°C, for 45 minutes.

Wrap each of the onions in a square of foil. Remove the roasting pan from the oven and season the lamb shanks with salt. Return the pan to the oven and place the onions on the shelf next to it. Roast for an additional 1–1¼ hours, until the lamb is very tender.

Meanwhile, bring a large pan of water to a boil. Add the carrot sticks and blanch for 1 minute. Drain and refresh under cold water.

Remove the roasting pan from the oven when the lamb is meltingly tender and transfer it to a warmed serving dish. Skim off any fat from the roasting pan and place it over medium heat. Add the carrots and cook for 2 minutes, then add the water, bring to a boil, and let simmer, stirring constantly and scraping up the glazed bits from the bottom of the roasting pan.

Transfer the carrots and sauce to the serving dish. Remove the onions from the oven and unwrap. Cut off and discard about ½ inch of the tops and add the onions to the dish. Serve immediately.

ingredients

14 oz. ready-made puff pastry

2 tbsp. all-purpose flour, for dusting

2 tbsp. butter, softened

$\frac{1}{3}$ cup brown sugar

$\frac{2}{3}$ cup currants

1 oz. candied peel, chopped

$\frac{1}{2}$ tsp. ground allspice (optional)

1 egg white, lightly beaten

1 tsp. superfine sugar

currant puffs

Preheat the oven to 425°F/220°C.

Roll out the pastry thinly, using the flour to dust the counter and the rolling pin.

Cut into rounds using a 3½-inch cutter. Fold the trimmings carefully, re-roll, and repeat the cuttings to give a total of 10–12 rounds.

In a bowl, mix together the butter and brown sugar until creamy, then add the dried fruit and allspice, if using.

Put a teaspoon of the filling in the center of each pastry round. Draw the edges of the circles together and pinch the edges over the filling. Reshape each puff into a round.

Turn the puffs over and lightly roll them with the rolling pin until the currants just show through. Score with a knife into a lattice pattern.

Place the puffs on a greased baking sheet and allow to rest for 10–15 minutes.

Brush the puffs with the egg white, sprinkle with the sugar, and bake at the top of the oven for about 15 minutes until golden brown and crisp.

Transfer to a wire rack and sprinkle with a little more sugar if desired. Delicious straight from the oven, they also keep well in an airtight container for a week and can be reheated before serving.

parmesan pumpkin

Heat the olive oil in a large pan, add the onion and garlic, and cook over low heat for 5 minutes, until softened. Stir in the strained tomatoes, basil, parsley, and sugar, and season with salt and pepper. Simmer for 10–15 minutes, until thickened.

Meanwhile, put the beaten eggs in a shallow dish and spread out the bread crumbs in another shallow dish. Dip the slices of pumpkin first in the egg, then in the bread crumbs to coat, shaking off any excess.

Grease a large ovenproof dish with butter. Melt the butter in a large, heavy-bottom skillet. Add the pumpkin slices, in batches, and cook until browned all over. Transfer the slices to the dish. Pour the sauce over them and sprinkle with the Parmesan.

Bake in a preheated oven 350°F/180°C, for 30 minutes, until the cheese is bubbling and golden. Serve immediately.

ingredients

2 tbsp. extra virgin olive oil

1 onion, chopped finely

1 garlic clove, chopped finely

1¾ cups strained tomatoes

10 fresh basil leaves, shredded

2 tbsp. chopped fresh
  flat-leaf parsley

1 tsp. sugar

salt and pepper

2 eggs, beaten lightly

½ cup dried, uncolored
  bread crumbs

3½ lb. pumpkin, peeled, seeded,
  and sliced

2 tbsp. butter, plus extra for
  greasing

½ cup freshly grated
  Parmesan cheese

NOVEMBER 7

SERVES 6

greek sausages

Put all the ingredients in a bowl and mix well together. Cover and let marinate in the fridge overnight or for about 12 hours.

Preheat the broiler. Stir the mixture and then, with damp hands, form the mixture into 24 small sausage shapes, about 2 inches long, and place on a broiler pan.

Broil the sausages for about 15 minutes, turning several times, until brown all over. Serve hot, garnished with lemon wedges.

ingredients

12 oz. ground pork

4 oz. ground beef

1 garlic clove, crushed

½ tsp. ground cinnamon

¼ tsp. dried savory or thyme

grated rind of 1 small orange

8 black peppercorns, crushed

⅓ cup dry red wine

lemon wedges, to garnish

NOVEMBER 8

MAKES ABOUT 24

risotto with sole & tomatoes

Bring the stock to a boil in a pan, then reduce the heat and keep simmering gently over a low heat while you are cooking the risotto.

Heat 1 tablespoon of the oil with 1 tablespoon of the butter in a deep pan over a medium heat until the butter has melted. Stir in the onion and cook, stirring occasionally, for 5 minutes, or until soft and starting to turn golden. Do not brown.

Reduce the heat, add the rice, and mix to coat in oil and butter. Cook, stirring constantly, for 2–3 minutes, or until the grains are translucent.

Gradually add the hot stock, a ladle at a time. Stir constantly and add more liquid as the rice absorbs each addition. Increase the heat to medium so that the liquid bubbles. Cook for 20 minutes, or until all the liquid is absorbed and the rice is creamy. Season to taste.

While the risotto is cooking, heat the remaining oil in a large skillet. Add the fresh and sun-dried tomatoes. Stir well and cook over a medium heat for 10–15 minutes, or until soft and slushy.

Stir in the tomato paste and wine. Bring the sauce to a boil, then reduce the heat until it is just simmering.

Cut the fish into strips and add to the sauce. Stir gently. Cook for 5 minutes, or until the fish flakes when checked with a fork. Most of the liquid should be absorbed, but if it isn't, remove the fish and then increase the heat to reduce the sauce.

Remove the risotto from the heat when all the liquid has been absorbed and add the remaining butter. Mix well, then stir in the Parmesan until it melts.

Place the risotto on serving plates and arrange the fish and tomato sauce on top. Garnish with fresh cilantro and serve immediately.

ingredients

2½ pints fish or chicken stock

3 tbsp. olive oil

2 tbsp. butter

1 small onion, finely chopped

10 oz. risotto rice

1 lb. tomatoes, peeled, seeded
    and cut into strips

6 sun-dried tomatoes in olive oil,
    drained and thinly sliced

3 tbsp. tomato paste

¼ cup red wine

1 lb. sole or plaice fillets, skinned

salt and pepper

4 oz. freshly grated Parmesan or
    Grana Padano cheese

2 tbsp. finely chopped fresh
    cilantro, to garnish

pad thai

Soak the noodles in a bowl of warm water for about
20 minutes. Drain in a colander and set aside. In a bowl,
combine the peanuts, lime juice, sugar, fish sauce, and hot
chili sauce and set aside. Rinse the bean curd in cold water,
then place between layers of paper towels and pat dry.

Heat the oil for deep-frying in a large wok or skillet. Deep-fry
the bean curd over a medium heat for 2 minutes, or until light
brown and crisp. Remove from the heat, lift the bean curd out
with a slotted spoon and set aside on paper towels to drain.

Heat a large wok or skillet and add the peanut oil, garlic, onion,
red bell pepper, and chicken strips. Cook for 2–3 minutes. Stir
in the beansprouts and snow peas and cook for 1 minute.
Then add the shrimp, noodles, eggs, and bean curd and stir-fry
for 4–5 minutes. Add the peanut and lime juice mixture and
cook for 3–4 minutes. Transfer to warm dishes and garnish,
then serve.

ingredients

3 cups rice noodles

generous ½ cup peanuts,
    chopped coarsely

2 tbsp. lime juice

1 tbsp. superfine sugar

6 tbsp. fish sauce

1 tsp. hot chili sauce, or to taste

9 oz. firm bean curd, cubed

vegetable oil, for deep frying

3 tbsp. peanut oil

1 garlic clove, crushed

1 onion, sliced finely

1 red bell pepper, sliced thinly

9 oz. chicken breast, cut into
    thin strips

3 oz. beansprouts

4½ oz. snow peas

6 oz. shrimp, shelled, then cut
    in half lengthwise

3 eggs, beaten

GARNISH

1 lemon, cut into wedges

4 scallions, chopped finely

2 tbsp. chopped peanuts

1 tbsp. chopped fresh basil

potato, fontina & rosemary tart

Preheat the oven to 375°F/190°C. Roll out the dough on a lightly floured counter into a round about 10 inches in diameter and put on a baking sheet.

Peel the potatoes and slice as thinly as possible so that they are almost transparent – use a mandolin if you have one. Arrange the potato slices in a spiral, overlapping the slices to cover the pastry, leaving a ¾-inch margin around the edge.

Arrange the cheese and onion over the potatoes, scatter with the rosemary, and drizzle over the oil. Season to taste with salt and pepper and brush the edges with the egg to glaze.

Bake in the preheated oven for 25 minutes, or until the potatoes are tender and the pastry is brown and crisp.

ingredients

14 oz. ready-made puff pastry

all-purpose flour, for dusting

FILLING

3–4 waxy potatoes

10½ oz. fontina cheese,
    cut into cubes

1 red onion, thinly sliced

3 large fresh rosemary sprigs

2 tbsp. olive oil

1 egg yolk

salt and pepper

cold weather vegetable casserole

Melt the butter in a large, heavy-bottom pan over a low heat. Add the leeks, carrots, potatoes, rutabaga, zucchini, and fennel and cook, stirring occasionally, for 10 minutes. Stir in the flour and cook, stirring constantly, for 1 minute. Stir in the can juice from the beans, the stock, tomato paste, thyme, and bay leaves and season to taste with salt and pepper. Bring to a boil, stirring constantly, then cover and simmer for 10 minutes.

Meanwhile, make the dumplings. Sift the flour and salt into a bowl. Stir in the suet and parsley, then add enough water to bind to a soft dough. Divide the dough into 8 pieces and roll into balls.

Add the lima beans and dumplings to the pan, cover, and simmer for a further 30 minutes. Remove and discard the bay leaves before serving.

ingredients

¼ cup butter

2 leeks, sliced

2 carrots, sliced

2 potatoes, cut into bite-size pieces

1 rutabaga, cut into bite-size pieces

2 zucchini, sliced

1 fennel bulb, halved and sliced

2 tbsp. all-purpose flour

15 oz. canned lima beans

2½ cups vegetable stock

2 tbsp. tomato paste

1 tsp. dried thyme

2 bay leaves

salt and pepper

generous ¾ cup self-rising flour

pinch of salt

½ cup vegetarian suet

2 tbsp. chopped fresh parsley

about 4 tbsp. water

VARIATION

If you like, you could replace the rutabaga with 2 parsnips, sliced, and the lima beans with canned kidney beans.

lamb stew with chickpeas

Heat 4 tablespoons of oil in a large, heavy-bottom flameproof casserole over medium-high heat. Reduce the heat, add the chorizo, and cook for 1 minute; set aside. Add the onions to the casserole and cook for 2 minutes, then add the garlic and continue cooking for 3 minutes, or until the onions are soft, but not brown. Remove from the casserole and set aside.

Heat an additional 2 tablespoons of oil in the casserole. Add the lamb cubes in a single layer without overcrowding the casserole, and cook until browned on each side; work in batches, if necessary.

Return the onion mixture to the casserole with all the lamb. Stir in the stock, wine, vinegar, tomatoes with their juices, and salt and pepper to taste. Bring to a boil, scraping any glazed bits from the bottom of the casserole. Reduce the heat and stir in the thyme, bay leaves, and paprika.

Transfer to a preheated oven, 325°F/170°C, and cook, covered, for 40–45 minutes until the lamb is tender. Stir in the chickpeas and return to the oven, uncovered, for 10 minutes, or until they are heated through and the juices reduced. Taste and adjust the seasoning. Garnish with thyme and serve.

ingredients

olive oil

8 oz. chorizo sausage, cut into ¼-in. thick slices, casings removed

2 large onions, chopped

6 large garlic cloves, crushed

2 lb. boned leg of lamb, cut into 2-in. chunks

scant 1¼ cups lamb stock or water

½ cup red wine, such as Rioja or Tempranillo

2 tbsp. sherry vinegar

1 lb. 12 oz. canned chopped tomatoes

salt and pepper

4 sprigs fresh thyme

2 bay leaves

½ tsp. sweet Spanish paprika

1 lb. 12 oz. canned chickpeas, rinsed and drained

sprigs fresh thyme, to garnish

spiced banana milkshake

NOVEMBER 14

Pour the milk into a food processor and add the allspice. Add half of the banana ice cream and process gently until combined, then add the remaining ice cream and process until well blended.

When the mixture is well combined, add the bananas and process until smooth. Pour the mixture into tall glasses, add straws, and serve at once.

ingredients

1¼ cups milk

½ tsp. allspice

5½ oz. banana ice cream

2 bananas, sliced and frozen

SERVES 2

ginger chicken with noodles

NOVEMBER 15

Heat the oil in a wok and stir-fry the onion, garlic, gingerroot, and carrots for 1–2 minutes, until softened. Add the chicken and stir-fry for 3–4 minutes, until the chicken is cooked through and lightly browned.

Add the stock, soy sauce, and bamboo shoots, and gradually bring to a boil. Let simmer for 2–3 minutes. Meanwhile, soak the noodles in boiling water for 6–8 minutes. Drain well. Garnish with the scallions and cilantro and serve immediately, with the chicken stir-fry.

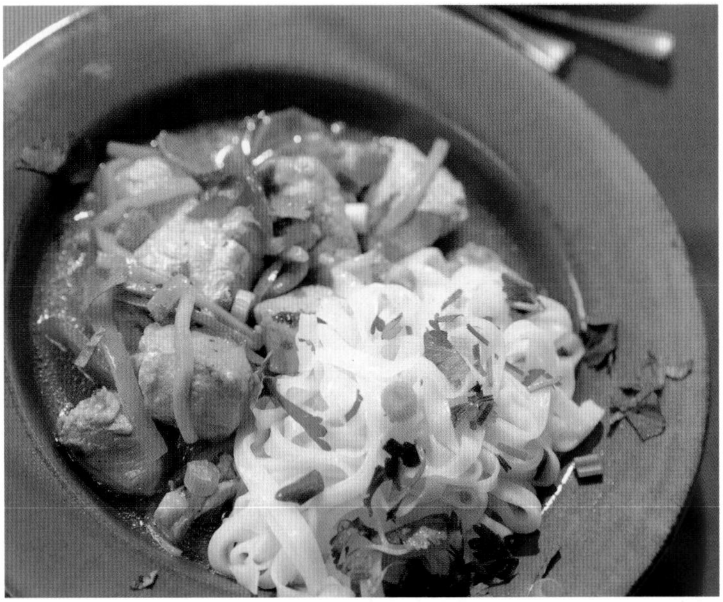

ingredients

2 tbsp. vegetable or peanut oil

1 onion, sliced

2 garlic cloves, chopped finely

2-inch piece fresh gingerroot, sliced thinly

2 carrots, sliced thinly

4 skinless, boneless chicken breasts, cut into cubes

1¼ cups chicken stock

4 tbsp. Thai soy sauce

8 oz. canned bamboo shoots, drained and rinsed

2¾ oz. flat rice noodles

FOR THE GARNISH

4 scallions, chopped

4 tbsp. chopped fresh cilantro

SERVES 4

ingredients

1 lb. 9 oz. neck of lamb

4 pints water

2 oz. pearl barley

2 onions, chopped

1 garlic clove, finely chopped

3 small turnips, cut into small dice

3 carrots, peeled and finely sliced

2 celery stalks, sliced

2 leeks, sliced

salt and pepper

2 tbsp. chopped fresh parsley,
    to garnish

lamb and barley soup

Cut the meat into small pieces, removing as much fat as possible. Put into a large pan and cover with the water. Bring to a boil over a medium heat and skim off any scum that appears.

Add the pearl barley, reduce the heat, and cook gently, covered, for 1 hour.

Add the prepared vegetables and season well with salt and pepper. Continue to cook for a further hour. Remove from the heat and allow to cool slightly.

Remove the meat from the pan using a slotted spoon and strip the meat from the bones. Discard the bones and any remaining fat or gristle. Place the meat back in the pan and let cool thoroughly, then refrigerate overnight.

Scrape the solidified fat off the surface of the soup. Reheat, season with salt and pepper to taste, and serve hot, garnished with the parsley scattered over the top.

pesto & cheese pastries

Preheat the oven to 400°F/200°C, then grease a cookie sheet. On a floured counter, roll out the pastry to a 14 x 6-inch rectangle and trim the edges with a sharp knife. Spread the pesto evenly over the pastry.

Roll up the ends tightly to meet in the center of the pastry. Wrap in plastic wrap and chill in the refrigerator for 20 minutes, until firm, then remove from the refrigerator and unwrap. Brush with the beaten egg yolk on all sides. Cut across into ½-inch thick slices.

Place the slices on the prepared cookie sheet. Bake in the oven for 10 minutes, or until crisp and golden. Remove from the oven and immediately sprinkle over the Parmesan cheese. Serve the pastries warm or transfer to a rack and let cool to room temperature.

ingredients

butter, for greasing

all-purpose flour, for dusting

9 oz. ready-made puff pastry

3 tbsp. green or red pesto

1 egg yolk, beaten with 1 tbsp water

¼ cup freshly grated
  Parmesan cheese

roasted garlic creamed potatoes

Preheat the oven to 350°F/180°C.

Separate the garlic cloves, place on a large piece of foil, and drizzle with the oil. Wrap the garlic in the foil and roast in the oven for about 1 hour, or until very tender. Let cool slightly.

Twenty minutes before the end of the cooking time, cut the potatoes into chunks, then cook in a pan of lightly salted boiling water for 15 minutes, or until tender.

Meanwhile, squeeze the cooled garlic cloves out of their skins and push through a strainer into a pan. Add the milk, butter, and salt and pepper to taste and heat gently until the butter has melted.

Drain the cooked potatoes, then cream in the pan until smooth. Pour in the garlic mixture and heat gently, stirring, until the ingredients are combined. Serve hot.

ingredients

2 whole garlic bulbs

1 tbsp. olive oil

2 lb. mealy potatoes, peeled

½ cup milk

2 tbsp. butter

salt and pepper

COOK'S TIP

When roasted, garlic loses its pungent acidity and acquires a delicious, full-flavored sweetness. So although using two whole bulbs may seem excessive, you will be surprised at the uniquely mellow flavor. In addition, roasted garlic leaves very little trace of its smell on the breath.

ingredients

2¼ cups lean ground beef

1 onion, grated

1 cup fresh white bread crumbs

1 egg, beaten lightly

2 tbsp. fresh parsley, chopped finely

salt and pepper

olive oil

2 large onions, sliced thinly

1 recipe Tomato and Bell Pepper
    Sauce (see page 66, March 8)

1½ cups frozen peas

meatballs with peas

Put the meat in a bowl with the grated onion, bread crumbs, egg, parsley, and salt and pepper to taste. Use your hands to squeeze all the ingredients together. Cook a small piece of the mixture and taste to see if the seasoning needs adjusting.

With wet hands, shape the mixture into 12 balls. Put on a plate and chill for at least 20 minutes.

When ready to cook, heat a small amount of the oil in 1 or 2 large skillets: the exact amount needed will depend on how much fat there is in the beef. Arrange the meatballs in a single layer, without overcrowding, and cook, stirring, for about 5 minutes until brown on the outside; work in batches if necessary.

Set the meatballs aside and remove all but 2 tablespoons of oil from the skillet. Add the sliced onions and cook for about 5 minutes until soft, but not brown. Return the meatballs to the skillet.

Stir the Tomato and Bell Pepper Sauce into the skillet and bring to a boil, gently spooning the sauce and onions over the meatballs. Reduce the heat, cover, and let simmer for 20 minutes. Add the peas and continue simmering for 7–10 minutes until the peas are tender and the meatballs cooked through. Serve at once.

tomato pilaf

SERVES 4

Heat the oil in a large, heavy-bottom pan, add the onion and garlic, and fry for 5 minutes, until softened. Add the rice and cook for 2–3 minutes, stirring all the time, until the rice looks transparent.

Add the tomatoes with their juice, the sugar, stock, mint, salt, and pepper. Bring to a boil then cover the pan with a tightly fitting lid and simmer for about 15 minutes, until the rice is tender and the liquid has been absorbed. Do not stir during cooking. When cooked, gently stir in the pine nuts.

Remove the lid, cover the pan with a clean dish towel, replace the lid, and leave in a warm place for 10 minutes to dry out. Stir with a fork to separate the grains and serve with lemon wedges to squeeze over.

ingredients

3 tbsp. olive oil

1 onion, chopped finely

1 garlic clove, chopped finely

generous 1 cup long-grain white rice

14 oz. canned chopped tomatoes
    in juice

pinch of sugar

2½ cups chicken or
    vegetable stock

1 tsp. dried mint

salt and pepper

2 tbsp. pine nuts

lemon wedges, to serve

VARIATION

An additional scattering of toasted pine kernels would enhance this pilaf. To prepare these, heat 1 tablespoon olive oil in a skillet, add 2 oz pine kernels and fry until golden brown shaking the pan constantly.

shrimp & vegetable bisque

Melt the butter in a large pan over medium heat. Add the garlic and onion and cook, stirring, for 3 minutes, until slightly softened. Add the carrot and celery and cook for another 3 minutes, stirring. Pour in the stock and red wine, then add the tomato paste and bay leaf. Season with salt and pepper.

Bring to a boil, then lower the heat and simmer for 20 minutes. Remove from the heat and let cool for 10 minutes, then remove and discard the bay leaf.

Transfer half of the soup into a food processor and blend until smooth (you may need to do this in batches). Return to the pan with the rest of the soup. Add the shrimp and cook the soup over low heat for 5–6 minutes.

Stir in the cream and cook for another 2 minutes, then remove from the heat and ladle into serving bowls. Garnish with swirls of light cream and whole cooked shrimp, and serve at once.

ingredients

3 tbsp. butter

1 garlic clove, chopped

1 onion, sliced

1 carrot, peeled and chopped

1 celery stalk, trimmed and sliced

5 cups fish stock

4 tbsp. red wine

1 tbsp. tomato paste

1 bay leaf

salt and pepper

1 lb. 5 oz. shrimp, peeled
 and deveined

scant ½ cup heavy cream

GARNISH

swirls of light cream

whole cooked shrimp

roast turkey with two stuffings

SERVES 4

Preheat the oven to 425°F/220°C.

Wipe the turkey inside and out with paper towels. Season, both inside and out, with salt and pepper.

To make the celery and walnut stuffing, fry the onion in the butter in a skillet until soft. In a bowl, mix together the bread crumbs, celery, apple, apricots, and walnuts. Add the cooked onion and season to taste with salt and pepper. Stir in the chopped parsley.

To make the chestnut stuffing, cook the bacon and onion in the butter in a skillet until soft. Add the mushrooms and cook for 1–2 minutes, then remove from the heat. In a bowl, mix together the chestnut purée with the parsley and lemon rind and season well with salt and pepper. Add the contents of the skillet to the bowl and mix well. Cool before using to stuff the turkey.

Stuff the body cavity of the turkey with the celery and walnut stuffing and the neck with the chestnut stuffing. Secure the neck skin with metal skewers and the legs with string.

Cover the bird all over with the butter and squeeze some under the breast skin. Use a little to grease the roasting pan. Place the bird in the pan, season again with salt and pepper, and cover the turkey breast with the bacon strips.

Cover the bird with foil and roast in the oven for 30 minutes. Reduce the oven temperature to 350°F/180°C and continue to cook for 2½–3 hours, basting the turkey every 30 minutes with the pan juices.

Forty-five minutes before the end of the cooking time, remove the foil and allow the turkey to brown, basting from time to time. Remove the bacon strips when crispy and keep warm.

ingredients

10 lb. turkey

salt and pepper

4 tbsp. butter, softened

10 lean bacon strips

CELERY AND WALNUT STUFFING

2 onions, finely chopped

2 tbsp. butter

²/₃ cup fresh whole wheat
    bread crumbs

4 celery stalks, chopped

2 apples, cored and roughly
    chopped

4 oz. no-soak apricots, chopped

4 oz. walnuts, chopped

salt and pepper

2 tbsp. chopped fresh parsley

CHESTNUT STUFFING

4 oz. lean bacon, diced

1 onion, finely chopped

2 tbsp. butter

4 oz. white mushrooms, sliced

8 oz. chestnut purée

2 tbsp. chopped fresh parsley

grated rind of 2 lemons

salt and pepper

GRAVY

2 tbsp. all-purpose flour

4 cups stock, if possible made from
    the giblets

½ cup red wine or sherry

Test that the turkey is cooked by piercing the thickest part of the leg with a sharp knife or skewer to make sure the juices run clear. Also, pull a leg slightly away from the body; it should feel loose.

Remove the turkey from the roasting pan and place on a warm serving plate, cover with foil, and let rest whilst you complete the remainder of the meal. Don't worry, you can leave it for up to 1 hour!

To make the gravy, drain the fat from the pan and place over a low heat on top of the stove. Sprinkle in the flour, stir well using a small whisk to make a smooth paste, and cook for 1 minute. Add the stock a little at a time, whisking constantly, until you have a smooth gravy. Add the wine and bubble together until the gravy is slightly reduced. Season to taste. When you carve the turkey some meat juices will escape: add these to the gravy and stir.

Carefully pour the gravy into a warmed serving bowl and serve with slices of carved turkey and the spare stuffing spooned into a warm dish.

pasta with green vegetables

Bring a large, heavy-bottom pan of lightly salted water to a boil. Add the pasta, return to the boil, and cook for about 8–10 minutes, or until tender but still firm to the bite. Drain the pasta in a colander, return to the pan, cover and keep warm.

Steam the broccoli, zucchini, asparagus spears, and snow peas over a pan of boiling, salted water until just beginning to soften. Remove from the heat and plunge into cold water to prevent further cooking. Drain and reserve. Cook the peas in boiling, salted water for 3 minutes, then drain. Refresh in cold water and drain again.

Place the butter and vegetable stock in a pan over a medium heat. Add all the vegetables except for the asparagus spears and toss carefully with a wooden spoon to heat through, taking care not to break them up. Stir in the cream, allow the sauce to heat through, and season to taste with salt, pepper, and nutmeg.

Transfer the pasta to a warmed serving dish and stir in the chopped parsley. Spoon the sauce over, and sprinkle on the freshly grated Parmesan. Arrange the asparagus spears in a pattern on top. Serve hot.

ingredients

8 oz. dried gemelli or other pasta
   shapes
2 tbsp. chopped fresh parsley
2 tbsp. freshly grated Parmesan
   cheese

SAUCE

1 head green broccoli, cut
   into florets
2 zucchini, sliced
8 oz. asparagus spears, trimmed
4½ oz snow peas
4½ oz frozen peas
1 tbsp. butter
3 tbsp. vegetable stock
5 tbsp. heavy cream
salt and pepper
large pinch of freshly grated nutmeg

SERVES 4

SERVES 4

thai baked fish

Reserve a few fresh basil leaves for garnish and tuck the rest inside the body cavity of the fish. Heat 1 tablespoon oil in a wide skillet and fry the fish quickly to brown, turning once. Place the fish on a large piece of foil in a roasting pan and spoon over the fish sauce. Wrap the foil over the fish loosely and bake in a preheated oven, 375°F/190°C, for about 25–30 minutes until just cooked through.

Meanwhile, heat the remaining oil and fry the garlic, galangal, and chilies for 30 seconds. Add the bell pepper and stir-fry for a further 2–3 minutes until softened, but not browned. Stir in the sugar, rice vinegar, and water, then add the tomatoes and bring to a boil over low heat. Remove the pan from the heat.

Remove the fish from the oven and transfer to a warmed serving plate. Add the fish juices to the pan, stir in, then spoon the sauce over the fish, and sprinkle with the reserved basil leaves. Serve immediately.

ingredients

handful of fresh sweet basil leaves

1 lb. 10 oz. whole red snapper, sea bass, or tilapia, cleaned

2 tbsp. peanut oil

2 tbsp. Thai fish sauce

2 garlic cloves, crushed

1 tsp. finely grated fresh galangal or gingerroot, finely grated

2 large fresh red chilies, sliced diagonally

1 yellow bell pepper, deseeded and diced

1 tbsp. palm sugar

1 tbsp rice vinegar

2 tbsp. water or fish stock

2 tomatoes, deseeded and sliced into thin wedges

SERVES 4–6

roasted root vegetables

Preheat the oven to 425°F/220°C.

Arrange all the vegetables in a single layer in a large roasting pan. Scatter over the garlic and the herbs. Pour over the oil and season well with salt and pepper.

Toss all the ingredients together until they are well mixed and coated with the oil (you can let them marinate at this stage to allow the flavors to be absorbed).

Roast the vegetables at the top of the oven for 50–60 minutes until they are cooked and nicely browned. Turn the vegetables over halfway through the cooking time.

Serve with a good handful of fresh herbs scattered on top and a final sprinkling of salt and pepper to taste.

ingredients

3 parsnips, cut into 2-inch chunks

4 baby turnips, quartered

3 carrots, cut into 2-inch chunks

1 lb. butternut squash, peeled and cut into 2-inch chunks

1 lb. sweet potatoes, peeled and cut into 2-inch chunks

2 garlic cloves, finely chopped

2 tbsp. chopped fresh rosemary

2 tbsp. chopped fresh thyme

2 tsp. chopped fresh sage

3 tbsp. olive oil

salt and pepper

2 tbsp. chopped fresh mixed herbs, such as parsley, thyme, and mint, to garnish

baked lamb & potatoes

Preheat the oven to 325°F/160°C.

Trim the chops of any excess fat. Cut the kidneys in half, remove the core, and cut into quarters. Season all the meat well with salt and pepper.

Butter a large, shallow ovenproof dish or deep roasting pan with half the butter and arrange a layer of potatoes in the bottom. Layer up the onions and meat, seasoning well with salt and pepper, and sprinkling in the herbs between each layer. Finish with a neat layer of overlapping potatoes.

Pour in most of the stock so that it covers the meat.

Melt the remaining butter and brush the top of the potato with it. Reserve any remaining butter. Cover with foil and cook in the oven for 2 hours.

Uncover the dish and brush the potatoes again with the melted butter.

Return the dish to the oven and cook for a further 30 minutes, allowing the potatoes to get brown and crisp. You may need to increase the temperature if not browning sufficiently, or pop under a hot broiler.

ingredients

2 lb. lamb chops

3 lambs' kidneys

salt and pepper

2 tbsp. butter

2 lb. mealy potatoes, peeled
    and sliced

3 onions, halved and finely sliced

2 tsp. fresh thyme leaves

1 tsp. finely chopped fresh rosemary

3 cups chicken stock

SERVES 4

chicken teriyaki

Place the chicken strips in a large, shallow dish. Mix the tamari, rice wine, sherry, sugar, and orange rind together in a measuring cup, stirring until the sugar has dissolved. Pour the marinade over the chicken, stir to coat, cover, and let marinate for 15 minutes.

Meanwhile, place the rice in a large, heavy-bottom pan. Pour in the water, add the salt, and bring to a boil. Stir once, reduce the heat, cover tightly, and let simmer very gently for 10 minutes. Remove the pan from the heat, but do not remove the lid.

Heat a wok or large, heavy-bottom skillet. Add the chicken and the marinade and cook, stirring constantly, for 5 minutes, or until the chicken is cooked through and tender. Remove the lid from the rice and fork through the grains to fluff up, then serve immediately with the chicken.

ingredients

1 lb. skinless, boneless chicken breasts, thinly sliced into strips

2 tbsp. tamari or dark soy sauce

1 tbsp. Chinese rice wine

1 tbsp. dry sherry

1 tsp. sugar

grated rind of 1 orange

generous 1 cup long-grain rice

scant 2½ cups water

pinch of salt

SERVES 4

creamy rice dessert

Preheat the oven to 325°F/160°C. Grease a 3½-cup ovenproof dish with butter. Put the golden raisins, sugar, and rice into a mixing bowl, then stir in the milk and vanilla extract.

Transfer to the prepared dish, sprinkle over the grated lemon zest and the nutmeg, then bake in the preheated oven for 2½ hours.

Remove from the oven and transfer to individual serving bowls. Decorate with chopped pistachios and serve.

ingredients

1 tbsp. butter, for greasing

½ cup golden raisins

5 tbsp. superfine sugar

3¼ oz. sweet rice

5 cups milk

1 tsp. vanilla extract

finely grated zest of 1 large lemon

pinch of nutmeg

chopped pistachios, to decorate

potato & cheese pancake

Heat half the olive oil and half the butter in a 9–10-inch skillet.

Peel the potatoes if necessary (you don't need to peel small new potatoes). Slice thinly using a mandolin or food processor. Rinse the slices quickly in cold water and dry thoroughly using a dish towel or paper towels.

Remove the oil and butter from the heat and arrange the sliced potato in the base of the skillet. Build up layers of potato, onion, and cheese, seasoning well with salt and pepper between each layer. Finish with a layer of potato and dot the remaining butter over the top.

Return to the heat and cook over a medium heat for 15–20 minutes. The base should become brown but not burn. Place a large plate over the skillet and invert the potato onto the plate by tilting the skillet. Add the remaining oil to the skillet and slip the potato back in, cooking the other side for a further 15 minutes until the bottom is crusty.

Remove from the heat and serve at once on a warm plate.

SERVES 4

ingredients

4 tbsp. olive oil

2 tbsp. butter

1 lb. firm potatoes or waxy
   new potatoes

8 oz. onions, halved and thinly sliced

1 cup grated Cheddar cheese

salt and pepper

COOK'S TIP

If preferred, the dish can be made in a shallow 10-inch gratin dish and cooked in the top of the oven at 350ºF/180ºC for 45–50 minutes until hot and golden brown.

upside-down cake

Preheat the oven to 350°F/180°C. Grease a 10-inch cake pan and line the base with parchment paper.

Cream 2 tablespoons of the butter with the brown sugar and spread over the base of the pan.

Place a hazelnut in each apricot half and invert onto the base. The apricots should cover the whole surface.

Cream the raw sugar together with the remaining butter until pale and fluffy, then beat in the eggs gradually. Fold in the flour and the ground hazelnuts, together with the milk, and spread the mixture over the apricots.

Bake in the center of the oven for about 45 minutes until the cake is golden brown and well risen. Run a knife around the edge of the cake and invert onto a warm serving plate. Serve warm with cream.

ingredients

8 tbsp. unsalted butter

⅓ cup brown sugar

14–16 hazelnuts

1 lb. 5 oz. canned apricot halves, drained

¾ cup raw sugar

3 eggs, beaten

1 cup self-rising flour

2 oz. ground hazelnuts

2 tbsp. milk

cream, to serve

VARIATIONS
You could use slices of pineapple and candied cherries as the topping, and ground almonds instead of hazelnuts in the sponge. Alternatively, use pear halves with walnuts or canned cherries and add 2 tablespoons cocoa instead of the nuts to make a chocolate sponge. To make a ginger sponge, add 1 tablespoon ground ginger to the mixture and use rhubarb. Add the grated zest of l lemon to the sponge mixture to make a lemon sponge and pair with strawberries or raspberries.

CHAPTER

12

December

SERVES 4

ingredients

4 tbsp. sweet butter, plus 1 tsp.
   extra for greasing

4 tbsp. dark brown sugar, plus
   2 tsp. extra for sprinkling

¾ cup cranberries, thawed if frozen

1 large tart apple

2 eggs, lightly beaten

⅔ cup self-rising flour

3 tbsp. unsweetened cocoa

SAUCE

6 oz. dark chocolate, broken into
   pieces

1¾ cups evaporated milk

1 tsp. vanilla extract

½ tsp. almond extract

chocolate cranberry sponge

Grease a 5-cup ovenproof bowl, sprinkle with brown sugar to coat the sides, and tip out any excess. Put the cranberries in a bowl. Peel, core, and dice the apple and mix with the cranberries. Put the fruit in the prepared ovenproof bowl.

Place the butter, brown sugar, and eggs in a large bowl. Strain in the flour and cocoa and beat well until thoroughly mixed. Pour the mixture into the ovenproof bowl on top of the fruit, cover the top with foil, and tie with string. Steam for about 1 hour, until risen, topping up with boiling water if necessary.

Meanwhile, to make the sauce, put the dark chocolate and milk in the top of a double boiler or a heatproof bowl set over a pan of barely simmering water. Stir until the chocolate has melted, then remove from the heat. Whisk in the vanilla and almond extracts and continue to beat until the sauce is thick and smooth.

To serve, remove the sponge from the heat and discard the foil. Run a round-bladed knife around the side of the bowl, place a serving plate on top of the sponge and, holding them together, invert. Serve immediately, handing the sauce separately.

vietnamese rolls with caramelized pork & noodles

MAKES 16 ROLLS

Blend the soy sauce and maple syrup together in a shallow dish. Add the pork and turn to coat in the mixture. Cover and let marinate in the refrigerator for at least 1 hour or preferably overnight.

Heat a grill pan over a medium-high heat until hot, add a little oil to cover the base, and cook the pork for 4–6 minutes each side, depending on the thickness of the fillets, until cooked and caramelized on the outside. Remove from the pan and slice into fine strips.

Fill a heatproof bowl with water that is just off a boil. Put 2 rice paper pancakes on top of one another (you will need 2 per roll as they are very thin and fragile) and soak in the water for 20 seconds, or until they turn pliable and opaque. Carefully remove using a spatula, drain for a second, and place flat on a plate.

Spread a spoonful of hoisin sauce over the pancake and top with a small bundle of noodles and a few strips of pork, cucumber, and scallion. Fold in the ends and sides of the pancake to resemble an egg roll. Set aside while you make the remaining rolls. Slice in half on the diagonal and serve with a little more hoisin sauce, if liked.

ingredients

2 tbsp. soy sauce or tamari

1½ tsp. maple syrup

1 lb. 2 oz. lean pork fillet

vegetable oil, for frying

32 rice paper pancakes

2½ oz. rice vermicelli noodles,
    cooked

TO SERVE

hoisin sauce

strips of cucumber

strips of scallion

italian steak heroes

Heat the oil in a pan over medium heat, add the onion, garlic, bell pepper, and mushrooms, and cook for 5–10 minutes until soft and beginning to brown.

Add the steak and cook, stirring and breaking up any lumps, for 5 minutes, or until brown on all sides. Add the wine, tomato paste, and salt and pepper and simmer for 10 minutes, stirring occasionally. Remove from the heat.

Split the rolls and brush both halves with extra virgin olive oil. Put the bottom halves on a piece of foil and spoon the sauce on top. Arrange the cheese on the sauce, add the basil, and cover with the tops of the rolls. Press down gently and wrap in the foil. Leave for at least 1 hour before serving.

ingredients

1 tbsp. olive oil

1 small onion, finely chopped

1 garlic clove, finely chopped

1 small red bell pepper, cored, seeded, and finely chopped

3½ oz. white mushrooms, finely chopped

⅞ cup freshly ground steak

½ cup red wine

2 tbsp. tomato paste

salt and pepper

4 ciabatta rolls

extra virgin olive oil, for brushing

2¾ oz. mozzarella cheese, sliced

2 tbsp. torn fresh basil leaves

stir-fried beef & snow peas

Put the strips of beef in a bowl, add the soy sauce, hoisin sauce, and sherry and stir together. Let marinate while you are cooking the vegetables.

Add a little of the oil to a large nonstick wok. Add the onion, garlic, gingerroot, carrot, and snow peas and stir-fry for 5 minutes, or until softened. Add the beef and marinade to the wok and stir-fry for 2–3 minutes, or until tender. Add the bamboo shoots and stir-fry for a further minute, until hot. Transfer to a warm serving dish, garnish with cilantro, and serve with cooked rice or noodles.

ingredients

1 lb. round or sirloin steak, sliced thinly

2 tbsp. soy sauce

5 tbsp. hoisin sauce

2 tbsp. dry sherry

vegetable oil

1 onion, sliced thinly

1 tsp. chopped fresh garlic

1 tsp. chopped fresh gingerroot

1 carrot, sliced thinly

1 lb snow peas

8 oz. canned sliced bamboo shoots, drained

fresh sprigs of cilantro, to garnish

cooked rice or noodles, to serve

buttered chicken parcels

Melt half of the butter in a skillet over medium heat. Add the shallots and cook, stirring, for 4 minutes. Remove from the heat and let cool for 10 minutes.

Preheat the oven to 350°F/180°C. Using your hands, squeeze out as much moisture from the thawed spinach as possible. Transfer the spinach into a large bowl, add the shallots, cheese, egg, herbs, and seasoning. Mix together well.

Halve each chicken breast and pound lightly to flatten each piece. Spoon some cheese mixture into the center of each piece, then roll them up. Wrap each roll in a slice of prosciutto and secure with a toothpick. Transfer to a roasting dish and dot with the remaining butter.

Bake in the preheated oven for 30 minutes until golden. Divide the baby spinach leaves between 4 serving plates. Remove the chicken from the oven and place 2 chicken rolls on each bed of spinach. Garnish with fresh chives and serve.

ingredients

4 tbsp. butter

4 shallots, finely chopped

10½ oz. frozen spinach, thawed

1 lb. blue cheese, such as
    Stilton, crumbled

1 egg, lightly beaten

1 tbsp. chopped fresh chives

1 tbsp. chopped fresh oregano

pepper

4 large, skinless chicken breasts

8 slices prosciutto

fresh chives, to garnish

baby spinach leaves, to serve

ingredients

1 piece of pork loin, weighing
    3 lb. 8 oz., boned and rolled
4 garlic cloves, thinly sliced
    lengthwise
1½ tsp. finely chopped fennel
    greenery or ½ tsp. dried fennel
4 cloves
salt and pepper
1¼ cups dry white wine
1¼ cups water

slow-roasted pork

Preheat the oven to 300°F/150°C.

Use a small, sharp knife to make incisions all over the pork, opening them out slightly to make little pockets. Place the garlic slices in a small strainer and rinse under cold running water to moisten. Spread out the fennel on a saucer and roll the garlic slices in it to coat. Slide the garlic slices and the cloves into the pockets in the pork. Season the meat all over to taste with salt and pepper.

Place the pork in a large ovenproof dish or roasting pan. Pour in the wine and water. Cook in the oven, basting the meat occasionally, for 2½–2¾ hours, until the pork is tender but still quite moist.

If you are serving the pork hot, transfer it to a carving board, cover with foil, and let rest before cutting it into slices. If you are serving it cold, leave it to cool completely in the cooking juices before removing and slicing.

paprika-spiced almonds

Put the sea salt and paprika in a mortar and grind with the pestle to a fine powder, or use a mini spice blender (the amount is too small to process in a full-size processor).

Place the almonds on a baking sheet and toast in a preheated oven, 400°F/200°C, for 8–10 minutes, stirring occasionally, until golden brown and giving off a toasted aroma: watch carefully after 7 minutes because they burn quickly. Immediately pour into a heatproof bowl.

Drizzle over about 1 tablespoon of oil and stir to ensure all the nuts are lightly and evenly coated; add extra oil, if necessary. Sprinkle with the salt and paprika mixture and stir again. Transfer to a small bowl and serve at room temperature.

ingredients

1½ tbsp. coarse sea salt

½ tsp. smoked sweet Spanish paprika, or hot paprika, to taste

3½ cups blanched almonds

extra virgin olive oil

DECEMBER

7

SERVES 4

COOK'S TIP

It is best, and more economical, to buy unblanched almonds and blanch them as and when required, because they start to dry out as soon as the thin, brown skin is removed. Put the unblanched almonds in a heatproof bowl. Pour over boiling water and let stand for 1 minute. Drain well, then pat dry and slip off the skins.

mulled wine

Put the wine, sherry, cloves, cinnamon, allspice, and honey into a pan and stir together well. Warm over low heat, stirring, until just starting to simmer, but do not let it boil. Remove from the heat and pour through a strainer. Discard the cloves and cinnamon stick.

Return the wine to the pan with the orange and lemon wedges. Warm gently over very low heat, but do not let it boil. Remove from the heat, pour into heatproof glasses, and serve hot.

ingredients

3 cups red wine

3 tbsp. sherry

8 cloves

1 cinnamon stick

½ tsp. ground allspice

2 tbsp. clear honey

1 seedless orange, cut into wedges

1 lemon, cut into wedges

DECEMBER

8

SERVES 4

split pea dip

Rinse the split peas under cold running water. Put in a pan and add the coarsely chopped onion, the garlic, and plenty of cold water. Bring to a boil then simmer for about 45 minutes, until very tender.

Drain the split peas, reserving a little of the cooking liquid, and put in a food processor. Add 5 tablespoons of the olive oil and blend until smooth. If the mixture seems too dry, add enough of the reserved liquid to form a smooth, thick purée. Add the oregano and season with salt and pepper.

Turn the mixture into a serving bowl and sprinkle with the finely chopped onion and extra oregano if desired. Drizzle over the remaining oil. Serve warm or cold with pita bread.

ingredients

9 oz. yellow split peas

2 small onions, 1 chopped coarsely
   and 1 chopped very finely

1 garlic clove, chopped coarsely

6 tbsp. extra virgin olive oil

1 tbsp. chopped fresh oregano

salt and pepper

warm pita bread, to serve

sesame crackers

Put the flour, 2 tablespoons sesame seeds, the lemon rind, thyme, salt, and pepper in a bowl. Cut the butter into small pieces and rub into the mixture until it resembles fine bread crumbs. Gradually stir in the water until the mixture forms a firm dough.

Turn the mixture onto a lightly floured surface and roll out thinly. Using a 2¼-inch round cookie cutter, cut the dough into rounds and place on baking sheets.

Brush the crackers with the egg white and sprinkle with the remaining sesame seeds. Bake in a preheated oven, 350°F/180°C, for 20–25 minutes, until lightly browned. Cool on a wire rack. Store the crackers in an airtight tin.

MAKES ABOUT 30

ingredients

⅔ cup plus 1 tbsp. all-purpose flour

3 tbsp. sesame seeds

finely grated rind of 1 lemon

2 tbsp. chopped fresh thyme

½ tsp. salt

freshly ground pepper

2 tbsp. butter

3–4 tbsp. cold water

1 small egg white

MAKES 20

COOK'S TIP

The tartlet shells can be made up to a week in advance and stored in an airtight container. Make the salsa just before serving. When the cases are filled, serve them straightaway, otherwise they will go soft.

phyllo tartlets with avocado salsa

Preheat the oven to 350°F/180°C. To make the tartlet shells, working with 1 sheet of phyllo pastry at a time and keeping the rest covered with a cloth, brush the pastry sheet with melted butter. With a sharp knife, cut the sheet into 2-inch squares.

Grease 20 cups in mini muffin pans and line each one with 3 buttered phyllo pastry squares, setting each one at an angle to the others. Repeat until all the pastry is used up. Bake in the preheated oven for 6–8 minutes, or until crisp and golden. Carefully transfer to a wire rack to cool.

To make the salsa, peel the avocado and remove the stone. Cut the flesh into small cubes and place in a bowl with the onion, chili, tomatoes, lime juice, and cilantro, and add salt and pepper to taste. Divide the avocado salsa among the tartlet shells and serve immediately.

ingredients

TARTLET CASES

2½ oz. ready-made phyllo pastry

3 tbsp. melted butter, plus extra
   for greasing

AVOCADO SALSA

1 large avocado

1 small red onion, finely chopped

1 fresh chili, seeded and finely
   chopped

2 tomatoes, peeled, seeded and
   finely chopped

juice of 1 lime

2 tbsp. chopped fresh cilantro

salt and pepper

fiery chicken vindaloo

Put the cumin, cinnamon, mustard, ground coriander, and cayenne pepper into a bowl. Add the vinegar and sugar and mix well.

Heat the oil in a large skillet. Add the garlic and onions and cook, stirring, over medium heat for 5 minutes. Add the chicken and cook for another 3 minutes, then add the chilies, potatoes, chopped tomatoes and tomato paste, and a few drops of red food coloring.

Stir in the spice mixture, season generously with salt and pepper, and bring to a boil. Lower the heat, cover the pan, and simmer, stirring occasionally, for 1 hour.

Arrange the cooked rice on a large serving platter. Remove the pan from the heat, spoon the chicken mixture over the rice, and serve.

ingredients

1 tsp. ground cumin

1 tsp. ground cinnamon

2 tsp. mustard powder

1½ tsp. ground coriander

1 tsp. cayenne pepper

5 tbsp. red wine vinegar

1 tsp. brown sugar

⅔ cup vegetable oil

8 garlic cloves, crushed

3 red onions, sliced

4 skinless chicken breasts, cut into
   bite-size chunks

2 small red chilies, seeded and
   chopped

1 lb. potatoes, peeled and chopped

1 lb. 12 oz. canned chopped
   tomatoes

1 tbsp. tomato paste

a few drops of red food coloring

salt and pepper

freshly boiled rice, to serve

sticky toffee dessert

To make the sponge, put the fruits and baking soda into a heatproof bowl. Cover with boiling water and set aside to soak. Preheat the oven to 350°F/180°C. Grease a round cake pan, 8 inches in diameter, with butter.

Put the remaining butter in a separate bowl, add the sugar, and mix well. Beat in the eggs then fold in the flour. Drain the soaked fruits, add to the bowl, and mix. Spoon the mixture into the cake pan. Transfer to the preheated oven and bake for 35–40 minutes. The sponge is cooked when a skewer inserted into the center comes out clean.

About 5 minutes before the end of the cooking time, make the sauce. Melt the butter in a pan over medium heat. Stir in the cream and sugar and bring to a boil, stirring constantly. Lower the heat and simmer for 5 minutes. Turn out the sponge onto a serving plate and pour over the sauce. Decorate with grated orange zest and serve with whipped cream.

ingredients

SPONGE

scant ½ cup golden raisins

generous ¾ cup stoned dates, chopped

1 tsp. baking soda

2 tbsp. butter, plus extra for greasing

1 cup brown sugar

2 eggs

scant 1½ cups self-rising flour, sifted

grated orange zest, to decorate

freshly whipped cream, to serve

STICKY TOFFEE SAUCE

2 tbsp. butter

¾ cup heavy cream

1 cup brown sugar

salmon tartare

Put the salmon into a shallow glass dish. Combine the sea salt, sugar, and dill, then rub the mixture into the fish until well coated. Season the salmon with plenty of pepper. Cover with plastic wrap and refrigerate for at least 48 hours, turning once.

When ready to serve, put the chopped tarragon into a mixing bowl with the mustard and lemon juice. Season well. Remove the salmon from the refrigerator, chop into small pieces, then add to the bowl. Stir until the salmon is well coated.

SERVES 4

To make the topping, put the cream cheese, chives, and paprika into a separate bowl and mix well. Place a 4-inch steel cooking ring or circular cookie cutter on each of 4 small serving plates. Divide the salmon among the 4 steel rings so that each ring is half-full. Level the surface of each one, then top with the cream cheese mixture. Smooth the surfaces, then carefully remove the steel rings. Garnish with sprigs of fresh dill and serve.

ingredients

1lb. 2 oz. salmon fillet, skin removed

2 tbsp. sea salt

1 tbsp. superfine sugar

2 tbsp. chopped fresh dill

pepper

1 tbsp. chopped fresh tarragon

1 tsp. Dijon mustard

juice of 1 lemon

TOPPING

1¾ cups cream cheese

1 tbsp. chopped fresh chives

pinch of paprika

sprigs of fresh dill, to garnish

green chicken curry

Heat the oil in a wok or large skillet and stir-fry the onion and garlic for 1–2 minutes, until starting to soften. Add the curry paste and stir-fry for 1–2 minutes.

Add the coconut milk, stock, and lime leaves, bring to a boil and add the chicken. Reduce the heat and let simmer gently for 15–20 minutes, until the chicken is tender.

Add the fish sauce, soy sauce, lime rind and juice, and sugar. Cook for 2–3 minutes, until the sugar has dissolved. Serve immediately, garnished with chopped cilantro.

ingredients

1 tbsp. vegetable or peanut oil

1 onion, sliced

1 garlic clove, chopped finely

2–3 tbsp. green curry paste

1¾ cups coconut milk

⅔ cup chicken stock

4 kaffir lime leaves

4 skinless, boneless chicken breasts, cut into cubes

1 tbsp. fish sauce

2 tbsp. Thai soy sauce

grated rind and juice of ½ lime

1 tsp. jaggery or brown sugar

4 tbsp. chopped fresh cilantro, to garnish

brazil nut brittle

Brush the bottom of an 8-inch square cake pan with oil and line with parchment paper. Melt half the semisweet chocolate and spread in the prepared pan. Sprinkle with the chopped Brazil nuts, white chocolate, and fudge.

Melt the remaining semisweet chocolate pieces and pour over the top. Let the brittle set, then break up into jagged pieces using the tip of a strong knife.

ingredients

oil, for brushing

12 oz. semisweet chocolate, broken into pieces

scant ¾ cup shelled Brazil nuts, chopped

6 oz. white chocolate, coarsely chopped

6 oz. fudge, coarsely chopped

COOK'S TIP

Put the brittle on a serving plate or in an airtight container and keep, covered, in a cool place. Alternatively, you can store it in the refrigerator for up to 3 days.

roasted garlic-&-rosemary lamb with potatoes

Rub the garlic cloves with a little oil in your hands so they are coated. Place the garlic in a small roasting pan and roast in a preheated oven, 400°F/200°C, for 20 minutes, or until very soft; cover the garlic with foil, shiny side in, if the cloves start to brown too much.

As soon as the garlic is cool enough to handle, peel the cloves. Use the back of a fork, or a mortar and pestle, to pound the garlic into a coarse paste with ½ teaspoon of oil. Make small incisions all over the lamb, then rub in the garlic paste. Let marinate for at least 2 hours in a cool place.

When you are ready to cook, place the lamb in a roasting pan on a bed of rosemary sprigs, and season with salt and pepper. Rub the potatoes with oil and place round the lamb. Sprinkle with more rosemary and season with salt and pepper to taste. Roast in a preheated oven, 450°F/230°C, for 10 minutes, then reduce the heat to 350°F/180°C for 15 minutes per pound plus an extra 15 minutes for medium, or until the temperature reaches 160°F/70°C on an internal meat thermometer.

Transfer the lamb to a carving plate and let stand for 10 minutes before carving. The potatoes should be tender at this point, but if not, return them to the oven in a separate dish while you deglaze the pan.

Set aside the rosemary sprigs and skim off any fat in the pan. Pour the wine into the pan and bring to a boil, scraping up any glazed bits from the bottom. Continue boiling until reduced to half. Taste and adjust the seasoning.

Slice the lamb and serve with the potatoes and juices spooned over.

ingredientss

15 garlic cloves, unpeeled, but
   separated into cloves
olive oil
1 leg of lamb, about 3 lb.
handful of fresh, tender
   rosemary sprigs
salt and pepper
24 new potatoes, scrubbed, but
   left whole
scant 1¼ cups full-bodied red wine

ingredients

2 lb. baking potatoes, scrubbed

2 tbsp. vegetable oil

1 tsp. coarse sea salt

4 tbsp. butter

1 small onion, chopped

salt and pepper

1 cup grated Cheddar cheese or
   crumbled blue cheese

OPTIONAL

4 tbsp. canned, drained corn kernels

4 tbsp. cooked mushrooms,
   zucchini, or peppers

snipped fresh chives, to garnish

stuffed baked potatoes

Preheat the oven to 375°F/190°C. Prick the potatoes in several places with a fork and put on a baking sheet. Brush with the oil and sprinkle with the sea salt. Bake in the preheated oven for 1 hour, or until the skins are crispy and the insides are soft when pierced with a fork.

Meanwhile, melt 1 tablespoon of the butter in a small skillet over a medium–low heat. Add the onion and cook, stirring occasionally, for 8–10 minutes until soft and golden. Set aside.

Cut the potatoes in half lengthwise. Scoop the flesh into a large bowl, leaving the skins intact. Reserve the skins. Increase the oven temperature to 400°F/200°C.

Roughly mash the potato flesh and mix in the onion and remaining butter. Add salt and pepper to taste and stir in any of the optional ingredients, if using. Spoon the mixture back into the reserved potato skins. Top with the cheese.

Cook the filled potato skins in the oven for 10 minutes, or until the cheese has melted and is beginning to brown. Garnish with chives and serve at once.

stilton & walnut tartlets

Lightly grease a 3-inch, 12-hole muffin pan. Sift the flour with the celery salt into a food processor, add the butter, and process until the mixture resembles bread crumbs. Tip into a large bowl and add the walnuts and a little cold water, just enough to bring the dough together.

Turn out onto a lightly floured counter and cut the dough in half. Roll out the first piece and cut out 3½-inch rounds. Roll out each round to 4½ inches in diameter and use to line the muffin holes. Repeat with the remaining dough. Line each hole with parchment paper and fill with dried beans. Chill in the refrigerator for 30 minutes. Meanwhile, preheat the oven to 400°F/200°C. Bake the tartlet cases for 10 minutes. Remove from the oven, then remove the paper and beans.

MAKES 12 TARTLETS

To make the filling, melt the butter in a skillet over a medium-low heat, add the celery and leek and cook, stirring occasionally, for 15 minutes until very soft. Add the 2 tablespoons of cream, crumble in the cheese, and mix well. Season to taste with salt and pepper. Put the remaining cream in a pan and bring to simmering point. Pour onto the egg yolks in a heatproof bowl, stirring constantly. Mix in the cheese mixture and spoon into the tartlet cases. Bake for 10 minutes, then turn the pan around in the oven and bake for a further 5 minutes. Leave the tartlets to cool in the tin for 5 minutes. Serve garnished with parsley.

ingredients

WALNUT PASTRY

1½ cups all-purpose flour, plus extra
    for dusting

pinch of celery salt

4 tbsp. cold butter, diced,
    plus extra for greasing

1 oz. walnut halves, chopped

ice-cold water

FILLING

1 tbsp. butter

2 celery stalks, finely chopped

1 small leek, finely chopped

1 cup heavy cream plus
    2 tbsp.

7 oz. Stilton cheese

salt and pepper

3 egg yolks

fresh parsley, to garnish

candied fruit ice cream

Put the golden raisins and raisins into a bowl and pour over 4 tablespoons of the almond liqueur. Cover with plastic wrap and set aside to soak.

Beat the egg yolks and sugar together in a large bowl until fluffy. In a separate bowl, whisk together the cream and remaining almond liqueur, then whisk the mixture into the beaten egg yolks.

In a separate bowl, whisk the egg whites until stiff peaks form, then fold into the cream mixture along with the soaked fruit, cherries, candied peel, and almonds. Transfer to a large ovenproof bowl, cover, and freeze for 4–5 hours until set.

To serve, dip the bowl in hot water to loosen the ice cream, then turn it out onto a serving plate. Decorate with candied peel and serve.

ingredients

scant ½ cup golden raisins

scant ½ cup raisins

6 tbsp. almond liqueur, such as Amaretto

4 eggs, separated

½ cup superfine sugar

2½ cups heavy cream

½ cup candied cherries

1¾ oz. candied citrus peel

½ cup blanched almonds, chopped

strips of candied peel, to decorate

chorizo & quail's eggs

Preheat the broiler to high. Arrange the slices of bread on a baking sheet and broil until golden brown on both sides.

Cut or fold the chorizo slices to fit on the toasts; set aside.

Heat a thin layer of oil in a large skillet over medium heat until a cube of day-old bread sizzles—this takes about 40 seconds. Break the eggs into the skillet and cook, spooning the fat over the yolks, until the whites are set and the yolks are cooked to your liking.

Remove the cooked eggs from the skillet and drain on paper towels. Immediately transfer to the chorizo-topped toasts and dust with paprika. Sprinkle with salt and pepper to taste, and serve at once.

ingredients

12 slices French bread, sliced on the diagonal, about ¼ in. thick

about 1½ oz. cured, ready-to-eat chorizo, cut into 12 thin slices

olive oil

12 quail's eggs

mild paprika

salt and pepper

DECEMBER

21

MAKES 12

COOK'S TIP

Despite their delicate appearance, quail's eggs can be difficult to crack because of a relatively thick membrane under the shell. It is useful to have a pair of scissors handy to cut through the membrane as you break the eggs into the skillet.

brussels sprouts with buttered chestnuts

Bring a large pan of salted water to a boil. Add the Brussels sprouts and cook for 5 minutes. Drain thoroughly.

Melt the butter in a large pan over medium heat. Add the Brussels sprouts and cook, stirring, for 3 minutes, then add the chestnuts and nutmeg. Season with salt and pepper and stir well. Cook for another 2 minutes, stirring, then remove from the heat. Transfer to a serving dish, scatter over the slivered almonds, and serve.

ingredients

12 oz. Brussels sprouts, trimmed

3 tbsp. butter

3½ oz. canned whole chestnuts

pinch of nutmeg

salt and pepper

½ cup slivered almonds, to garnish

DECEMBER

22

SERVES 4

white chocolate truffles

Put the chocolate pieces into a heatproof glass bowl and place over a pan of hot but not simmering water. When it starts to melt, stir gently until completely melted. Do not overheat, or the chocolate will separate. Remove from the heat and gently stir in the butter, then the cream and brandy. Let cool, then cover with plastic wrap and refrigerate for 2–2½ hours until set.

Remove the chocolate mixture from the refrigerator. Using a teaspoon, scoop out small pieces of the mixture, then use your hands to roll them into balls.

To decorate, roll the balls in the grated white chocolate. To store, transfer to an airtight container and refrigerate for up to 12 days.

ingredients

4¼ oz. white chocolate, broken into small, even-size pieces

4 tbsp. butter, softened to room temperature

2 tbsp. heavy cream

½ tsp. brandy

grated white chocolate, to decorate

herbed salmon with hollandaise sauce

Preheat the broiler to medium. Rinse the fish fillets under cold running water and pat dry with paper towels. Season with salt and pepper. Combine the olive oil with the dill and chives, then brush the mixture over the fish. Transfer to the broiler and cook for about 6–8 minutes, turning once and brushing with more oil and herb mixture, until cooked to your taste.

Meanwhile, to make the sauce, put the egg yolks in a heatproof bowl over a pan of boiling water. Add the water and season with salt and pepper. Lower the heat and simmer, whisking constantly, until the mixture begins to thicken. Whisk in the butter, cube by cube, until the mixture is thick and shiny. Whisk in the lemon juice, then remove from the heat.

Remove the fish from the broiler and transfer to individual serving plates. Pour over the sauce and garnish with chopped fresh chives. Serve with freshly boiled new potatoes and snow peas.

ingredients

4 salmon fillets, about 6 oz. each, skin removed

salt and pepper

2 tbsp. olive oil

1 tbsp. chopped fresh dill

1 tbsp. chopped fresh chives, plus extra to garnish

HOLLANDAISE SAUCE

3 egg yolks

1 tbsp. water

salt and pepper

1 cup butter, cut into small cubes

juice of 1 lemon

TO SERVE

freshly boiled new potatoes

freshly cooked snow peas

ingredients

1 oven-ready turkey, weighing 11 lb.

1 garlic clove, finely chopped

3½ fl oz. red wine

3 tbsp. butter

STUFFING

3½ oz. white mushrooms

1 onion, chopped

1 garlic clove, chopped

3 tbsp. butter

1¼ cups fresh bread crumbs

2 tbsp. finely chopped fresh sage

1 tbsp. lemon juice

salt and pepper

PORT AND CRANBERRY SAUCE

½ cup sugar

1 cup port

6 oz. fresh cranberries

traditional roast turkey with wine & mushrooms

Preheat the oven to 400°F/200°C.

To make the stuffing, clean and chop the mushrooms, put them in a pan with the onion, garlic, and butter and cook for 3 minutes. Remove from the heat and stir in the remaining stuffing ingredients. Rinse the turkey and pat dry with paper towels. Fill the neck end with stuffing and truss with string.

Put the turkey in a roasting pan. Rub the garlic over the bird and pour the wine over. Add the butter and roast in the oven for 30 minutes. Baste, then reduce the temperature to 350°F/180°C and roast for a further 40 minutes. Baste again and cover with foil. Roast for a further 2 hours, basting regularly. Check that the bird is cooked by inserting a knife between the legs and body. If the juices run clear, it is cooked. Remove from the oven, cover with foil, and let stand for 25 minutes.

Meanwhile, put the sugar, port, and cranberries in a pan. Heat over a medium heat until almost boiling. Reduce the heat, simmer for 15 minutes, stirring, then remove from the heat. Serve with the turkey.

roast ham

Place the ham in a large pan, cover with cold water, and gradually bring to a boil over a low heat. Cover and simmer very gently for 1 hour. Preheat the oven to 400°F/200°C.

Remove the ham from the pan and drain. Remove the rind from the ham and discard. Score the fat into a diamond-shape pattern with a sharp knife.

Spread the mustard over the fat. Mix the sugar and ground spices together on a plate and roll the ham in it, pressing down to coat evenly.

Stud the diamond shapes with cloves and place the ham in a roasting pan. Roast in the oven for 20 minutes until the glaze is a rich golden colour.

To serve hot, cover with foil and let stand for 20 minutes before carving. If the ham is to be served cold, it can be cooked a day ahead.

To make the Cumberland sauce, using a citrus zester, remove the zest from the oranges and reserve. Place the red currant jelly, port, and mustard in a small pan and heat gently until the jelly has melted. Squeeze the juice from the oranges into the pan. Add the orange zest and season to taste with salt and pepper. Serve cold with the ham. The sauce can be kept in a screw-top jar in the refrigerator for up to 2 weeks.

1 boneless ham, weighing 3 lb., presoaked if necessary
2 tbsp. Dijon mustard
½ cup raw sugar
½ tsp. ground cinnamon
½ tsp. ground ginger
18 whole cloves

CUMBERLAND SAUCE
2 oranges, halved
4 tbsp. red currant jelly
4 tbsp. port
1 tsp. mustard
salt and pepper

feta cheese & cranberry tarts

Preheat the oven to 350°F/180°C. Heat 2 tablespoons of oil in a skillet over medium heat. Add the onion and cook, stirring, for 3 minutes, until slightly softened. Remove from the heat and stir in the olives and cranberries. Core and chop the apple and add it to the pan with the lemon juice. Stir well and set aside.

Brush the phyllo squares with the remaining oil and use them to line 4 muffin pans. Place 4 sheets in each pan, staggering them so that the overhanging corners make a decorative star shape. Divide the cranberry filling between the four tart shells. Scatter over the feta cheese and bake in the center of the preheated oven for about 10 minutes until golden. Serve hot.

ingredients

4 tbsp. olive oil

1 onion, chopped

8 black olives, pitted and chopped

generous ¾ cup cranberries

1 eating apple

1 tbsp. lemon juice

8 sheets of phyllo pastry, cut
    into 16 squares measuring
    5 inches across

4½ oz. feta cheese (drained weight),
    cut into small cubes

turkey tortillas with sour cream

Heat the oil in a skillet over medium heat. Add the onion, garlic, and zucchini and cook, stirring, for 4 minutes. Add the tomatoes, chili, and red wine, cook for another 5 minutes, then remove from the heat. Arrange the warm tortillas on a clean counter and spoon some tomato and zucchini into each one.

Add some shredded turkey and a spoonful of sour cream, then roll up the tortillas and arrange them on serving plates. Garnish with salad greens and serve with the rolls.

ingredients

1 tbsp. olive oil

1 onion, chopped

1 garlic clove, chopped

1 zucchini, trimmed and sliced

2 tomatoes, sliced

1 small red chili, seeded and
    finely chopped

1 tbsp. red wine

8 flour tortillas, warmed

12 oz. cooked turkey meat,
    shredded

½ cup sour cream

fresh salad greens, to garnish

crusty wholewheat rolls, to serve

panettone dessert

Grease a 3½-cup shallow ovenproof dish. Butter the slices of panettone and arrange in the dish.

Place the milk, cream, and vanilla bean in a pan over low heat until the mixture reaches boiling point.

Place the eggs and sugar in a bowl and beat together, then pour in the milk mixture and beat together. Pour the custard through a strainer over the buttered panettone. Let stand for 1 hour so that the panettone soaks up the custard.

Preheat the oven to 325°F/160°C. Bake the dessert in the oven for 40 minutes, then drizzle the apricot jelly over the top. If the top crusts of the dessert are not crisp and golden, heat under a preheated hot broiler for 1 minute before serving.

ingredients

3 tbsp. butter, softened, plus extra
    for greasing

9 oz. panettone, cut into slices

scant 1 cup milk

scant 1 cup heavy cream

1 vanilla bean, split

3 eggs

generous ½ cup superfine sugar

2 tbsp. apricot jelly, warmed
    and strained

COOK'S TIP

The vanilla bean used in this recipe may be rinsed clean and patted dry with paper towels and used again in another recipe.

turkey, leek & cheese soup

Melt the butter in a pan over medium heat. Add the onion and cook, stirring, for 4 minutes, until slightly softened. Add the leek and cook for another 3 minutes. Add the turkey to the pan and pour in the stock. Bring to a boil, then reduce the heat and simmer gently, stirring occasionally, for about 15 minutes. Remove from the heat and let cool a little.

Transfer half of the soup into a food processor and blend until smooth. Return the mixture to the pan with the rest of the soup, stir in the Stilton, cream, and tarragon, and season with pepper. Reheat gently, stirring.

Remove from the heat, pour into 4 warm soup bowls, garnish with tarragon and croûtons, and serve.

ingredients

4 tbsp. butter

1 large onion, chopped

1 leek, trimmed and sliced

11½ oz. cooked turkey meat, sliced

2½ cups chicken stock

5½ oz. Stilton or any strong cheese

⅔ cup heavy cream

1 tbsp chopped fresh tarragon

pepper

GARNISH

fresh tarragon leaves

croûtons

boned & stuffed roast duck

Wipe the duck with paper towels both inside and out. Lay it skin-side down on a board and season with salt and pepper.

Mix together the sausage meat, onion, apple, apricots, walnuts, and parsley and season well with salt and pepper. Form into a large sausage shape.

Lay the duck breast(s) on the whole duck and cover with the stuffing. Wrap the whole duck around the filling and tuck in any leg and neck flaps.

Preheat the oven to 375°F/190°C.

Sew the duck up the back and across both ends with fine string. Try to use one piece of string so that you can remove it in one go. Mold the duck into a good shape and place, sewn-side down, on a rack over a roasting pan.

Roast for 1½–2 hours, basting occasionally. Pour off some of the fat in the pan. When it is cooked, the duck should be golden brown and crispy.

Carve the duck into thick slices at the table and serve with the apricot sauce.

ingredients

4 lb. duck (dressed weight), ask your butcher to bone the duck and cut off the wings at the first joint

1 large or 2 smaller duck breasts, skin removed

salt and pepper

1 lb. flavored sausage meat, such as Duck & Mango or Pork & Apricot

1 small onion, finely chopped

1 apple, cored and finely chopped

3 oz. no-soak dried apricots, finely chopped

3 oz. chopped walnuts

2 tbsp. chopped fresh parsley

Apricot Sauce (see Accompaniment), to serve

SERVES 6–8

ACCOMPANIMENT

To make the Apricot Sauce, purée 14 oz. canned apricot halves in syrup in a blender. Pour the purée into a pan and add ⅔ cup stock, ½ cup Marsala, ½ teaspoon ground cinnamon and ½ teaspoon ground ginger, and season with salt and pepper. Stir over a low heat, simmering for 2–3 minutes. Serve warm.

index

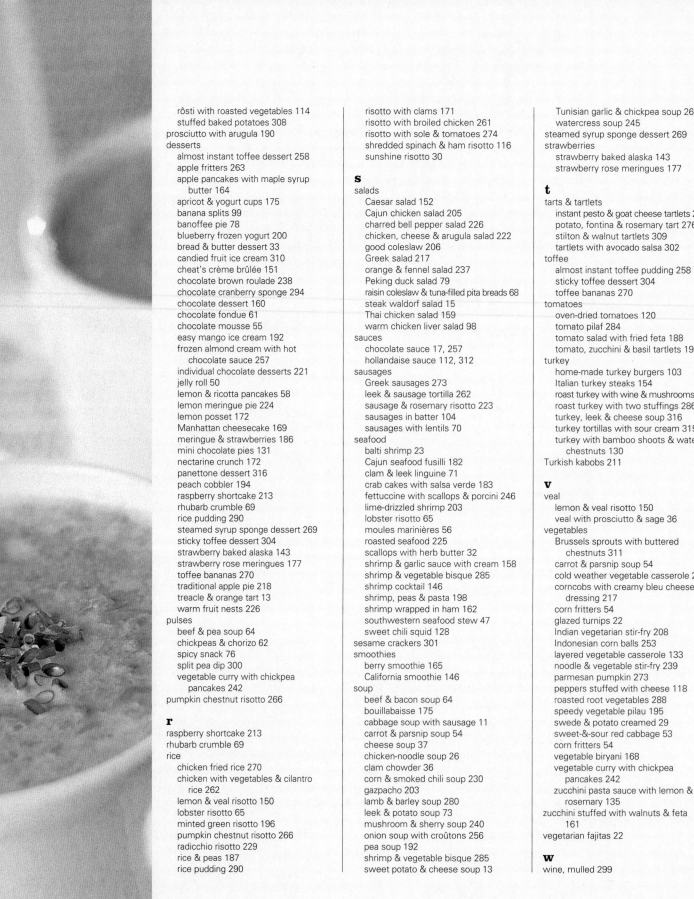